AF538920

Time Management, Time Allocation and Time Discipline

Time Management, Time Allocation and Time Discipline

Ms. Kalpana Taing

RANDOM PUBLICATIONS
NEW DELHI - 110 002 (INDIA)

Time Management, Time Allocation and Time Discipline

ISBN 978-93-5111-308-9

© Reserved

All Rights Reserved. No Part of this book may be reproduced in any manner without written permission.

Published in 2014 in India by
RANDOM PUBLICATIONS
4376-A/4B, Gali Murari Lal, Ansari Road
New Delhi-110 002
Phone: +9111-43580356, 23289044
E-mail: randomexports@gmail.com; sales@randompublications.com; info@randompublications.com

Type Setting by: Friends Media, Delhi-110089
Printed at : Thomson Press (India) Ltd

Preface

Time management is the act or process of planning and exercising conscious control over the amount of time spent on specific activities, especially to increase effectiveness, efficiency or productivity. Time management may be aided by a range of skills, tools, and techniques used to manage time when accomplishing specific tasks, projects and goals complying with a due date. Initially, time management referred to just business or work activities, but eventually the term broadened to include personal activities as well. A time management system is a designed combination of processes, tools, techniques, and methods. Time management is usually a necessity in any project development as it determines the project completion time and scope. Time management is often considered necessary because:

(1) available time is limited,
(2) time cannot be stored: if unused it is lost forever,
(3) one's goals are usually multiple, sometimes conflict, and not all goals are of equal priority,
(4) goals cannot be accomplished without the application of effort, which requires the use of time.

Time Management is the control and focus of a person's actions for the purpose of improving efficiency.

Time management techniques typically involve setting goals, establishing priorities, budgeting the amount of time allotted to a given activity, and planning and scheduling the steps needed to achieve goals. Generally, time management refers to the development of processes and tools that increase efficiency and productivity. When we think of time management, we tend to think of personal time management, loosely defined as managing our time to waste less time on doing the things we have to do so we have more time to do the things that we want to do. Therefore, time management is often thought of or presented as a set of time management skills; the theory is that once we master the time management skills, we'll be more organised, efficient, and happier. Personal time management skills include:

- Goal Setting

- Planning
- Prioritizing
- Decision-making
- Delegating
- Scheduling

The first step in effective time management is analysing how you currently spend your time and deciding how you want to change how you spend your time. Unless time is managed properly, nothing worthwhile can be accomplished. Time is a unique resource. It is indispensable, intangible, irreplaceable, irretrievable and therefore invaluable. It is equitably and uniformly distributed. A day of every one consists of 24 hours only, no more and no less. Every piece of work requires time. Time without energy has not much value; for instance, if one is seriously ill the time duration of illness is practically useless. Time is money. Time is also a measure of effort.

This book titled, "Time Management, Time Allocation and Time Discipline: Models, Theories, Methods, Tips and Skills", provides readers with an introductory overview of time management. An introduction to major elements and dimensions of time management is given. An overview of time perception, allocation and time discipline is discussed in detail. An analysis of the interrelationship between information management and time management is provided herein. Efforts have been made to know the modern time management tips and skills. In addition, this book is helpful in discussing the major time management models, theories and methods. Efforts are made towards estimating the time management tools and strategies. A detailed bibliography and elaborate index make this publication user-friendly.

—Editor

Contents

1

Time Management: An Introductory Overview

"I am definitely going to take a course on time management... just as soon as I can work it into my schedule."

—*Louis E. Boone*

INTRODUCTION TO TIME MANAGEMENT

This study provides some excellent tips for effective time management. While students can learn information to prepare them for the certification exam, emphasize that they can also make some important changes in their life to make it run more smoothly. As you begin, tell students that time management is an ongoing process, not a quick fix. Time management is the act or process of exercising conscious control over the amount of time spent on specific activities, especially to increase efficiency or productivity. Time management may be aided by a range of skills, tools, and techniques used to manage time when accomplishing specific tasks, projects and goals.

This set encompasses a wide scope of activities, and these include planning, allocating, setting goals, delegation, analysis of time spent, monitoring, organizing, scheduling, and prioritizing. Initially, time management referred to just business or work activities, but eventually the term broadened to include personal activities as well. A time management system is a designed combination of processes, tools, techniques, and methods. Usually time management is a necessity in any project development as it determines the project completion time and scope.

Categorization

Stephen R. Covey has offered a categorization scheme for the hundreds of time management approaches that they reviewed:

- First generation: reminders based on clocks and watches, but with computer implementation possible; can be used to alert a person when a task is to be done.
- Second generation: planning and preparation based on calendar and appointment books; includes setting goals.
- Third generation: planning, prioritizing, controlling (using a personal organizer, other paper-based objects, or computer or PDA-based systems) activities on a daily basis. This approach implies spending some time in clarifying values and priorities.
- Fourth generation: being efficient and proactive using any of the above tools; places goals and roles as the controlling element of the system and favours importance over urgency.

Time management literature can be paraphrased as follows:

- "Get Organized" - paperwork and task triage
- "Protect Your Time" - insulate, isolate, delegate
- "Set gravitational goals" - that attract actions automatically
- "Achieve through Goal management Goal Focus" - motivational emphasis
- "Work in Priority Order" - set goals and prioritize
- "Use Magical Tools to Get More Out of Your Time" - depends on when written
- "Master the Skills of Time Management"
- "Go with the Flow" - natural rhythms, Eastern philosophy
- "Recover from Bad Time Habits" - recovery from underlying psychological problems, e.g. procrastination

More unconventional time usage techniques, such as those discussed in "Where Did Time Fly," include concepts that can be paraphrased as "Less is More," which de-emphasizes the importance of squeezing every minute of your time, as suggested in traditional time management schemes. In recent years, several authors have discussed time management as applied to the issue of digital information overload, in particular, Tim Ferriss with "The 4 hour workweek", and Stefania Lucchetti with "The Principle of Relevance"

Time Management and Related Concepts

Time management has been considered as subsets of different concepts such as:

- Project management. Time Management can be considered as

a project management subset and is more commonly known as project planning and project scheduling. Time Management has also been identified as one of the core functions identified in project management.

- Attention management: Attention Management relates to the management of cognitive resources, and in particular the time that humans allocate their mind (and organizations the minds of their employees) to conduct some activities.
- Personal knowledge management or Personal time management.

Conceptual Effect on Labor

Professor Stephen Smith, of BYUI, is among recent sociologists that have shown that the way workers view time is connected to social issues such as the institution of family, gender roles, and the amount of labor by the individual.

Personal Time Management

Time management strategies are often associated with the recommendation to set personal goals. These goals are recorded and may be broken down into a project, an action plan, or a simple task list. For individual tasks or for goals, an importance rating may be established, deadlines may be set, and priorities assigned. This process results in a plan with a task list or a schedule or calendar of activities. Authors may recommend a daily, weekly, monthly or other planning periods associated with different scope of planning or review. This is done in various ways, as follows. Time management also covers how to eliminate tasks that don't provide the individual or organization value.

Task List

A task list (also *to-do list* or *things-to-do*) is a list of tasks to be completed, such as chores or steps toward completing a project. It is an inventory tool which serves as an alternative or supplement to memory. Task lists are used in self-management, grocery lists, business management, project management, and software development. It may involve more than one list. When one of the items on a task list is accomplished, the task is *checked* or *crossed* off. The traditional method is to write these on a piece of paper with a pen or pencil, usually on a note pad or clip-board.

Writer Julie Morgenstern suggests "do's and don'ts" of time management that include:

- Map out everything that is important, by making a task list
- Create "an oasis of time" for one to control
- Say "No"
- Set priorities
- Don't drop everything
- Don't think a critical task will get done in spare time.

Numerous digital equivalents are now available, including PIM (Personal information management) applications and most PDAs. There are also several web-based task list applications, many of which are free.

Task List Organization

Task lists are often tiered. The simplest tiered system includes a general to-do list (or task-holding file) to record all the tasks the person needs to accomplish, and a daily to-do list which is created each day by transferring tasks from the general to-do list. Task Lists are often Prioritized:

- An early advocate of "ABC" prioritization was Alan Lakein. In his system "A" items were the most important ("A-1" the most important within that group), "B" next most important, "C" least important.
- A particular method of applying the *ABC method* assigns "A" to tasks to be done within a day, "B" a week, and "C" a month.
- To prioritize a daily task list, one either records the tasks in the order of highest priority, or assigns them a number after they are listed ("1" for highest priority, "2" for second highest priority, etc.) which indicates in which order to execute the tasks. The latter method is generally faster, allowing the tasks to be recorded more quickly.
- A completely different approach which argues *against* prioritising altogether was put forward by British author Mark Forster in his book "Do It Tomorrow and Other Secrets of Time Management". This is based on the idea of operating "closed" to-do lists, instead of the traditional "open" to-do list. He argues that the traditional never-ending to-do lists virtually guarantees that some of your work will be left undone. This approach advocates getting all your work done, every day, and if you are unable to achieve it helps you diagnose where you are going wrong and what needs to change.

Software Applications

Modern task list applications may have built-in task hierarchy (tasks are composed of subtasks which again may contain subtasks), may support multiple methods of filtering and ordering the list of tasks, and may allow one to associate arbitrarily long notes for each task. In contrast to the concept of allowing the person to use multiple filtering methods, at least one new software product additionally contains a mode where the software will attempt to dynamically determine the best tasks for any given moment. Many of the software products for time management support multiple users. It allows the person to give tasks to other users and use the software for communication. In law firms, law practice management software may also assist in time management. Task list applications may be thought of as lightweight personal information manager or project management software.

Attention Deficit Disorder

Excessive and chronic inability to manage time effectively may be a result of Attention Deficit Disorder (ADD). Diagnostic criteria include: A sense of underachievement, difficulty getting organized, trouble getting started, many projects going simultaneously and trouble with follow-through.

- Prefrontal cortex: The prefrontal cortex is the most recently evolved part of the brain. It controls the functions of attention span, impulse control, organization, learning from experience and self-monitoring, among others. Some authors argue that changing the way the prefrontal cortex works is possible and offers a solution.

Caveats

Dwelling on the Lists

- According to Sandberg, task lists “aren’t the key to productivity [that] they’re cracked up to be”. He reports an estimated “30% of listers spend more time managing their lists than [they do] completing what’s on them”.
- This could be caused by procrastination by prolonging the planning activity. This is akin to analysis paralysis. As with any activity, there’s a point of diminishing returns.

Rigid Adherence

- Hendrickson asserts that rigid adherence to task lists can create a “tyranny of the to-do list” that forces one to “waste time on unimportant activities”.

- Again, the point of diminishing returns applies here too, but toward the size of the task. Some level of detail must be taken for granted for a task system to work. Rather than put “clean the kitchen”, “clean the bedroom”, and “clean the bathroom”, it is more efficient to put “housekeeping” and save time spent writing and reduce the system’s administrative load (each task entered into the system generates a cost in time and effort to manage it, aside from the execution of the task). The risk of consolidating tasks, however, is that “housekeeping” in this example may prove overwhelming or nebulously defined, which will either increase the risk of procrastination, or a mismanaged project.
- Listing routine tasks wastes time. If you are in the habit of brushing your teeth every day, then there is no reason to put it down on the task list. The same goes for getting out of bed, fixing meals, etc. If you need to track routine tasks, then a standard list or chart may be useful, to avoid the procedure of manually listing these items over and over.
- To remain flexible, a task system must allow for disaster. A disaster occurs constantly whether it is personal or business-related. A company must have a cushion of time ready for a disaster. Even if it is a small disaster, if no one made time for this situation, it can blow up bigger, causing the company to bankruptcy just because of poor time management.
- To avoid getting stuck in a wasteful pattern, the task system should also include regular (monthly, semi-annual, and annual) planning and system-evaluation sessions, to weed out inefficiencies and ensure the user is headed in the direction he or she truly desires.
- If some time is not regularly spent on achieving long-range goals, the individual may get stuck in a perpetual holding pattern on short-term plans, like staying at a particular job much longer than originally planned.

Techniques for Setting Priorities

There are several ways to set priorities.

ABC Analysis

A technique that has been used in business management for a long time is the categorization of large data into groups. These groups are often marked A, B, and C—hence the name. Activities are ranked upon these general criteria:

- A – Tasks that are perceived as being urgent and important,
- B – Tasks that are important but not urgent,
- C – Tasks that are neither urgent nor important.

Each group is then rank-ordered in priority. To further refine priority, some individuals choose to then force-rank all "B" items as either "A" or "C". ABC analysis can incorporate more than three groups. ABC analysis is frequently combined with Pareto analysis.

Pareto Analysis

This is the idea that 80% of tasks can be completed in 20% of the disposable time. The remaining 20% of tasks will take up 80% of the time. This principle is used to sort tasks into two parts. According to this form of Pareto analysis it is recommended that tasks that fall into the first category be assigned a higher priority. The 80-20-rule can also be applied to increase productivity: it is assumed that 80% of the productivity can be achieved by doing 20% of the tasks.

Similarly, 80% of results can be attributed to 20% of activity. If productivity is the aim of time management, then these tasks should be prioritized higher. It depends on the method adopted to complete the task. There is always a simpler and easy way to complete the task. If one uses a complex way, it will be time consuming. So, one should always try to find out the alternate ways to complete each task.

The Eisenhower Method

All tasks are evaluated using the criteria important/unimportant and urgent/not urgent and put in according quadrants. Tasks in unimportant/not urgent are dropped, tasks in important/urgent are done immediately and personally, tasks in unimportant/urgent are delegated and tasks in important/not urgent get an end date and are done personally. This method is said to have been used by US President Dwight D. Eisenhower, and is outlined in a quote attributed to him: *What is important is seldom urgent and what is urgent is seldom important.*

POSEC Method

POSEC is an acronym for *Prioritize by Organizing, Streamlining, Economizing and Contributing*. The method dictates a template which emphasizes an average individual's immediate sense of emotional and monetary security. It suggests that by attending to one's personal responsibilities first, an individual is better positioned to shoulder collective responsibilities. Inherent in the acronym is a hierarchy of self-realization which mirrors Abraham Maslow's "Hierarchy of needs".

1. Prioritize - Your time and define your life by goals.
2. Organizing - Things you have to accomplish regularly to be successful. (Family and Finances)
3. Streamlining - Things you may not like to do, but must do. (Work and Chores)
4. Economizing - Things you should do or may even like to do, but they're not pressingly urgent. (Pastimes and Socializing)
5. Contributing - By paying attention to the few remaining things that make a difference. (Social Obligations).

Effective Time Management

Rakesh is a senior executive in a top firm, eminently qualified for his job. He is ambitious and does not easily trust his subordinates, afraid of being let down by them. He, therefore, tries to do everything himself and is left with little time to think over larger issues. He remains immersed in files and carries work home. The last time he took the family for an outing appears to be years ago. Shiv, also in a senior position in the same firm, heads another department. However, the ambience here is different. Everyone goes about his job with a song on his lips and Shiv is always at hand, easily accessible to anyone. He packs for home on time and frequents the golf course in the afternoon. Holidays with the family help him to unwind further, which brings in added zip to his job.

Difference Between Two Executives

Most people seldom have enough time to do all the things they want to do. They have to work late in the offices, carry papers home for disposal and spend all their energy in the drudgery of daily routine. They have, therefore, no time to plan and execute jobs requiring their personal attention. Nor do they have adequate time for selfdevelopment. One's control over time is directly related to the hierarchical position one holds in an organization. Of all the resources—human, material, financial and the like—time is the scarcest. It is rightly said that time is money.

An executive earning Rs 40,000 per month has his time cost him Rs. 1,818 per day and Rs 227 per hour. This works out to Rs four every minute of his working time, including lunch and coffee breaks. Time must, therefore, be utilized with utmost care and on a priority basis. In the competitive environment prevailing in all spheres of life, the one who manages his time effectively will have the cutting edge.

How Time is Spent ?

The failure to manage time is the result of poor planning and is related to how managers feel about themselves. Broadly speaking, the pattern of time spent in a work situation is closely related to the personal values and priority system of an individual. An analysis indicates that most of the time spent will be on items:

- Which one is directly responsible for.
- Which are easy to perform.
- Which have brought due recognition and satisfaction in the past.
- Which give a chance for the display of certain special skills and talents

Management of Time

Personal traits: Time is often wasted due to various reasons and personality traits given below.

Indecision: Inability to decide what to do and when as also the inability to take a decision when required.

Procrastination: Decision is postponed or avoided whenever possible.

Perfectionist: Trying to be a perfectionist and doing a perfect job without taking care of the time schedule. Too much reliance on written records: Tendency to be over cautious.

Tension: Too much tension, mostly due to inability to accomplish tasks in time.

Self Organization: An individual should organize himself and his activities in order to make the most effective use of time by the following methods:

Priorities: The key to optimizing your time is to decide what is important to you. Generally, the priorities for many people have been family, health and well-being, career, money and intellectual growth. A lot depends on your outlook towards life, but more of that later. Wrong priority delays accomplishment of urgent jobs that contribute to your overall and immediate goals. Ironically, if you have too many priorities it becomes self-defeating because they can't all be priorities. You can prioritize only if you are clear about your personal and work objectives. Once you have prioritized, pay attention to critical and urgent jobs. Manage by exception and handle unusual cases instead of each one.

Planning: This involves realistic allocation of time and ability to dispose of matters according to time schedule. Always plan ahead. Set aside some time for planning the next day. Review mid-day your goals for the day. Develop routines whenever possible. People who get the most of their limited time prefer to plan the upcoming week, month and even further ahead.

Taking Decisions: Complicating the decision-making process is the fact that we are faced with more choices in most things—education, lifestyle, place of residence, career, marriage...all through your life you will have to face the problem of taking decisions squarely. Approach decision-making with a positive frame of mind. Don't consider decisions to be taken as some sort of a problem, although some management experts view it just like that. Consider decisionmaking as a challenge and an opportunity or an avenue. With such a positive outlook you will also be able to put your intuition to good use and take reasonably good decisions—and work to let them pay. Intuition is not guess work or wishful thinking.

It is defined as instinctive knowledge—in other words knowledge or perception not gained by reasoning and intelligence. It will be worthwhile to do the low-level decisions quickly and work on the big ones, for which you may have to consult one or more experts to garner their views. Then go ahead and decide what's the best course for you to adopt. One thing at a time: The tendency to skip from one job to another should be avoided. Complete one task in hand before taking up another.

This involves doing first things first and one thing at a time—something you can achieve only if you have prioritized and planned well. Your attempt always should be to create "chunks" of time instead of "driblets".

Delegation: It will help you to avoid doing everything yourself. You will be surprised at the amount of delegation you could do. This will free your time to deal with more important matters. Delegation, however, doesn't mean just palming off responsibility to others. It implies training your subordinates to undertake jobs with the requisite authority given to them.

Clarify responsibility: It will help if your subordinates know what is their responsibility and what decisions they can take. Excessive control and cross checking will make your subordinates ineffective, a situation which can easily be avoided.

Conferences: Some people habitually waste too much time on conferences and meetings. Decide on who are really required to attend and have the agenda set out properly. It will help to develop good conference leadership. Completed homework: Instead of going to your boss for decisions, go to him with recommendations for action. He doesn't have enough time to think through all the items with which you are familiarÑand he will just take up his time and yours by reviewing.

Aids to Effective Utilization of Time

A good memory: Reduce the need for reliance on written records. Always try to keep a notebook and pencil handy to jot down points. Good ideas seldom repeat themselves.

Flexibility in work: Do not entirely depend upon precedents before deciding an issue.

Self-confidence: Develop the ability to handle matters independently.

Physical fitness: The ability to stand physical and mental strain and to take reasonably good decisions is important.

Speed-reading: Develop the ability to go through a paper an grasp the essentials quickly.

Congenial environment: A work environment of mutual cooperation and rapport instead of competition and conflict is conductive to efficiency. It would be a good idea to remember that people who feel good about themselves produce good results. This depends upon your outlook towards life, which in turn will determine your ability to create quality time.

Outlook Towards Life

Life is not all about careerism. It is a mix of making money, spending quality time with your family, socializing adequately, and taking time out for yourself to recharge your batteries. Once you have these priorities right, you will find everything falling into place. You will set less tighter deadlines that will not affect your health and which will allow you to keep pace with the demands on your time. You will find yourself taking occasional breaks for a holiday that will fire you with fresh ideas and enthusiasm back into your work with enhanced doses of creativity. Uppermost for a rational attitude towards life is the concern for one's health. Poor health and tight schedules result in much wasted time without corresponding productivity. It is prudent to devote the right time and effort to maintain your physical health so that you are not only able to optimize your available time but also reap the benefits of enhanced productivity and wealth. A right balance in life is thus essential to boost efficiency, no matter what your calling.

Getting Away

In the workplace you will find many distractions that makes it not the ideal environment to do all your tasks with ideal effect and in quick time. Many people find it profitable to get away from the office distractions by working in the library, conference room or even out in the lawn. Such a change of scene and environment is essential when you feel the need to do some deep and conceptual thinking that can come about only when you create some quiet space for yourself. An ability to get away from colleagues, subordinates and even one's boss is a boon.

It depends upon one's own perceived sense of "importance" and ego. Getting tied down to the telephone isn't really a sign of how important we are. Even if you are the top boss, you needn't remain tied up to the telephone. People who need to reach out to you for a decision will do so in their own way and time. To be able to create the "chunk of time" that we had spoken of earlier, one must be able to control and minimize one's interruptions. This will give you enhanced control over your work, apart from giving you a sense of control over your own time and life.

Learning to Say No

Whether you are a student or a career person, there will be many expectations from you from many quarters—your boss, colleagues, friends and family. If you are one of those who silently fall into the trap of committing yourself and later curse because you feel that you are being 'used', then you have to learn to say 'no' politely—and not feel bad about it. To deal with your boss you have to be diplomatic but firm. If you find your boss is overloading you with work, it would not be out of place to give him an account of the tasks currently in your hand. Then you might add that since you are over-committed at the moment, and if you take that additional task on you would not be able to do it justice. Do of course thank him for the confidence he has in you. In dealing with your family members who put in constant demands on your time, it is better to explain how your diversion of time would affect your main projects, research, studies, exam, or whatever. Do also let them know how and when you would be available to help them out at other times and in a different way. If you plan to spend "quality time" with your family, you will easily maintain the essential bonding. In dealing with a score of other people who constantly badger you for "work or favours", a firm "no" will do the trick. Once the word gets around that you don't divert from your main tasks easily, people will be glad to leave you alone.

Personal Time

If you want to get ahead in life, deep thinking is what you will have to constantly engage in. It is a leadership trait that can be cultivated by creating personal time and using it effectively. All great men have realized the importance of personal time. Such people isolate themselves for varying periods at a time of their own choosing every day. Even the most brilliant executives, or students for that matter, need to set aside time for deep thinking, to read, write and enhance their knowledge base so that they widen their faculties. The grievance of most people is that they hardly get time to think, and it gets reflected in their work output.

Such people allow themselves to drift along with the situation and time. But those who do create time for deep thinking find themselves in charge of the situation and time that they use to their own advantage. Such people go about creating their personal time first and then allocating time for the remaining activities. A major advantage of this is that one is able to prioritize judiciously which results in a marked saving of time and the tackling of really important tasks first. In sum, the principles of time management are few and simple. One must carefully analyse how one's time is spent. To be effective, one has to devote adequate attention to proper planning and utilization of time. It will be useful to plan the day, week and further ahead. Clarity about one's personal and work objectives and allocation of priorities to the task in hand must be turned into second nature.

This involves change in the attitude and pattern of work habits. In today's world where one gets involved in multifarious activities, a conscious attempt to manage time will be very rewarding. Irrespective of one's calling, these can be applied profitably resulting in a more orderly, more efficient and effective existence, added satisfaction with more time to think and enjoy life. All successful men have always managed their time well.

REFERENCES

Albert Hamilton (2004). *Handbook of Project Management Procedures.* TTL Publishing, Ltd.

Apostolou, D.; Karapiperis, S.; Stojanovic, N. (2008). "On Managing Users' Attention in Knowledge-Intensive Organizations". In G.A. Tsihrintzis et al.. *New Directions in Intelligent Interactive Multimedia, SCI 142*. Springer. pp. 239–248.

Apshvalka, Dace; Wendorff, Peter (2005), *A Framework of Personal Knowledge Management in the Context of Organizational Knowledge Management*, ECKM 2005, pp. 34–41.

Avery, Susan; Brooks, Randy; O'Conner, Michael (2001), *Personal Knowledge Management: Framework for Integration and Partnerships*, In ASCUE 2001, http://www.millikin.edu/pkm/pkm_ascue.html

Bernhard Schlagheck (2000). Objektorientierte Referenzmodelle für das Prozess- und Projektcontrolling. Grundlagen - Konstruktionen – Anwendungsmöglichkeiten.

Bjarne Kousholt (2007). *Project Managementý –. Theory and practice..* Nyt Teknisk Forlag. ISBN 87-571-2603-8. p.59.

Buck, M. L., Lee, M. D., MacDermid, S., & Smith S. C. (2000). Reduced load work and the experience of time among professionals and managers: Implications for personal and organizational life. In C. Cooper & D. Rousseau (Eds.), Trends in Organizational Behaviour (Vol. 7). New York: John Wiley & Sons.

Change Your Brain Change Your Life: The Breakthrough Program for Conquering Anxiety, Depression, Obsessiveness, Anger, and Impulsiveness 1998.

Dace Apshvalka, Peter Wendorff: A Framework of Personal Knowledge Management in the Context of Organizational Knowledge Management.

Davenport, T.H.; Beck, J.C. (2001). *The Attention Economy: Understanding the New Currency of Business*. Harvard Business School Press.

David I. Cleland, Roland Gareis (2006). *Global project management handbook*. "Chapter 1: "The evolution of project management". McGraw-Hill Professional, 2006.

David I. Cleland, Roland Gareis (2006). *Global project management handbook*. McGraw-Hill Professional, 2006.

Dennis Lock (2007) *Project management* (9e ed.) Gower Publishing, Ltd., 2007.

Dorsey, Paul A. (2001), *Personal Knowledge Management: Educational Framework for Global Business*, Tabor School of Business, Millikin University, http://www.millikin.edu/pkm/pkm_istanbul.html

Efimova, L. (2005) "Understanding personal knowledge management: A weblog case". Enschede: Telematica Instituut.

F.L. Harrison, Dennis Lock (2004). *Advanced project management: a structured approachý*. Gower Publishing, Ltd., 2004.

Forster, Mark (2006-07-20). *Do It Tomorrow and Other Secrets of Time Management*. Hodder & Stoughton Religious. pp. 224.

Frand, Jason; Hixon, Carol (1999), "Personal Knowledge Management : Who, What, Why, When, Where, How?", *Working paper, UCLA Anderson School of Management*.

Grundspenkis, J. (2007), "Agent based approach for organization and personal knowledge modelling: knowledge management perspective", *Journal of Intelligent Manufacturing* 18 (4): 451–457.

Harold Kerzner (2003). *Project Management: A Systems Approach to Planning, Scheduling, and Controlling* (8th Ed. ed.). Wiley.

Huberman, Bernardo A.; Wu, Fang (2008). "The Economics of Attention: Maximizing User Value in Information Rich Environments". *Advances in Complex Systems* 11 (4): 487–496.

James P. Lewis (2000). *The project manager's desk reference: : a comprehensive guide to project planning, scheduling, evaluation, and systems.* p.185.

Jörg Becker, Martin Kugeler, Michael Rosemann (2003). Process management: a guide for the design of business processes.

Joseph Phillips (2003). *PMP Project Management Professional Study Guide*. McGraw-Hill Professional, 2003.

Kebinger, J. (2005). "Current research in workplace interruption management". *Paper COMP171.*

Lakein, Alan (1973). *How to Get Control of Your Time and Your Life..* New York: P.H. Wyden.

Lewis R. Ireland (2006) *Project Management*. McGraw-Hill Professional, 2006.

Maglio, P.P.; Barrett, R.; Campbell, C.S.; Selker, T. (2000). "SUITOR: An attentive information system". In G.A. Tsihrintzis et al.. *Proceedings of the International Conference on Intelligent User Interfaces 2000*. ACM Press. pp. 169–176.

Martin Stevens (2002). *Project Management Pathways*. Association for Project Management. APM Publishing Limited, 2002.

Max Völkel (2007) "From Documents to Knowledge Models" in Proc. of the 4th Conference on Professional Knowledge Management, volume 2, pp. 209–216. GITO mbh, Berlin, March 2007.

Morgen Witzel (2003). *Fifty key figures in managementý*. Routledge, 2003.

Morgenstern, Julie (2004). *Time Management from the Inside Out: The Foolproof System for Taking Control of Your Schedule—and Your Life* (2nd ed.). New York: Henry Holt/Owl Books. pp. 285.

Nabeth, Thierry (2008). "User Profiling for Attention Support for School and Work". In Mireille Hildebrandt and Serge Gutwirth. *Profiling the European Citizen*. Springer. pp. 185–200.

Nonaka, Ikujiro; von Krogh, Georg (2009), "Tacit Knowledge and Knowledge Conversion: Controversy and Advancement in Organizational Knowledge Creation Theory", *Organization Science* 20 (3): 635–652.

Paul C. Dinsmore et al (2005) *The right projects done right!* John Wiley and Sons, 2005.

Pauleen, David (2009), "Personal knowledge management: putting the 'person' back into the knowledge equation", *Online Information Review* 33 (2): 221–224.

Pollard, Dave (2008), *PKM: A bottom-up approach to knowledge management. In Knowledge Management in Practice: Connections and Context, ed. T.K. Srikantaiah and M.E.D. Koenig*, Information Today, pp. 95–114.

Project Management Institute (2004). *A Guide to the Project Management Body of Knowledge (PMBOK Guide)*.

Roda, Claudia; Nabeth, Thierry (2008). "Attention management in organizations: Four levels of support in information systems". In A. Bounfour. *Organizational Capital: Modelling, Measuring and Contextualising. Routledge (advanced research series in management)*. Routledge. pp. 214–233.

Rosen, Christine (2008). "The Myth of Multitasking". *The New Atlantis, Spring 2008* 20: 105–110.

Sandberg, Jared (2004-09-10). "Though Time-Consuming, To-Do Lists Are a Way of Life". The Wall Street Journal.

Sheridan, William (2008), *How to Think like a knowledge worker*, United Nations Public Administration Network.

Smedley, Jo (2009), "Modelling personal knowledge management", *OR Insight* 22 (4): 221–233.

Snowden, David; Pauleen, David J. (2008), *Knowledge management and the individual: it's nothing personal—an interview with Dave Snowden by David J. Pauleen*, http://pauleen.massey.ac.nz

Steinle, Bruch, Lawa (1995). Projektmanagement. FAZ Verlagsbereich Wirtschaftsbücher. p.136-143.

Stellman, Andrew; Greene, Jennifer (2005). *Applied Software Project Management.* O'Reilly Media.

The Principle of Relevance, Stefania Lucchetti, RT Publishing, Hong Kong 2010 http://www.stefanialucchetti.com

The Seven Habits of Highly Effective People, Stephen Covey, Fireside 1990.

VA Office of Information and Technology (2003) Project Management Guide US DEPARTMENT OF VETERANS AFFAIRS. March 3, 2005.

Vertegaal, Roel (2003). "Attentive User Interfaces". *Communications of the ACM* 46 (3).

Vertegaal, Roel; Shell, J.S.; Chen, D.; Mamuji, A. (2006). "Designing for augmented attention: Towards a framework for attentive user interfaces". *Computers in Human Behaviour* 22 (4): 771–789.

Völkel, Max; Abecker, Andreas (2008), *Cost-Benefit Analysis for the Design of Personal Knowledge Management Systems*, Proc. of 10th International Conference on Enterprise Information Systems.

Winston W. Royce (1970). "Managing the Development of Large Software Systems" in: In: *Technical Papers of Western Electronic Show and Convention* (WesCon) August 25–28, 1970, Los Angeles, USA.

Wolpers, Martin; Najjar, Jehad; Verbert, Katrien; Duval, Erik (2007). "Tracking Actual Usage: the Attention Metadata Approach". *International Journal Educational Technology and Society* 10 (3 Special Issue on "Advanced Technologies for Life-Long Learning).

Wright, Kirby (2005), "Personal knowledge management: supporting individual knowledge worker performance", *Knowledge Management Research and Practice* 3 (3): 156–165.

Wright, Kirby (2007), *Rethinking Knowledge Work: Supporting Work and Learning through Personal Knowledge Management*, KRW Knowledge Resources.

Young-Hoon Kwak (2005). "A brief history of Project Management". In: *The story of managing projects.* Elias G. Carayannis et al. (9 eds), Greenwood Publishing Group, 2005.

Zhang, Zuopeng (Justin) (2009), "Personalising organizational knowledge and organizationalising personal knowledge", *Online Information Review* 33 (2): 237–256.

2

Major Elements and Dimensions of Time Management

PROJECT MANAGEMENT

Project management is the discipline of planning, organizing, securing and managing resources to bring about the successful completion of specific project goals and objectives. It is sometimes conflated with program management, however technically that is actually a higher level construction: a group of related and somehow interdependent projects. A project is a temporary endeavor, having a defined beginning and end (usually constrained by date, but can be by funding or deliverables), undertaken to meet unique goals and objectives, usually to bring about beneficial change or added value. The temporary nature of projects stands in contrast to business as usual (or operations), which are repetitive, permanent or semi-permanent functional work to produce products or services. In practice, the management of these two systems is often found to be quite different, and as such requires the development of distinct technical skills and the adoption of separate management. The primary challenge of project management is to achieve all of the project goals and objectives while honoring the preconceived project constraints. Typical constraints are scope, time, and budget. The secondary—and more ambitious—challenge is to optimize the allocation and integration of inputs necessary to meet pre-defined objectives.

History

Project management has been practiced since early civilization. Until 1900 civil engineering projects were generally managed by creative architects and engineers themselves, among those for example Vitruvius (1st century BC), Christopher Wren (1632–1723), Thomas Telford (1757–1834) and Isambard Kingdom Brunel (1806–1859). It was in the 1950s that organizations started to systematically apply project management tools and techniques to complex engineering projects. As a discipline, Project Management developed from several fields of application including civil construction, engineering, and heavy defense activity. Two forefathers of project management are Henry Gantt, called the father of planning and control techniques, who is famous for his use of the Gantt chart as a project management tool; and Henri Fayol for his creation of the 5 management functions which form the foundation of the body of knowledge associated with project and program management. Both Gantt and Fayol were students of Frederick Winslow Taylor's theories of scientific management. His work is the forerunner to modern project management tools including work breakdown structure (WBS) and resource allocation. The 1950s marked the beginning of the modern Project Management era where core engineering fields come together working as one. Project management became recognized as a distinct discipline arising from the management discipline with engineering model. In the United States, prior to the 1950s, projects were managed on an *ad hoc* basis using mostly Gantt Charts, and informal techniques and tools. At that time, two mathematical project-scheduling models were developed.

The "Critical Path Method" (CPM) was developed as a joint venture between DuPont Corporation and Remington Rand Corporation for managing plant maintenance projects. And the "Program Evaluation and Review Technique" or PERT, was developed by Booz Allen Hamilton as part of the United States Navy's (in conjunction with the Lockheed Corporation) Polaris missile submarine program; These mathematical techniques quickly spread into many private enterprises. At the same time, as project-scheduling models were being developed, technology for project cost estimating, cost management, and engineering economics was evolving, with pioneering work by Hans Lang and others. In 1956, the American Association of Cost Engineers (now AACE International; the Association for the Advancement of Cost Engineering) was formed by early practitioners of project management and the associated specialties of planning and scheduling, cost estimating, and cost/schedule control (project control). AACE continued its pioneering work and in 2006 released the first integrated process for portfolio, program and project management (Total Cost Management Framework).

The International Project Management Association (IPMA) was founded in Europe in 1967, as a federation of several national project management associations. IPMA maintains its federal structure today and now includes member associations on every continent except Antarctica. IPMA offers a Four Level Certification program based on the IPMA Competence Baseline (ICB). The ICB covers technical competences, contextual competences, and behavioural competences. In 1969, the Project Management Institute

(PMI) was formed in the USA. PMI publishes *A Guide to the Project Management Body of Knowledge* (PMBOK Guide), which describes project management practices that are common to "most projects, most of the time." PMI also offers multiple certifications.

Approaches

There are a number of approaches to managing project activities including agile, interactive, incremental, and phased approaches. Regardless of the methodology employed, careful consideration must be given to the overall project objectives, timeline, and cost, as well as the roles and responsibilities of all participants and stakeholders.

The Traditional Approach

A traditional phased approach identifies a sequence of steps to be completed. In the "traditional approach", we can distinguish 5 components of a project (4 stages plus control) in the development of a project:

- Project initiation stage;
- Project planning and design stage;
- Project execution and construction stage;
- Project monitoring and controlling systems;
- Project completion.

Not all the projects will visit every stage as projects can be terminated before they reach completion. Some projects do not follow a structured planning and/or monitoring stages. Some projects will go through steps 2, 3 and 4 multiple times. Many industries use variations on these project stages. For example, when working on a brick and mortar design and construction, projects will typically progress through stages like Pre-Planning, Conceptual Design, Schematic Design, Design Development, Construction Drawings (or Contract Documents), and Construction

Administration. In software development, this approach is often known as the waterfall model, i.e., one series of tasks after another in linear sequence. In software development many organizations have adapted the Rational Unified Process (RUP) to fit this methodology, although RUP does not require or explicitly recommend this practice. Waterfall development works well for small, well defined projects, but often fails in larger projects of undefined and ambiguous nature.

The Cone of Uncertainty explains some of this as the planning made on the initial phase of the project suffers from a high degree of uncertainty. This becomes especially true as software development is often the realization of a new or novel product. In projects where requirements have not been finalized and can change, requirements management is used to develop an accurate and complete definition of the behaviour of software that can serve as the basis for software development. While the terms may differ from industry to industry, the actual stages typically follow common steps to problem solving — "defining the problem, weighing options, choosing a path, implementation and evaluation."

Critical Chain Project Management

Critical Chain Project Management (CCPM) is a method of planning and managing projects that puts more emphasis on the resources (physical and human) needed in order to execute project tasks. The most complex part involves engineering professionals of different fields (Civil, Electrical, Mechanical etc.) working together. It is an application of the Theory of Constraints (TOC) to projects. The goal is to increase the rate of throughput (or completion rates) of projects in an organization.

Applying the first three of the five focusing steps of TOC, the system constraint for all projects is identified as are the resources. To exploit the constraint, tasks on the critical chain are given priority over all other activities. Finally, projects are planned and managed to ensure that the resources are ready when the critical chain tasks must start, subordinating all other resources to the critical chain. Regardless of project type, the project plan should undergo Resource Leveling, and the longest sequence of resource-constrained tasks should be identified as the critical chain. In multi-project environments, resource leveling should be performed across projects.

However, it is often enough to identify (or simply select) a single "drum" resource—a resource that acts as a constraint across projects—and stagger projects based on the availability of that single resource.

Extreme Project Management

In critical studies of Project Management, it has been noted that several of these fundamentally PERT-based models are not well suited for the multi-project company environment of today. Most of them are aimed at very large-scale, one-time, non-routine projects, and nowadays all kinds of management are expressed in terms of projects. Using complex models for "projects" (or rather "tasks") spanning a few weeks has been proven to cause unnecessary costs and low maneuverability in several cases. Instead, project management experts try to identify different "lightweight" models, such as Agile Project Management methods including Extreme Programming for software development and Scrum techniques.

The generalization of Extreme Programming to other kinds of projects is extreme project management, which may be used in combination with the process modeling and management principles of human interaction management.

Event Chain Methodology

Event chain methodology is another method that complements critical path method and critical chain project management methodologies. Event chain methodology is an uncertainty modeling and schedule network analysis technique that is focused on identifying and managing events and event chains that affect project schedules. Event chain methodology helps to mitigate the negative impact of psychological heuristics and biases, as well as to allow for easy modeling of uncertainties in the project schedules. Event chain methodology is based on the following principles.

- Probabilistic moment of risk: An activity (task) in most real life processes is not a continuous uniform process. Tasks are affected by external events, which can occur at some point in the middle of the task.
- Event chains: Events can cause other events, which will create event chains. These event chains can significantly affect the course of the project. Quantitative analysis is used to determine a cumulative effect of these event chains on the project schedule.
- Critical events or event chains: The single events or the event chains that have the most potential to affect the projects are the "critical events" or "critical chains of events." They can be determined by the analysis.
- Project tracking with events: Even if a project is partially completed and data about the project duration, cost, and events occurred is available, it is still possible to refine information about future potential events and helps to forecast future project performance.

- Event chain visualization: Events and event chains can be visualized using event chain diagrams on a Gantt chart.

Prince 2

PRINCE2 is a structured approach to project management, released in 1996 as a generic project management method. It combined the original PROMPT methodology (which evolved into the PRINCE methodology) with IBM's MITP (managing the implementation of the total project) methodology. PRINCE2 provides a method for managing projects within a clearly defined framework. PRINCE2 describes procedures to coordinate people and activities in a project, how to design and supervise the project, and what to do if the project has to be adjusted if it does not develop as planned. In the method, each process is specified with its key inputs and outputs and with specific goals and activities to be carried out.

This allows for automatic control of any deviations from the plan. Divided into manageable stages, the method enables an efficient control of resources. On the basis of close monitoring, the project can be carried out in a controlled and organized way. PRINCE2 provides a common language for all participants in the project. The various management roles and responsibilities involved in a project are fully described and are adaptable to suit the complexity of the project and skills of the organization.

Process-Based Management

Also furthering the concept of project control is the incorporation of process-based management. This area has been driven by the use of Maturity models such as the CMMI (Capability Maturity Model Integration) and ISO/IEC15504 (SPICE - Software Process Improvement and Capability Estimation).

Agile Project Management

Agile Project Management approaches based on the principles of human interaction management are founded on a process view of human collaboration. This contrasts sharply with the traditional approach. In the agile software development or flexible product development approach, the project is seen as a series of relatively small tasks conceived and executed as the situation demands in an adaptive manner, rather than as a completely pre-planned process.

Processes

Traditionally, project management includes a number of elements: four to five process groups, and a control system. Regardless of the methodology or terminology used, the same basic project management processes will be used. Major process groups generally include:

- Initiation
- Planning or development
- Production or execution
- Monitoring and controlling
- Closing

In project environments with a significant exploratory element (e.g., Research and development), these stages may be supplemented with decision points (go/no go decisions) at which the project's continuation is debated and decided. An example is the Stage-Gate model.

Initiation

The initiation processes determine the nature and scope of the project. If this stage is not performed well, it is unlikely that the project will be successful in meeting the business' needs. The key project controls needed here are an understanding of the business environment and making sure that all necessary controls are incorporated into the project. Any deficiencies should be reported and a recommendation should be made to fix them. The initiation stage should include a plan that encompasses the following areas:

- Analyzing the business needs/requirements in measurable goals
- Reviewing of the current operations
- Financial analysis of the costs and benefits including a budget
- Stakeholder analysis, including users, and support personnel for the project
- Project charter including costs, tasks, deliverables, and schedule

Planning and Design

After the initiation stage, the project is planned to an appropriate level of detail. The main purpose is to plan time, cost and resources adequately to estimate the work needed and to effectively manage risk during project execution. As with the Initiation process group, a failure to adequately plan greatly reduces the project's chances of successfully accomplishing its goals. Project planning generally consists of

- determining how to plan (e.g. by level of detail or rolling wave);
- developing the scope statement;
- selecting the planning team;
- identifying deliverables and creating the work breakdown structure;

- identifying the activities needed to complete those deliverables and networking the activities in their logical sequence;
- estimating the resource requirements for the activities;
- estimating time and cost for activities;
- developing the schedule;
- developing the budget;
- risk planning;
- gaining formal approval to begin work.

Additional processes, such as planning for communications and for scope management, identifying roles and responsibilities, determining what to purchase for the project and holding a kick-off meeting are also generally advisable. For new product development projects, conceptual design of the operation of the final product may be performed concurrent with the project planning activities, and may help to inform the planning team when identifying deliverables and planning activities.

Executing

Executing consists of the processes used to complete the work defined in the project management plan to accomplish the project's requirements. Execution process involves coordinating people and resources, as well as integrating and performing the activities of the project in accordance with the project management plan. The deliverables are produced as outputs from the processes performed as defined in the project management plan.

Monitoring and Controlling

Monitoring and controlling consists of those processes performed to observe project execution so that potential problems can be identified in a timely manner and corrective action can be taken, when necessary, to control the execution of the project. The key benefit is that project performance is observed and measured regularly to identify variances from the project management plan. Monitoring and Controlling includes:

- Measuring the ongoing project activities ('where we are');
- Monitoring the project variables (cost, effort, scope, etc.) against the project management plan and the project performance baseline (*where we should be*);
- Identify corrective actions to address issues and risks properly (*How can we get on track again*);
- Influencing the factors that could circumvent integrated change control so only approved changes are implemented

In multi-phase projects, the monitoring and control process also provides feedback between project phases, in order to implement corrective or preventive actions to bring the project into compliance with the project management plan. Project Maintenance is an ongoing process, and it includes:

- Continuing support of end users
- Correction of errors
- Updates of the software over time

In this stage, auditors should pay attention to how effectively and quickly user problems are resolved. Over the course of any construction project, the work scope may change. Change is a normal and expected part of the construction process. Changes can be the result of necessary design modifications, differing site conditions, material availability, contractor-requested changes, value engineering and impacts from third parties, to name a few. Beyond executing the change in the field, the change normally needs to be documented to show what was actually constructed. This is referred to as Change Management. Hence, the owner usually requires a final record to show all changes or, more specifically, any change that modifies the tangible portions of the finished work. The record is made on the contract documents – usually, but not necessarily limited to, the design drawings. The end product of this effort is what the industry terms as-built drawings, or more simply, "as built."

The requirement for providing them is a norm in construction contracts. When changes are introduced to the project, the viability of the project has to be re-assessed. It is important not to lose sight of the initial goals and targets of the projects. When the changes accumulate, the forecasted result may not justify the original proposed investment in the project.

Closing

Closing includes the formal acceptance of the project and the ending thereof. Administrative activities include the archiving of the files and documenting lessons learned. This phase consists of:

- Project close: Finalize all activities across all of the process groups to formally close the project or a project phase
- Contract closure: Complete and settle each contract (including the resolution of any open items) and close each contract applicable to the project or project phase.

Project Controlling and Project Control Systems

Project controlling should be established as an independent function in project management. It implements verification and controlling function during the processing of a project in order to reinforce the defined performance and formal goals. The tasks of project controlling are also:

- creation of infrastructure for the supply of the right information and its update
- establishment of a way to communicate disparities of project parameters
- development of project information technology based on an intranet or the determination of a project key performance index system (KPI)
- divergence analyses and generation of proposals for potential project regulations
- the establishment of methods to accomplish an appropriate the project structure, project workflow organization, project control and governance
- creation of transparency among the project parameters

Fulfillment and implementation of these tasks can be achieved by applying specific methods and instruments of project controlling. The following methods of project controlling can be applied:

- investment analysis
- cost-benefit analyses
- value benefit Analysis
- expert surveys
- simulation calculations
- risk profile analyses
- surcharge calculations
- milestone trend analysis
- cost trend analysis
- target/actual-comparison

Project control is that element of a project that keeps it on-track, on-time and within budget. Project control begins early in the project with planning and ends late in the project with post-implementation review, having a thorough involvement of each step in the process. Each project should be assessed for the appropriate level of control needed: too much control is too time consuming, too little control is very risky. If project control is not implemented correctly, the cost to the business should be clarified in terms of errors, fixes, and additional audit fees. Control systems are needed for cost, risk, quality, communication, time, change, procurement, and human resources.

In addition, auditors should consider how important the projects are to the financial statements, how reliant the stakeholders are on controls, and how many controls exist. Auditors should review the development process and procedures for how they are implemented. The process of development and the quality of the final product may also be assessed if needed or requested. A business may want the auditing firm to be involved throughout the process to catch problems earlier on so that they can be fixed more easily. An auditor can serve as a controls consultant as part of the development team or as an independent auditor as part of an audit. Businesses sometimes use formal systems development processes. These help assure that systems are developed successfully.

A formal process is more effective in creating strong controls, and auditors should review this process to confirm that it is well designed and is followed in practice. A good formal systems development plan outlines:

- A strategy to align development with the organization's broader objectives
- Standards for new systems
- Project management policies for timing and budgeting
- Procedures describing the process
- Evaluation of quality of change

Topics

Project Managers

A project manager is a professional in the field of project management. Project managers can have the responsibility of the planning, execution, and closing of any project, typically relating to construction industry, engineering, architecture, computing, or telecommunications. Many other fields in the production engineering and design engineering and heavy industrial also have project managers. A project manager is the person accountable for accomplishing the stated project objectives. Key project management responsibilities include creating clear and attainable project objectives, building the project requirements, and managing the triple constraint for projects, which is cost, time, and scope. A project manager is often a client representative and has to determine and implement the exact needs of the client, based on knowledge of the firm they are representing. The ability to adapt to the various internal procedures of the contracting party, and to form close links with the nominated representatives, is essential in ensuring that the key issues of cost, time, quality and above all, client satisfaction, can be realized.

Project Management Triangle

Like any human undertaking, projects need to be performed and delivered under certain constraints. Traditionally, these constraints have been listed as "scope," "time," and "cost". These are also referred to as the "project management triangle", where each side represents a constraint. One side of the triangle cannot be changed without affecting the others. A further refinement of the constraints separates product "quality" or "performance" from scope, and turns quality into a fourth constraint. The time constraint refers to the amount of time available to complete a project. The cost constraint refers to the budgeted amount available for the project.

The scope constraint refers to what must be done to produce the project's end result. These three constraints are often competing constraints: increased scope typically means increased time and increased cost, a tight time constraint could mean increased costs and reduced scope, and a tight budget could mean increased time and reduced scope. The discipline of project management is about providing the tools and techniques that enable the project team (not just the project manager) to organize their work to meet these constraints.

Work Breakdown Structure

The work breakdown structure (WBS) is a tree structure, which shows a subdivision of effort required to achieve an objective; for example a program, project, and contract. The WBS may be hardware, product, service, or process oriented. A WBS can be developed by starting with the end objective and successively subdividing it into manageable components in terms of size, duration, and responsibility (e.g., systems, subsystems, components, tasks, subtasks, and work packages), which include all steps necessary to achieve the objective. The work breakdown structure provides a common framework for the natural development of the overall planning and control of a contract and is the basis for dividing work into definable increments from which the statement of work can be developed and technical, schedule, cost, and labor hour reporting can be established.

Project Management Framework

The Program (Investment) Life Cycle integrates the project management and system development life cycles with the activities directly associated with system deployment and operation. By design, system operation management and related activities occur after the project is complete and are not documented within this guide. In the US United States Department of Veterans Affairs (VA) the program management life cycle is depicted and describe in the overall VA IT Project Management Framework to address the integration of OMB Exhibit 300 project (investment) management activities and the overall project budgeting process.

The VA IT Project Management Framework diagram illustrates Milestone 4 which occurs following the deployment of a system and the closing of the project. The project closing phase activities at the VA continues through system deployment and into system operation for the purpose of illustrating and describing the system activities the VA considers part of the project. The figure illustrates the actions and associated artifacts of the VA IT Project and Program Management process.

International Standards

There have been several attempts to develop Project Management standards, such as:

- Capability Maturity Model from the Software Engineering Institute.
- GAPPS, Global Alliance for Project Performance Standards- an open source standard describing COMPETENCIES for project and program managers.
- A Guide to the Project Management Body of Knowledge
- HERMES method, Swiss general project management method, selected for use in Luxembourg and international organizations.
- The ISO standards ISO 9000, a family of standards for quality management systems, and the ISO 10006:2003, for Quality management systems and guidelines for quality management in projects.
- PRINCE2, PRojects IN Controlled Environments.
- Team Software Process (TSP) from the Software Engineering Institute.
- Total Cost Management Framework, AACE International's Methodology for Integrated Portfolio, Program and Project Management)
- V-Model, an original systems development method.
- The Logical framework approach, which is popular in international development organizations.

- IAPPM, The International Association of Project & Program Management, guide to Project Auditing and Rescuing Troubled Projects.

Project Portfolio Management

An increasing number of organizations are using, what is referred to as, project portfolio management (PPM) as a means of selecting the right projects and then using project management techniques as the means for delivering the outcomes in the form of benefits to the performing private or not-for-profit organization.

ATTENTION MANAGEMENT

Attention management refers to models and tools for supporting the management of attention at the individual or at the collective level (cf. attention economy), and at the short-term (quasi real time) or at a longer term (over periods of weeks or months).

Approaches for Attention Support

Different studies have been conducted in using ICT for supporting attention, and in particular, models have been elaborated for supporting attention (Davenport, Beck 2001) (Roda & Nabeth 2008). Supporting the management of attention objective is to bring a certain number of solutions to:

- people perception cognitive limitations, such as the limited capacity of the human short-term memory (a maximum number of 7 items ±2 can be managed at a given time), or the theoretical cognitive limit to the number of people with whom one can maintain stable social relationships (the Dunbar's number of 150).
- information overload
- social interaction overload (that may for instance originate from the online social networking services from which people get a lot of solicitations)
- interruption (Kebinger 2005)
- multitasking (Rosen 2008)

Tools can been designed for supporting attention:

- at the organizational level, by supporting organization processes (Apostolou, Karapiperis & Stojanovic 2008)
- at the collective level

- at the individual level, for instance using attentive user interfaces (Vertegaal 2003) (Vertegaal et al. 2006) (Huberman & Wu 2008).
- at the individual level by helping people to assess and analyze their attention related practices (for instance with the tool AttentionScape (Davenport, Beck 2001)).

These tools are often adaptive hypermedia, and often rely on profiling the user (Nabeth 2008) in order determine how to better support people's attention.

Projects

A certain number of projects have been conducted to investigate how to use ICT to support attention such as:

- AtGentive – Attentive Agents for Collaborative Learners.
- SAKE – Semantic-enabled Agile Knowledge-based eGovernment (IST 027128)
- SUITOR (Maglio et al. 2000)

PERSONAL KNOWLEDGE MANAGEMENT

Personal knowledge management (PKM) refers to a collection of processes that an individual carries out to gather, classify, store, search, retrieve, and share knowledge in his/her daily activities (Grundspenkis 2007) and how these processes support work activities (Wright 2005). It is a response to the idea that knowledge workers increasingly need to be responsible for their own growth and learning (Smedley 2009) and represents a bottom-up approach to knowledge management, as opposed to more traditional, top-down KM (Pollard 2008).

History and Background

Although as early as 1998 Davenport wrote on the importance to worker productivity of understanding individual knowledge processes (cited in (Zhang 2009)), the term *personal knowledge management* appears to be relatively new. Its origin can be traced in a working paper by Frand and Hixon (Frand & Hixon 1999). PKM integrates personal information management (PIM), focused on individual skills, with knowledge management (KM) in addition to input from a variety of disciplines such as cognitive psychology, management, and philosophy (Pauleen 2009). From an organizational perspective, understanding of the field has developed in light of expanding knowledge about human cognitive capabilities and the permeability of organizational boundaries. From a metacognitive perspective, it compares various modalities within human cognition as to their competence and efficacy (Sheridan 2008). It is an underresearched area (Pauleen 2009).

PKM Models

Dorsey (2000) identified information retrieval, assessment and evaluation, organization, analysis, presentation, security, and collaboration as essential to PKM (cited in (Zhang 2009)). Wright's model involves four interrelated domains: analytical, information, social, and learning. The analytical domain involves competencies such as interpretation, envisioning, application, creation, and contextualization. The information dimension comprises the sourcing, assessment, organization, aggregation, and communication of information. The social dimension involves finding and collaborating with people, development of both close networks and extended networks, and dialogue.

The learning dimension entails expanding pattern recognition and sensemaking capabilities, reflection, development of new knowledge, improvement of skills, and extension to others. This model stresses the importance of both bonding and bridging networks (Wright 2007). In Nonaka and Takeuchi's SECI model of knowledge creation, knowledge can be tacit or explicit, with the interaction of the two resulting in new knowledge (Nonaka & Takeuchi 1995). Smedley has developed a PKM model based on Nonaka and colleagues' model in which an expert provides direction and a community of practice provides support for personal knowledge creation (Smedley 2009). Trust is central to knowledge sharing in this model.

Nonaka has recently returned to his earlier work in an attempt to further develop his ideas about knowledge creation (Nonaka & von Krogh 2009) Personal knowledge management can also be viewed along two main dimensions, personal knowledge and personal management (Zhang 2009). Zhang has developed a model of PKM in relation to organizational knowledge management (OKM) that considers two axes of knowledge properties and management perspectives, either organizational or personal. These aspects of organizational and personal knowledge are interconnected through the OAPI process (organizationalize, aggregate, personalize, and individualize), whereby organizational knowledge is personalized and individualized and personal knowledge is aggregated and operationalized as organizational knowledge (Zhang 2009).

Criticisms of PKM

Not everyone agrees that the focus on the individual is a good thing, or that PKM is anything more than a new wrapper around personal information management (PIM). William Jones argues that only personal information as tangible resource can be managed, whereas personal knowledge cannot. Dave Snowden has asserted that most individuals cannot manage their knowledge in the traditional sense of "managing" and has advocated thinking in terms of sensemaking rather than PKM (Snowden & Pauleen 2008). Most notably, some argue that knowledge is never an individual product - that it emerges through connections, dialog and social interaction.

However, in Wright's model, PKM involves the application to problem solving of analytical, information, social, and learning dimensions, which are interrelated (Wright 2007), and so is inherently social. An aim of PKM is "helping individuals to be more effective in personal, organizational and social environments" ((Pauleen 2009), p. 221), often through the use of technology such as networking software. It has been argued, however, that equation of PKM with technology has limited the value and utility of the concept (e.g., (Pollard 2008) (Snowden & Pauleen 2008)).

PKM Skills

Skills associated with personal knowledge management.

- Reflection. Continuous improvement on how the individual operates.
- Manage learning. Manage how and when the individual learns.
- Information literacy. Understanding what information is important and how to find unknown information.
- Organizational skills. Personal librarianship. Personal categorization and taxonomies.
- Networking with others. Knowing what your network of people knows. Knowing who might have additional knowledge and resources to help you
- Researching, canvassing, paying attention, interviewing and observational 'cultural anthropology' skills
- Communication skills. Perception, intuition, expression, visualization, and interpretation.
- Creative skills. Imagination, pattern recognition, appreciation, innovation, inference. Understanding of complex adaptive systems.
- Collaboration skills. Coordination, synchronization, experimentation, cooperation, and design.

PKM Tools

Some organizations are now introducing PKM 'systems' with some or all of four components:

- Just-in-time Canvassing - templates and e-mail canvassing lists that enable people to identify and connect with the appropriate experts and expertise quickly and effectively
- Knowledge harvesting - software tools that automatically collect appropriate knowledge residing on subject matter experts' hard drives
- Content management tools - taxonomy processes and desktop search tools that enable employees to subscribe to, find, organize, and publish information that resides on their desktops
- Personal Productivity Improvement - knowledge fairs and one-on-one training sessions to help each employee make more effective personal use of the knowledge, learning, and technology resources available in the context of their work

PKM has also been linked to these tools:

- social bookmarking and enterprise social bookmarking
- knowledge logs (K-logs)
- e-mail, calendars, task managers
- Online Web Assistants
- Wikis
  - o Desktop wikis
  - o Personal wikis
  - o Semantic Wikis

Other useful tools include Open Space Technology, cultural anthropology, stories and narrative, mindmaps, concept maps and eco-language, and single frames and similar visualization techniques. Individuals use these tools to capture and ideas, expertise, experience, opinions, or thoughts, and this 'voicing' will encourage cognitive diversity and promote free exchanges away from a centralized policed knowledge repository. The goal is to facilitate knowledge sharing and personal content management.

WORKING TIME

Working time is the period of time that an individual spends at paid occupational labor. Unpaid labors such as personal housework or caring for children/pets are not considered part of the working week. Many countries regulate the work week by law, such as stipulating minimum daily rest periods, annual holidays and a maximum number of working hours per week. Working time may vary from person to person often depending on location, culture, lifestyle choice, and the profitability of the individuals livelihood. For example someone who is supporting children and paying a large mortgage will need to work more hours to meet a basic cost of living than someone without children of the same earning power. As fewer people than ever are having children choosing part time is becoming more popular. Standard working hours (or normal working hours) refers to the legislation to limit the working hours per day, per week, per month or per year. If an employee needs to work overtime, the employer will need to pay overtime payments to employees as required in the law. Generally speaking, standard working hours of countries worldwide are around 40 to 44 hours per week, and the additional overtime payments are around 25% to 50% to the normal hourly payments. Maximum working hours refers to the maximum working hours of an employee. The employee cannot work more than the level specified in the maximum working hours law. Some economists have recommended moving to a 21 hour standard work week to address problems with unemployment, high carbon emissions, low well-being, entrenched inequalities, overworking, family care, and the general lack of free time. Actual work week lengths have been falling in the developed world.

Hunter-Gatherer

Since the 1960s, the consensus among anthropologists, historians, and sociologists has been that early hunter-gatherer societies enjoyed more leisure time than is permitted by capitalist and agrarian societies; For instance, one camp of !Kung Bushmen was estimated to work two-and-a-half days per week, at around 6 hours a day. Aggregated comparisons show that on average the working day was less than five hours. Subsequent studies in the 1970s examined the Machiguenga of the Upper Amazon and the Kayapo of Northern Brazil. These studies expanded the definition of work beyond purely hunting-gathering activities, but the overall average across the hunter-gatherer societies he studied was still below 4.86, while the maximum was below 8 hours. Popular perception is still aligned with the old academic consensus that hunter-gatherers worked far in-excess of modern human's forty-hour week.

History

The industrial revolution made it possible for a larger segment of the population to work year-round, because this labor was not tied to the season and artificial lighting made it possible to work longer each day. Peasants and farm laborers moved from rural areas to factories, and working time during the year increased significantly. Before collective bargaining and worker protection laws, there was a financial incentive for a company to maximize the return on expensive machinery by having long hours. Records indicate that work schedules as long as twelve to sixteen hours per day, six to seven days per week were practiced in some industrial sites.

The automobile manufacturer, Henry Ford, was an ardent proponent of shorter work hours, which he introduced unilaterally in his own factories. Ford stated that he pursued this policy for business rather than humanitarian reasons. He believed that workers (who were also the main consumers of products) needed adequate leisure time to consume products and thus perceive a need to purchase them. Recent articles supporting a four-day week have argued that reduced work hours would increase consumption and invigorate the economy. However, other articles actually state that consumption would decrease. Other arguments for the four-day week include improvements to worker's level of education (due to having extra time to take classes and courses) and improvements to worker's health (less work-related stress and extra time for exercise). Reduced hours also save money on day care costs and transportation, which in turn helps the environment with less carbon-related emissions. These benefits increase workforce productivity on a per-hour basis.

Over the 20th century, work hours declined by almost half, mostly due to rising wages brought about by renewed economic growth, with a supporting role from trade unions, collective bargaining, and progressive legislation. The workweek, in most of the industrialized world, dropped steadily, to about forty hours after World War II. The decline continued at a faster pace in Europe: for example, France adopted a 35-hour workweek in 2000. In 1995, China adopted a 40-hour week, eliminating half-day work on Saturdays (though this is not widely practiced). Working hours in industrializing economies like South Korea, though still much higher than the leading industrial countries, are also declining steadily.

Technology has also continued to improve worker productivity, permitting standards of living to rise as hours declined. In developed economies, as the time needed to manufacture goods has declined, more working hours have become available to provide services, resulting in a shift of much of the workforce between sectors. Economic growth in monetary terms tends to be concentrated in health care, education, government, criminal justice, corrections, and other activities that are regarded as necessary for society rather than those that contribute directly to the production of material goods. In the mid-2000s, the Netherlands was the first country to achieve an overall average working week of less than 30 hours.

Gradual Decrease in Working Hours

Most countries in the developed world have seen average hours worked decrease greatly. For example in the U.S in the late 19th century it was estimated that the average work week was over 60 hours per week. Today the average hours worked in the U.S is around 33, with the average man employed full-time for 8.4 hours per work day, and the average woman employed full-time for 7.7 hours per work day. The front runners for lowest average weekly work hours are the Netherlands with 27 hours, and France with 30 hours. At current rates the Netherlands is set to become the first country to reach an average work week under 21 hours. In a 2011 report of 26 OECD countries, Germany had the lowest average working hours per week at 25.6 hours.

The New Economics Foundation has recommended moving to a 21 hour standard work week to address problems with unemployment, high carbon emissions, low well-being, entrenched inequalities, overworking, family care, and the general lack of free time. Actual work week lengths have been falling in the developed world.

Factors that have contributed to lowering average work hours and increasing standard of living have been:

- Technological advances in efficiency such as mechanization, robotics and information technology.
- The increase of women equally participating in making income as opposed to previously being commonly bound to homemaking and childrearing exclusively.
- Dropping fertility rates leading to fewer hours needed to be worked to support children.

9-to-5

9-to-5 is a phrase used to describe a conventional and possibly tedious job. Negatively used, it connotes a tedious or unremarkable occupation. The phrase also indicates that a person is an employee, usually in a large company, rather than self-employed. More neutrally, it connotes a job with stable hours and low career risk, but still a position of subordinate employment.

The phrase is an expression in the United States originating from the traditional American business hours of 9:00 a.m. to 5:00 p.m., Monday through Friday, representing a workweek of five eight-hour days composing 40 hours in total. The actual time at work often varies between 35 and 48 hours in practice due to the inclusion, or lack of inclusion, of breaks. In many traditional white collar positions, employees were required to be in the office during these hours to take orders from the bosses, hence the relationship between this phrase and subordination. Workplace hours have become more flexible, but even still the phrase is commonly used. The structure of the work week varies considerably for different professions and cultures. Among salaried workers in the western world, the work week often consists of Monday through Friday or Saturday with the weekend set aside as a time of personal work and leisure. Sunday is set aside in the western world because it is the Christian sabbath.

Several countries have adopted a workweek from Monday morning until Friday noon, either due to religious rules (observation of shabbat in Israel whose workweek is Sunday to Friday afternoon) or the growing predominance of a 35–37.5 hour workweek in continental Europe. Several of the Muslim countries have a standard Sunday through Thursday or Saturday through Wednesday workweek leaving Friday for religious observance, and providing breaks for the daily prayer times.

Differences among Countries and Regions

South Korea and Japan

South Korea has the fastest declining working time in the OECD, which is the result of the government's proactive move to lower working hours at all levels to increase leisure and relaxation time, which introduced the mandatory forty-hour, five-day working week in 2004 for companies with over 1,000 employees. This expanded to companies with 300 employees or more in 2005, 100 employees or more in 2006, 50 or more in 2007, 20 or more in 2008 and a full inclusion to all workers nationwide in July 2011. The government has continuously increased public holidays to 16 days in 2013, more than the 10 days of the United States and double that of Britain's 8 days.

Work hours in Japan are decreasing, but many Japanese still work long hours. Recently, Japan's Ministry of Health, Labor and Welfare (MHLW) has issued a draft report recommending major changes to regulations that govern working hours. The centerpiece of the proposal is an exemption from overtime pay for white-collar workers.Japan enacts an 8-hour work day and 40-hour work week (44 hours in specified workplace). The overtime hour limits are: 15 hours in a week, 27 hours in two weeks, 43 hours in four weeks, 45 hours in a month, 81 hours in two months and 120 hours in three months. They get around this by working several hours a day without 'clocking in' whether physically or metaphorically. The overtime allowance should not be lower than 125% and not more than 150% of normal hourly rate.

European Union

In most European Union countries, working time is gradually decreasing. The European Union's working time directive imposes a 48 hour maximum working week that applies to every member state except the United Kingdom and Malta (which have an opt-out meaning that UK-based employees may work longer than 48 hours if they wish, but they cannot be forced to do so). France has enacted a 35-hour workweek by law, and similar results have been produced in other countries such as Germany through collective bargaining. A major reason for the low annual hours worked in Europe is a relatively high amount of paid annual leave. Fixed employment comes with four to six weeks of holiday as standard. For example, in the UK, full time employees are entitled to 28 days paid leave a year.

Mexico

Mexican laws mandate a maximum of 48 hours of work per week, but they are rarely observed or enforced due to loopholes in the law, the volatility of labor rights in Mexico, and its underdevelopment relative to other members countries of the Organization for Economic Co-operation and Development (OECD). Indeed, private sector employees often work overtime without receiving overtime compensation. Fear of unemployment and threats by employers explain in part why the 48-hour work week is disregarded.

Colombia

Articles 161 to 167 of the Substantive Work Code in Colombia provides for a maximum of 48 hours of work a week.

Australia

In Australia, between 1974 and 1997 no marked change took place in the average amount of time spent at work by Australians of "prime working age" (that is, between 25 and 54 years of age). Throughout this period, the average time spent at work by prime working-age Australians (including those who did not spend any time at work) remained stable at between 27 and 28 hours per week. This unchanging average, however, masks a significant redistribution of work from men to women. Between 1974 and 1997, the average time spent at work by prime working-age Australian men fell from 45 to 36 hours per week, while the average time spent at work by prime working-age Australian women rose from 12 to 19 hours per week. In the period leading up to 1997, the amount of time Australian workers spent at work outside the hours of 9 a.m. to 5 p.m. on weekdays also increased.

In 2009, a rapid increase in the number of working hours was reported in a study by The Australia Institute. The study found the average Australian worked 1855 hours per year at work. According to Clive Hamilton of The Australia Institute, this surpasses even Japan. The Australia Institute believes that Australians work the highest number of hours in the developed world. From January 1, 2010, Australia enacted the new maximum weekly hour regulation under a new system created by the Fair Work Act 2009. Unless the additional hours are reasonable, the maximum weekly hours of work of a full-time employee is 38 hours.

United States

In 2006, the average man employed full-time worked 8.4 hours per work day, and the average woman employed full-time worked 7.7 hours per work day. There is no mandatory minimum amount of paid time off for sickness or holiday. However, regular, full-time workers often have the opportunity to take about nine days off for various holidays, two weeks (10 business days) of sick leave and two weeks (10 business days) of paid holiday time, with some workers receiving additional time after several years. Because of the pressure of working, time is increasingly viewed as a commodity.

Recent History

By 1946 the United States government had inaugurated the 40-hour work week for all federal employees. Beginning in 1950, under the Truman Administration, the United States became the first known industrialized nation to explicitly (albeit secretly) and permanently forswear a reduction of working time. Given the military-industrial requirements of the Cold War, the authors of the then secret National Security Council Report 68 (NSC-68) proposed the US government undertake a massive permanent national economic expansion that would let it "siphon off" a part of the economic activity produced to support an ongoing military buildup to contain the Soviet Union. In his 1951 Annual Message to the Congress, President Truman stated: In terms of manpower, our present defense targets will require an increase of nearly one million men and women in the armed forces within a few months, and probably not less than four million more in defense production by the end of the year. This means that an additional 8 percent of our labor force, and possibly much more, will be required by direct defense needs by the end of the year. These manpower needs will call both for increasing our labor force by reducing unemployment and drawing in women and older workers, and for lengthening hours of work in essential industries.

According to the Bureau of Labor Statistics, the average non-farm private sector employee worked 34.5 hours per week as of June 2012. As President Truman's 1951 message had predicted, the share of working women rose from 30 percent of the labor force in 1950 to 47 percent by 2000 – growing at a particularly rapid rate during the 1970s. According to a Bureau of Labor Statistics report issued May 2002, "In 1950, the overall participation rate of women was 34 percent ... The rate rose to 38 percent in 1960, 43 percent in 1970, 52 percent in 1980, and 58 percent in

1990 and reached 60 percent by 2000. The overall labor force participation rate of women is projected to attain its highest level in 2010, at 62 percent." The inclusion of women in the work force can be seen as symbolic of social progress as well as of increasing American productivity and hours worked. Between 1950 and 2007 official price inflation was measured to 861 percent. President Truman, in his 1951 message to Congress, predicted correctly that his military buildup "will cause intense and mounting inflationary pressures." Using the data provided by the United State Bureau of Labor Statistics, Erik Rauch has estimated productivity to have increased by nearly 400%. According to Rauch, "if productivity means anything at all, a worker should be able to earn the same standard of living as a 1950 worker in only 11 hours per week." In the United States, the working time for upper-income professionals has increased compared to 1965, while total annual working time for low-skill, low-income workers has decreased. This effect is sometimes called the "leisure gap".

Overtime Rules

Many professional workers put in longer hours than the forty-hour standard. In professional industries like investment banking and large law firms, a forty-hour workweek is considered inadequate and may result in job loss or failure to be promoted. Medical residents in the United States routinely work long hours as part of their training. Workweek policies are not uniform in the U.S. Many compensation arrangements are legal, and three of the most common are *wage*, *commission*, and *salary* payment schemes. Wage earners are compensated on a per-hour basis, whereas salaried workers are compensated on a per-week or per-job basis, and commission workers get paid according to how much they produce or sell. Under most circumstances, wage earners and lower-level employees may be legally required by an employer to work more than forty hours in a week; however, they are paid extra for the additional work. Many salaried workers and commission-paid sales staff are not covered by overtime laws. These are generally called "exempt" positions, because they are exempt from federal and state laws that mandate extra pay for extra time worked. The rules are complex, but generally exempt workers are executives, professionals, or sales staff. For example, school teachers are not paid extra for working extra hours. Business owners and independent contractors are considered self-employed, and none of these laws apply to them.

Generally, workers are paid *time-and-a-half*, or 1.5 times the worker's base wage, for each hour of work past forty. California also applies this rule to work in excess of eight hours per day. In some states, firms are required to pay *double-time*, or twice the base rate, for each hour of work past 60, or each hour of work past 12 in one day in California. This provides an incentive for companies to limit working time, but makes these additional hours more desirable for the worker. It is not uncommon for overtime hours to be accepted voluntarily by wage-earning workers. Unions often treat overtime as a desirable commodity when negotiating how these opportunities shall bc partitioned among union members.

China

China enacts a 44-hour normal working week, 150% overtime payment with reference to the normal hourly pay, and a maximum of 48 hours of work per week. But in reality the law is rarely, if ever, enforced. Most people in China work much more than 44 hours per week, and when they work on weekends or on national holidays, they typically don't get any overtime payment.

Hong Kong

Until now, Hong Kong has no legislations regarding maximum and normal working hours. The average weekly working hours of full-time employees in Hong Kong is 49 hours. According to the Price and Earnings Report 2012 conducted by UBS, while the global and regional average were 1,915 and 2,154 hours per year respectively, the average working hours in Hong Kong is 2,296 hours per year, which ranked the fifth longest yearly working hours among 72 countries under study. In addition, from the survey conducted by the Public Opinion Study Group of the University of Hong Kong, 79% of the respondents agree that the problem of overtime work in Hong Kong is "severe", and 65% of the respondents support the legislation on the maximum working hours. In Hong Kong, 70% of surveyed do not receive any overtime remuneration. These show that people in Hong Kong concerns the working time issues. As Hong Kong implemented the minimum wage law in May 2011, the Chief Executive, Donald Tsang, of the Special Administrative Region pledged that the government will standardize working hours in Hong Kong.

On 26 November 2012, the Labour Department of the HKSAR released the "Report of the policy study on standard working hours". The report covers three major areas, including: (1) the regimes and experience of other places in regulating working hours, (2)latest working time situations of employees in different sectors, and (3) estimation of the possible impact of introducing standard working hour in Hong Kong. Under the selected parameters, from most loosen to most stringent, the estimated increase in labour cost vary from 1.1 billion to 55 billion HKD, and affect 957,100 (36.7% of total employees)to 2,378,900 (91.1%of total) employees. Various sectors of the community show concerns about the standard working hours in Hong Kong. The points are summarized as below:

Singapore

Singapore enacts an 8-hour normal work day, a 44-hour normal working week, and a maximum 48-hour work week. It is to note that if the employee works no more than five days a week, the employee's normal working day is 9-hour and the working week is 44 hours. Also, if the number of hours worked of the worker is less than 44 hours every alternate week, the 44-hour weekly limit may be exceeded in the other week. Yet, this is subjected to the pre-specification in the service contract and the maximum should not exceed 48 hours per week or 88 hours in any consecutive two week time. In addition, a shift worker can work up to 12 hours a day, provided that the average working hours per week do not exceed 44 over a consecutive 3-week time. The overtime allowance per overtime hour must not be less than 1.5 times of the employee's hour basic rates.

Other Countries

The Kapauku people of Papua think it is bad luck to work two consecutive days. The !Kung Bushmen work just two-and-a-half days per week, rarely more than six hours per day. The work week in Samoa is approximately 30 hours, and though average annual Samoan cash income is relatively low, by some measures, the Samoan standard of living is quite good. In India at the managerial level, particularly in smaller companies, someone generally works for 11 hours a day and 6 days a week. A typical office will open at 09:00 or 09:30 and officially end the work day at about 19:00. However, many workers and especially managers will stay later in the office due to additional work load. However, large Indian companies and MNC offices located in India tend to follow a 5-day, 8- to 9-hour per day working schedule. The Government of India in some of its offices also follows a 5-day week schedule. Nigeria has public servants work 35 hours per week. The work time in Brazil is 44 hours per week, usually 8 hours per day and 4 hours on Saturday or 8.8 hours per day, on duty jobs are 6 hours per day.

Recent Trends

Many modern workplaces are experimenting with accommodating changes in the workforce and the basic structure of scheduled work. Flextime allows office workers to shift their working time away from rush-hour traffic; for example, arriving at 10:00 am and leaving at 6:00 pm. Telecommuting permits employees to work from their homes or in satellite locations (not owned by the employer), eliminating or reducing long commute times in heavily populated areas. Zero-hour contracts establish work contracts without minimum-hour guarantees; workers are paid only for the hours they work.

Points in Favour of and against Standard Working Hours

Points in favour of standard working hours

- Longer working hours can result in higher pay
  - o Overtime pay boosts income
- Promote work-life balance
  - o Enjoy family life
  - o Increased time for leisure and resto
- Beneficial to health
  - o Can have more time to pursue further studies

Points against standard working hours

- Increased costs of running businesses
  - o Employers may use various measures to offset the cost increases, such as:
    - lowering average hourly/annual compensation
    - using part-time rather than full-time employees
    - lowering or canceling year-end bonuses, etc.
- When employees are forced to work part-time jobs, they may need to acquire additional employment to maintain standard of living.
- Lower production output
- Extend retirement age, the lifelong work hour may not change
- Standard working hours favour employer needs and can cause issues with achieving work-life balance.
- Forces employees to work overtime in some situations
- Appropriate standard working hours can vary across different industries based on the type of work performed.
  - o Certain professional positions are difficult to define in terms of appropriate working hours.
  - o May need different exclusions
- Issues can arise with employers expecting employees to work extra hours "off the clock" in order to keep costs down.

Agenda-Setting Theory

Agenda-setting theory describes the "ability [of the news media] to influence the salience of topics on the public agenda." That is, if a news item is covered frequently and prominently the audience will regard the issue as more important. Agenda-setting theory was formally developed by Dr. Max McCombs and Dr. Donald Shaw in a study on the 1968 presidential election. In the 1968 "Chapel Hill study," McCombs and Shaw demonstrated a strong correlation ($r > .9$) between what 100 residents of Chapel Hill, North Carolina thought was the most important election issue and what the local and national news media reported was the most important issue. By comparing the salience of issues in news content with the public's perceptions of the most important election issue, McCombs and Shaw were able to determine the degree to which the media determines public opinion. Since the 1968 study, published in a 1972 edition of *Public Opinion Quarterly*, more than 400 studies have been published on the agenda-setting function of the mass media, and the theory continues to be regarded as relevant.

Core Assumptions and Statements

Agenda-setting is the creation of public awareness and concern of salient issues by the news media. Two basic assumptions underlie most research on agenda-setting:

1. the press and the media do not reflect reality; they filter and shape it;
2. media concentration on a few issues and subjects leads the public to perceive those issues as more important than other issues.

One of the most critical aspects in the concept of an agenda-setting role of mass communication is the time frame for this phenomenon. In addition, different media have different agenda-setting potential.

The Cognitive Effects of Agenda-Setting

Agenda setting occurs through a cognitive process known as "accessibility." Accessibility implies that the more frequently and prominently the news media cover an issue, the more instances of that issue become accessible in audience's memories. When respondents are asked what the most important problem facing the country is, they answer with the most accessible news issue in memory, which is typically the issue the news media focused on the most. The agenda-setting effect is not the result of receiving one or a few messages but is due to the aggregate impact of a very large number of messages, each of which has a different content but all of which deal with the same general issue. Mass-media coverage in general and agenda-setting in particular also has a powerful impact on what individuals think that other people are thinking, and hence they tend to allocate more importance to issues that have been extensively covered by mass media. This is also called schemata theory.

Agenda-Setting vs. Agenda-Building

As more scholars published articles on agenda-setting theories it became evident that the process involves not only active role of media organizations, but also participation of the public as well as policymakers. Rogers and Dearing described the difference between agenda-setting and agenda-building based on the dominant role of media or public. Thus "setting" an agenda refers to the effect of the media agenda on society, transfer of the media agenda to the public agenda, while "building" an agenda includes "some degree of reciprocity" between the mass media and society where both media and public agendas influence public policy.

Berkowitz has implemented a more nuanced analysis of agenda-setting and agenda-building theories by introducing the terms policy agenda-setting and policy agenda-building. He argues that when scholars investigate only the linkage between media and policymakers, it is still appropriate to use the notion of policy agenda-setting. However, when the focus is placed not only on policymakers' personal agendas, but also on the broader salient issues where media represent only one indicator of public sentiment, Berkowitz suggests talking about policy agenda-building.

Three Types of Agenda-Setting

Rogers and Dearing identify three types of agenda setting:

1. public agenda setting, in which the public's agenda is the dependent variable (the traditional hypothesis)
2. media agenda setting, in which the media's agenda is treated as the dependent variable (aka agenda building)
3. policy agenda setting, in which elite policy makers' agendas are treated as the dependent variable (aka political agenda setting)

Mass communication research, Rogers and Dearing argue, has focused a great deal on public agenda setting - e.g., McCombs and Shaw, 1972 - and media agenda setting, but has largely ignored policy agenda setting, which is studied primarily by political scientists. As such, the authors suggest mass communication scholars pay more attention to how the media and public agendas might influence elite policy maker's agendas (i.e., scholars should ask where the President or members of the U.S. Congress get their news from and how this affects their policies). Writing in 2006, Walgrave and Van Aelst took up Rogers and Dearing's suggestions, creating a preliminary theory of political agenda setting, which examines factors that might influence elite policy makers' agendas.

Research

The Audience-Contingent Effects of Agenda-Setting

In an attempt to overcome mirror-image effects of agenda-setting that implied direct influence of media agenda on the audience, several scholars proposed that the model of agenda-setting should include individual/collective audience characteristics and/or real-world conditions that are likely to affect issue importance. They discovered that certain individual and group characteristics are likely to act as contingent conditions of media impact and proposed a model of "audience effects". According to the audience effects model media coverage interacts with the audience's pre-existing sensitivities to produce changes in issue concerns. Thus media effects are contingent on issue-specific audience characteristics. For instance, for high-sensitivity audiences who are most affected by a certain issue or a problem, the salience of this issue increases substantially with news exposure, while the same exposure has little effect on other groups. Erbring, Goldenberg and Miller have also demonstrated that people who do not talk about political issues are more subject to agenda-setting influence because they depend more heavily on media content than those who receive information from other sources, including their colleagues and friends.

Another factor that causes variations in the correlation between the media and public agenda is whether an issue is "obtrusive" or "unobtrusive" or in other terms have high or low issue threshold. Obtrusive or issues with low threshold are generally the ones that affect nearly everyone and with which we can have some kind of personal experience (e.g. city-wide crime or inflation at the gas pump). Because of their link to personal concerns, these issues almost compel attention from political elites as well as the news media. Moreover, with this type of issues the problem would be of general concern even without attention from the news media. Unobtrusive or high threshold issues are those issues that are generally remote from just about everyone (e.g. wrongdoing high up in the government like Watergate, plight of refugees from Syria). Research performed by Zucker suggests that an issue is obtrusive if most members of the public have had direct contact with it, and less obtrusive if audience members have not had direct experience. This means that the less direct experience people have with an issue, the greater is the news media's influence on public opinion on that issue

Moreover, unobtrusive or high threshold issues do not pertain into media agenda as quickly as obtrusive issues and therefore require a buildup, which is a function of more than the amount of space and/or time the media devote to the story. The latter may push the story past the threshold of inattention, but it is also important to look at the kind of coverage to explain how a certain incident becomes an issue.

Role of Policymakers in Agenda-Setting Process

Some groups have a greater ease of access than others and are thus more likely to get their demands placed on agenda than others. For instance, policymakers have been found to be more influential than the overall group of news sources because they often better understand journalists' needs for reliable and predictable information and their definition of newsworthiness. Cobb and Elder ascribed even more importance to decision makers, claiming that in order for an issue to attain agenda status, it must be supported by at least some of key decision makers as they act as guardians of the formal agenda. They also asserted that certain personages in the media can act as opinion leaders and bring media coverage to a particular issue. Government-affiliated news sources have higher success rates in becoming media agenda and have been found by a number of scholars to be the most frequently appearing of sources at the local, state, and national levels.

News sources can also provide definitions of issues, thus determining the terms of future discussion and framing problems in particular ways. What interpretation of "reality" will dominate public discourse has implications for the future of the social problem, for the interest groups and policymakers involved, and for the policy itself. For example, Gusfield argues that the highway deaths associated with alcohol consumption can be interpreted as a problem of irresponsible drunken drivers, insufficient automobile crash-worthiness, a transportation system overly dependent on cars, poor highway design, excessive emphasis on drinking in adult social life. Different ways of framing the situation may compete to be accepted as an authoritative version of reality, consequently spurring competition between sources of information for definition of an issue. Very powerful resources of information can even influence whether an issue receives media attention at all.

The relationship of media and policymakers is symbiotic and is controlled by shared culture of unofficial set of ground rules as journalists need access to official information and policymakers need media coverage; nevertheless the needs of journalists and policymakers are often incompatible because of their different orientation in time as powerful sources are at their best in routine situations and react more slowly when crisis or disaster occur. Consequently, policymakers who understand the rules of this culture the best will be most capable of setting their agendas and issue definitions. On the other hand, media also influence policymakers when government officials and politicians take the amount of media attention given to an issue as an indirect expression of public interest in the issue.

Need for Orientation

Agenda-setting studies typically show variability in the correlation between media and public agenda. To explain differences in the correlation, McCombs and colleagues created the concept of "need for orientation," which "describes individual differences in the desire for orienting cues and background information."

Two concepts: relevance and uncertainty, define an individual's need for orientation. Relevance suggests that an individual will not seek news media information if an issue is not personally relevant. Hence, if relevance is low, people will feel the need for less orientation. There are many issues in our country that are just not relevant to people, because they do not affect us. Many news organizations attempt to frame issues in a way that attempts to make them relevant to its audiences. This is their way of keeping their viewership/readership high. "Level of uncertainty is the second defining condition of need for orientation. Frequently, individuals already have all the information that they desire about a topic. Their degree of uncertainty is low." When issues are of high personal relevance and uncertainty low, the need to monitor any changes in those issues will be present and there will be a moderate the need for orientation. If at any point in time viewers/readers have high relevance and high uncertainty about any type of issue/event/election campaign there was a high need for orientation.

David Weaver(1977) adapted the concept of 'individual's need for orientation' defined regarding relevance and uncertainty. Research done by Weaver in 1977 suggested that individuals vary on their need for orientation. Need for orientation is a combination of the individual's interest in the topic and uncertainty about the issue. The higher levels of interest and uncertainty produce higher levels of need for orientation. So the individual would be considerably likely to be influenced by the media stories (psychological aspect of theory). Schonbach and Weaver(1985) 's study with a focus on need for orientation showed the strongest agenda setting effects at a moderate need for orientation(under conditions of low interest and high uncertainty).

Role of Public in Agenda-Building Process

The agenda-building perspective ascribes importance not only to mass media and policymakers, but also to social process, to mutually interdependent relation between the concerns generated in social environment and the vitality of governmental process. Thus according to

Cobb and Elder, the agenda-building framework makes allowances for continuing mass involvement and broaden the range of recognized influences on the public policy-making process. This idea of mass involvement has become more prominent with the advent of the Internet and its potential to make everyone a pamphleteer. Increase in the role of citizens in agenda setting sheds light on a new direction in the traditional agenda-building research.

Kim and Lee noted that the agenda-setting research on the Internet differs from traditional agenda-setting research with respect that the Internet is in competition with traditional media and has enormous capacity for contents' and users' interactivity. Lee, Lancendorfer and Lee argued that "various opinions about public issues are posted on the Internet bulletin boards or the Usenet newsgroup by Netizens, and the opinions then form an agenda in which other Netizens can perceive the salient issue". Scholars also stated that the Internet plays role in forming Internet user's opinion as well as the public space. Kim and Lee studied the pattern of the Internet mediated agenda-setting by conducting a case study of 10 cases that have a great ripple effect in Korea for 5 years (from 2000 until 2005). Scholars found that a person's opinion could be disseminated through various online channels and could synthesize public opinion that influences news coverage. Their study suggests 'reversed agenda effects', meaning that public agenda could set media agenda. Maxwell McCombs also mentioned "reverse agenda-setting" in his recent textbook as a situation where public concern sets the media agenda.

According to Kim and Lee, agenda-building through the Internet take the following three steps: 1) Internet-mediated agenda-rippling: an anonymous netizen's opinion spreads to the important agenda in the Internet through online main rippling channels such as blogs, personal homepages, and the Internet bulletin boards. 2) agenda diffusion in the Internet: online news or web-sites report the important agenda in the Internet that in turn leads to spreading the agenda to more online publics. 3) Internet-mediated reversed agenda-setting: traditional media report online agenda to the public so that the agenda spread to both offline and online publics.

However, scholars concluded that the Internet-mediated agenda-setting or agenda-building processes not always occur in consecutive order. For example, the agenda that was reported by traditional media can come to the fore again through the online discussion or the three steps can occur simultaneously in a short period of time. Several real-world examples provide evidence that the Internet-community, particularly bloggers, can push their own agenda into public agenda, then media agenda, and, eventually, into policy agenda. For instance, in 2005 Eason Jordan, the chief news executive at CNN, abruptly resigned after being besieged by the online community after saying, according to various witnesses, that he believed the United States military had aimed at journalists in Iraq and killed 12 of them. Similarly, in 2002 Senate majority leader Trent Lott had to resign due to his inappropriate racist remarks that were widely discussed in the blogosphere. However bloggers attract attention not only to oust journalists and politicians. An online investigation on technical problems with electronic voting machines started by an activist Bev Harris in 2003 eventually forced traditional media outlets to address issue of electronic voting malperformance. This in turn made Diebold, a company that produces these machines, to acknowledge its fault and take measures to fix it.

Framing or Second-Level Agenda-Setting?

As agenda setting theory has been developed, scholars pointed out attributes that describe the object. Each of the objects on an agenda has a lot of attributes containing cognitive components such as information that describes characteristics of the object, and an affective component including tones (positive, negative, neutral) of the characteristics on agenda. McCombs et al. (1998) demonstrated that agenda-setting research at the second level deals with the influence of 'attribute' salience, whereas the first level agenda-setting illustrates the influence of 'issue' salience. Balmas and Sheafer (2010) argued that the focus at the first level agenda-setting which emphasizes media's role in telling us "what to think about" is shifted to media's function of telling us "how to think about" at the second level agenda-setting. The second level of agenda-setting considers how the agenda of attributes affects public opinion (McCombs & Evatt, 1995). Furthermore, Ghanem(1997) demonstrated that the certain attributes agendas in the news with low psychological distance, drove compelling arguments for the salience of public agenda.

The second level agenda setting differs from traditional agenda setting in that it focus on attribute salience, and public's attribute agenda is regarded as one of the important variables. There is a debate over whether framing theory should be subsumed within agenda-setting as "second-level agenda-setting." McCombs, Shaw, Weaver and colleagues generally argue that framing is a part of agenda-setting that operates as a "second-level" or secondary effect. Dietram Schefuele has argued the opposite. Scheufele argues that framing and agenda-setting possess distinct theoretical boundaries, operate via distinct cognitive processes (accessibility vs. attribution), and relate to different outcomes (perceptions of issue importance vs. interpretation of news issue).

According to Weaver, framing and second-level agenda setting have the following characteristics:

Similarities:

- Both are more concerned with how issues or other objects are depicted in the media than with which issues or objects are more or less prominently reported.
- Both focus on most salient or prominent aspects of themes or descriptions of the objects of interest.
- Both are concerned with ways of thinking rather than objects of thinking

Difference:

- Framing does seem to include a broader range of cognitive processes – moral evaluations, causal reasoning, appeals to principle, and recommendations for treatment of problems – than does second-level agenda setting (the salience of attributes of an object)

Based on these shared characteristics, McCombs and colleagues recently argued that framing effects should be seen as the extension of agenda setting. In other words, according to them, the premise that framing is about selecting "a restricted number of thematically related attributes" for media representation can be understood as the process of transferring the salience of issue attributes (i.e., second-level agenda setting). That is, according to McCombs and colleagues' arguments, framing falls under the umbrella of agenda setting. According to Price and Tewksbury, however, agenda setting and framing are built on different theoretical premises: agenda setting is based on accessibility, while framing is concerned with applicability (i.e., the relevance between message features and one's stored ideas or knowledge). Accessibility-based explanation of agenda setting is also applied to second-level agenda setting. That is, transferring the salience of issue attributes (i.e., second-level agenda setting) is a function of accessibility.

For framing effects, empirical evidence shows that the impact of frames on public perceptions is mainly determined by perceived importance of specific frames rather than by the quickness of retrieving frames. That is, the way framing effects transpires is different from the way second-level agenda setting is supposed to take place (i.e., accessibility). On a related note, Scheufele and Tewksbury argues that, because accessibility and applicability vary in their functions of media effects, "the distinction between accessibility and applicability effects has obvious benefits for understanding and predicting the effects of dynamic information environments."

Taken together, it can be concluded that the integration of framing into agenda setting is either impossible because they are based on different theoretical premises or imprudent because merging the two concepts would result in the loss of our capabilities to explain various media effects.

Agenda Setting vs. Framing

Scheufele and Tewksbury argue that "framing differs significantly from these accessibility-based models [i.e., agenda setting and priming]. It is based on the assumption that how an issue is characterized in news reports can have an influence on how it is understood by audiences;" the difference between whether we think about an issue and how we think about it. Framing and agenda setting differs in their functions in the process of news production, information processing and media effects.

1. News production: Although "both frame building and agenda building refer to macroscopic mechanisms that deal with message construction rather than media effects," frame building is more concerned with the news production process than agenda building. In other words, "how forces and groups in society try to shape public discourse about an issue by establishing predominant labels is of far greater interest from a framing perspective than from a traditional agenda-setting one."
2. News processing: For framing and agenda setting, different conditions seem to be needed in processing messages to produce respective effects. Framing effect is more concerned with audience attention to news messages, while agenda setting is more with repeated exposure to messages.
3. Locus of effect: Agenda-setting effects are determined by the ease with which people can retrieve from their memory issues recently covered by mass media, while framing is the extent to which media messages fit ideas or knowledge people have in their knowledge store.

WORK–LIFE BALANCE

Work–life balance is a concept including proper prioritizing between "work" (career and ambition) and "lifestyle" (health, pleasure, leisure, family and spiritual development/meditation). Related, though broader, terms include "lifestyle calm balance" and "lifestyle choices".

History

The work-leisure dichotomy was invented in the mid-1800s. Paul Krassner remarked that anthropologists, use a definition of happiness that is to have as little separation as possible "between your work and your play". The expression "work–life balance" was first used in the United Kingdom in the late 1970s to describe the balance between an individual's work and personal life. In the United States, this phrase was first used in 1986. Most recently, there has been a shift in the workplace as a result of advances in technology. As Bowswell and Olson-Buchanan stated, "increasingly sophisticated and affordable technologies have made it more feasible for employees to keep contact with work". Employees have many methods, such as emails, computers, and cell phones, which enable them to accomplish their work beyond the physical boundaries of their office. Employees may respond to an email or a voice mail after-hours or during the weekend, typically while not officially "on the job". Researchers have found that employees who consider their work roles to be an important component of their identities will be more likely to apply these communication technologies to work while in their non-work domain.

Some theorists suggest that this blurred boundary of work and life is a result of technological control. Technological control "emerges from the physical technology of an organization". In other words, companies use email and distribute smartphones to enable and encourage their employees to stay connected to the business even when they are not in the office. This type of control, as Barker argues, replaces the more direct, authoritarian control, or simple control, such as managers and bosses. As a result, communication technologies in the temporal and structural aspects of work have changed, defining a "new workplace" in which employees are more connected to the jobs beyond the boundaries of the traditional workday and workplace.

The more this boundary is blurred, the higher work-to-life conflict is self-reported by employees. Many authors believe that parents being affected by work-life conflict will either reduce the number of hours one works where other authors suggest that a parent may run away from family life or work more hours at a workplace. This implies that each individual views work-life conflict differently. Employee assistance professionals say there are many causes for this situation ranging from personal ambition and the pressure of family obligations to the accelerating pace of technology.. According to a recent study for the Center for Work-Life Policy, 1.7 million people consider their jobs and their work hours excessive because of globalization.

Work Statistics

According to a survey conducted by the National Life Insurance Company, four out of ten U.S. employees state that their jobs are "very" or "extremely" stressful. Those in high-stress jobs are three times more likely than others to suffer from stress-related medical conditions and are twice as likely to quit. The study states that women, in particular, report stress related to the conflict between work and family. In the study, *Work-Family Spillover and Daily Reports of Work and Family Stress in the Adult Labor Force*, researchers found that with an increased amount of negative spillover from work to family, the likelihood of reporting stress within the family increased by 74%, and with an increased amount of negative spillover from family to work the likelihood to report stress felt at work increased by 47%.

Employee benefits in the United States –MARCH 2011 Paid leave benefits continued to be the most widely available benefit offered by employers, with paid vacations available to 91 percent of full-time workers in private industry in March 2011, the Bureau of Labor Statistics reported today. Access to these benefits, however, varied by employee and establishment characteristics. In private industry, paid vacation benefits were available to only 37 percent of part-time workers. Paid sick leave was available to 75 percent of full-time workers and 27 percent of part-time workers. Paid vacations were available to 90 percent of workers earning wages in the highest 10th percent of private industry employees and only to 38 percent of workers in the lowest 10 percent of private industry wage earners. Access to paid sick leave benefits ranged from 21 percent for the lowest wage category to 87 percent for the highest wage category. These data are from the National Compensation Survey (NCS), which provides comprehensive measures of compensation cost trends and incidence and provisions of employee benefit plans.

According to 2010 National Health Interview Survey Occupational Health Supplement data, 16% of U.S. workers reported difficulty balancing work and family. Imbalance was more prevalent among workers aged 30–44 (19%) compared with other age groups; non-Hispanic black workers

(19%) compared with non-Hispanic white workers (16%), and Hispanic workers (15%); divorced or separated workers (19%) compared with married workers (16%), widowed workers (13%), and never married workers (15%); and workers having a Bachelor's degree and higher (18%) compared with workers having a high school diploma or G.E.D. (16%), and workers with less than a high school education (15%). Workers in agriculture, forestry, fishing, and hunting industries (9%) had a lower prevalence rate of work-family imbalance compared to all employed adults (16%). Among occupations, a higher prevalence rate of work-family imbalance was found in legal occupations (26%), whereas a lower prevalence rate was observed for workers in office and administrative support (14%) and farming, forestry, and fishing occupations (10%).

Stress and Work-Life Balance

The number of stress-related disability claims by American employees has doubled according to the Employee Assistance Professionals Association in Arlington, Virginia. Seventy-five to ninety percent of physician visits are related to stress and, according to the American Institute of Stress, the cost to industry has been estimated at $200 billion-$300 billion a year. Steven L. Sauter, chief of the Applied Psychology and Ergonomics Branch of the National Institute for Occupational Safety and Health in Cincinnati, Ohio, states that recent studies show that "the workplace has become the single greatest source of stress". Michael Feuerstein, professor of clinical psychology at the Uniformed Services University of the Health Sciences at Bethesda Naval Hospital states, "We're seeing a greater increase in work-related neuroskeletal disorders from a combination of stress and ergonomic stressors". It is clear that problems caused by stress have become a major concern to both employers and employees. Symptoms of stress are manifested both physiologically and psychologically. Persistent stress can result in cardiovascular disease, sexual health problems, a weaker immune system and frequent headaches, stiff muscles, or backache. It can also result in poor coping skills, irritability, jumpiness, insecurity, exhaustion, and difficulty concentrating. Stress may also perpetuate or lead to binge eating, smoking, and alcohol consumption. According to James Campbell Quick, a professor of organizational behaviour at the University of Texas-Arlington, "The average tenure of presidents at land-grant universities in the past ten years has dropped from approximately seven to three-and-a-half years". The feeling that simply working hard is not enough anymore is acknowledged by many other American workers. "To get ahead, a seventy-hour work week is the new standard. What little time is left is often divvied up among relationships, kids, and sleep." [3] This increase in work hours over the past two decades means that less time will be spent with family, friends, and community as well as pursuing activities that one enjoys and taking the time to grow personally and spiritually.

Texas Quick, an expert witness at trials of companies who were accused of overworking their employees, states that "when people get worked beyond their capacity, companies pay the price." Although some employers believe that workers should reduce their own stress by simplifying their lives and making a better effort to care for their health, most experts feel that the chief responsibility for reducing stress should be management. According to Esther M. Orioli, president of Essi Systems, a stress management consulting firm, "Traditional stress-management programs placed the responsibility of reducing stress on the individual rather than on the organization-where it belongs. No matter how healthy individual employees are when they start out, if they work in a dysfunctional system, they'll burn out."

Formation of the "ideal worker" and Gender Differences

Work-life conflict is not gender-specific. According to the Center for American Progress, 90 percent of working mothers and 95 percent of working fathers report work-family conflict. However, because of the social norms surrounding each gender role, and how the organization views its ideal worker, men and women handle the work-life balance differently. Organizations play a large part in how their employees deal with work-life balance. Some companies have taken proactive measures in providing programs and initiatives to help their employees cope with work-life balance. Yet, the root of the work-life conflict may come from the organizational norms and ideologies. As a macro structure, the organization maintains the locus of power. Organizations, through its structure, practices, symbols and discourse, create and reproduce a dominant ideology. The dominant ideology is what drives organizational power and creates organizational norms. At the top of the organizational hierarchy, the majority of individuals are males, and assumptions can be made regarding their lack of personal experience with the direct and indirect effects of work-family conflict. For one, they may be unmarried and have no thought as to what "normal" family responsibilities entail. On the other hand, the high-level manager may be married, but his wife, due to the demands of the husband's position, has remained at home, tending solely to the house and children. Ironically, these are the individuals creating and reforming workplace policies. Workplace policies, especially regarding the balance between family/life and work, create an organizational norm in which employees must fall into. This type of organizational behaviour, according to Dennis Mumby, "contribut[es] in some ways to the structuring of organizational reality, and hence organizational power."

In other words, the reality of what employees experience, specifically in regards to work-life balance, is a direct result of power operating covertly through ideological controls. This is seen in the ideological norm of the "ideal worker." Many organizations view the ideal worker as one who is "committed to their work above all else". "Ideal workers" are those that demonstrate extra-role behaviours, which are seen as positive attributes.

Alternatively, those who are perceived as having to divide their time (and their commitments) are seen not as dedicated to the organization. As research has shown, a manager's perception of a subordinate's commitment to the organization is positively associated with the individual's promotability. Hoobler et al.'s (2009) findings mirrored the perceived commitment-to-promotabilty likelihood. Often, these perceptions are placed on the female worker. Managers who perceived their female employees of maintaining high work-family conflict were presumed as not as committed to the organization, therefore not worthy of advancement. This negatively impacts working mothers as they may be "inaccurately perceived to have less commitment to their organizations than their counterparts, their advancement in organizations may be unfairly obstructed". Working mothers often have to challenge perceptions and stereotypes that evolve as a working woman becomes a working mother. Working mothers are perceived as less competent and less worthy of training than childless women. Another study, focusing on professional jobs, found that mothers were 79 percent less likely to be hired and are typically held to a higher standard of punctuality and performance than childless women. The moment when she becomes a mother, a working woman is held at a completely different norm than her childless colleagues. In the same Cuddy et al. (2004) study, men who became fathers were not perceived as any less competent, and in fact, their perceived warmth increased.

The ways in which corporations have modeled the "ideal worker" does not compliment the family lifestyle, nor does it accommodate it. Long hours and near complete devotion to the profession makes it difficult for working mothers to participate in getting ahead in the workplace. A Fortune article found that among the most powerful women in business (female CEOs, presidents and managing directors of major corporations), 29 percent were childless compared to 90 percent of men who were parents (;). Should a woman seek a position of power within an organization, she must consider the toll on other facets of her life, including hobbies, personal relationships and families. As Jeffrey Pfeffer states: "Time spent on the quest for power and status is time you cannot spend on other things, such as ... family...The price seems to be particularly severe for women". Many executive jobs require a substantial amount of overtime, which as a mother, many cannot devote because of family obligations.

Consequently, it is nearly impossible for a working mother in a top management position to be the primary caretaker of her child.

Perceptions of Work-Life Balance and Gender Differences

This circumstance only increases the work-life balance stress experienced by many women employees. Research conducted by the Kenexa Research Institute (KRI), a division of Kenexa, evaluated how male and female workers perceive work-life balance and found that women are more positive than men in how they perceive their company's efforts to help them balance work and life responsibilities. The report is based on the analysis of data drawn from a representative sample of 10,000 U.S. workers who were surveyed through WorkTrends, KRI's annual survey of worker opinions. The results indicated a shift in women's perceptions about work-life balance. In the past, women often found it more difficult to maintain balance due to the competing pressures at work and demands at home.

"The past two decades have witnessed a sharp decline in men's provider role, caused in part by growing female labor participation and in part by the weakening of men's absolute power due to increased rates of unemployment and underemployment" states sociologist Jiping Zuo. She continues on to state that "Women's growing earning power and commitment to the paid workforce together with the stagnation of men's social mobility make some families more financially dependent on women. As a result, the foundations of the male dominance structure have been eroded."

Work-Life Balance Concerns of Men and Women Alike

Similar discrimination is experienced by men who take time off or reduce working hours for taking care of the family. For many employees today—both male and female—their lives are becoming more consumed with a host of family and other personal responsibilities and interests. Therefore, in an effort to retain employees, it is increasingly important for organizations to recognize this balance.

Young Generation Views on Work-Life Balance

According to Kathleen Gerson, Sociologist, young people "are searching for new ways to define care that do not force them to choose between spending time with their children and earning an income" and "are looking for definition of personal identity that do not pit their own development against creating committed ties to others" readily. Young adults believe that parents should get involved and support the children both economically and emotionally, as well as share labor equally. Young people do not believe work-life balance is possible and think it is dangerous to build a life dependent on another when relationships are unpredictable. They are looking for partners to share the house work and family work together. Men and women believe that women should have jobs before considering marriage, for better life and to be happy in marriage. Young people do not think their mother's generations were unhappy. They also do not think they were powerless because they were economically dependent.

Identity Through Work

By working in an organization, employees identify, to some extent, with the organization, as part of a collective group. Organizational values, norms and interests become incorporated in the self-concept as employees increase their identify with the organization. However, employees also identify with their outside roles, or their "true self". Examples of these might be parental/caretaker roles, identifications with certain groups, religious affiliations, align with certain values and morals, mass media etc. Employee interactions with the organization, through other employees, management, customers, or others, reinforces (or resists) the employee identification with the organization. Simultaneously, the employee must manage their "true self" identification. In other words, identity is "fragmented and constructed" through a number of interactions within and out of the organization; employees don't have just one self.

Most employees identify with not only the organization, but also other facets of their life (family, children, religion, etc.). Sometimes these identities align and sometimes they do not. When identities are in conflict, the sense of a healthy work-life balance may be affected. Organization members must perform identity work so that they align themselves with the area in which they are performing to avoid conflict and any stress as a result.

Women

Today there are many young women who do not want to just stay at home and do house work, but want to have careers. About 64% of mothers whose youngest child was under age six, and 77% of mothers with a youngest child age 6-17 were employed in 2010, indicating that the majority of women with dependent care responsibilities cannot or do not wish to give up careers. While women are increasingly represented in the work force, they still face challenges balancing work and home life. Both domestic and market labor compete for time and energy. "For women, the results show that that only time spent in female housework chores has a significant negative effect on wages".

Men

Men know that work alone may not provide their lives with meaning.

Young men can lose their meaning of life; they want a balance between paid work and personal attachments without being victimized at work. More men are realizing that work is not their only primary source of fulfillment from life. A new study on fatherhood (2010) shows that more men are looking for alternatives to their 40-hour workweek in order to spend more time with their family. Though working less means a smaller paycheck and higher stress levels, men are looking for flexibility just as much as women. However, with an ever-changing society, flexibility is becoming much more apparent. "It seems that some traditional stereotypes are starting to lessen just a bit in terms of who's responsible for care of the children" says human resource specialist Steve Moore. Traditionalism is becoming less frequent due to what's actually practical for each individual family. Men often face unequal opportunity to family life as they are often expected to be the financial supporter of the family unit, "The masculine ideal of a worker unencumbered by caregiving obligations is built into workplace structures and patterns of reward" (Thorne 2011).

Consequences of an Imbalance

Mental health is a balancing act that may be affected by four factors: the influence of unfavourable genes, by wounding trauma, by private pressures and most recently by the stress of working. Many people expose themselves unsolicited to the so-called job stress, because the "hard worker" enjoys a very high social recognition. These aspects can be the cause of an imbalance in the areas of life. But there are also other reasons which can lead to such an imbalance.

Remarkable is, for example, the increase in non-occupational activities with obligation character, which include mainly house and garden work, maintenance and support of family members or volunteer activities. All this can contribute to the perception of a chronic lack of time. This time pressure is, amongst others, influenced by their own age, the age and number of children in the household, marital status, the profession and level of employment as well as the income level. The psychological strain, which in turn affects the health, increases due to the strong pressure of time, but also by the complexity of work, growing responsibilities, concern for long-term existential protection and more. The mentioned stresses and strains could lead in the long term to irreversible, physical signs of wear as well as to negative effects on the human cardiovascular and immune systems. Prominent cultural beliefs that parenthood is the best avenue for a happy fulfilling life may not be justified. In, The Joys of Parenthood Reconsidered, what was found is the opposite, that parents actually suffer worse mental and physical health than childless adults. This is associated with the high costs of parenthood described in the article. Simon states that, "In America we lack institutional supports that would help ease the social and economic burdens associated with parenthood."

Psychoanalysts diagnose uncertainty as the dominant attitude to life in the postmodern society. This uncertainty can be caused by the pressure which is executed from the society to the humans. It is the uncertainty to fail, but also the fear of their own limits, not to achieve something what the society expects, and especially the desire for recognition in all areas of life. In today's society we are in a permanent competition. Appearance, occupation, education of the children - everything is compared to a media staged ideal. Everything should be perfect, because this deep-rooted aversion to all average, the pathological pursuit to excellence - these are old traditions. Who ever wants more - on the job, from the partner, from the children, from themselves - will one day be burned out and empty inside. He is then faced with the realization that perfection does not exist. Who is nowadays empty inside and burned out, is in the common language a Burnout. But due to the definitional problems Burnout is till this date not a recognized illness. An attempt to define this concept more closely, can be: a condition that gets only the passionate, that is certainly not a mental illness but only a grave exhaustion (but can lead to numerous sick days). It can benefit the term that it is a disease model which is socially acceptable and also, to some extent, the individual self-esteem stabilizing. This finding in turn facilitates many undetected depressed people, the way to a qualified treatment. According to experts in the field are, in addition to the ultra hard-working and the idealists mainly the perfectionist, the loner, the grim and the thin-skinned, especially endangered of a burnout. All together they usually have a lack of a healthy distance to work.

Another factor is also, that for example decision-makers in government offices and upper echelons are not allowed to show weaknesses or signs of disease etc., because this would immediately lead to doubts of the ability for further responsibility. Only 20% of managers (e.g. in Germany) do sports regularly and als only 2% keep regularly preventive medical check-up. In such a position other priorities seem to be set and the time is lacking for regular sports. Frightening is that the job has such a high priority, that people waive screening as a sign of weakness. In contrast to that, the burnout syndrome seems to be gaining popularity. There seems nothing to be ashamed to show weaknesses, but quite the opposite: The burnout is part of a successful career like a home for the role model family. Besides that the statement which describes the burnout as a "socially recognized precious version of the depression and despair that lets also at the moment of failure the self-image intact" fits and therefore concludes "Only losers become depressed, burnout against it is a diagnosis for winners, more precisely, for former winners." However, it is fact that four out of five Germans complain about too much stress.

One in six under 60 swallows at least once a week, a pill for the soul, whether it is against insomnia, depression or just for a bit more drive in the stressful everyday life. The phases of burnout can be described, among other things, first by great ambition, then follows the suppression of failure, isolation and finally, the cynical attitude towards the employer or supervisor. Concerned persons have very often also anxiety disorders and depressions, which are serious mental diseases. Depressions are the predominant causes of the nearly 10,000 suicides that occur alone each year in Germany. The implications of such imbalances can be further measured in figures: In 1993, early retirement due to mental illness still made 15.4 percent of all cases. In 2008, there were already 35.6 percent. Even in the days of illness, the proportion of failures due to mental disorders increased. Statisticians calculated that 41 million absent days in 2008 went to the account of these crises, which led to 3.9 billion euros in lost production costs.

Responsibility of the Employer

Companies have begun to realize how important the work-life balance is to the productivity and creativity of their employees. Research by Kenexa Research Institute in 2007 shows that those employees who were more favourable toward their organization's efforts to support work-life balance also indicated a much lower intent to leave the organization, greater pride in their organization, a willingness to recommend it as a place to work and higher overall job satisfaction.

Employers can offer a range of different programs and initiatives, such as flexible working arrangements in the form of part-time, casual and telecommuting work. More proactive employers can provide compulsory leave, strict maximum hours and foster an environment that encourages employees not to continue working after hours. It is generally only highly skilled workers that can enjoy such benefits as written in their contracts, although many professional fields would not go so far as to discourage workaholic behaviour. Unskilled workers will almost always have to rely on bare minimum legal requirements. The legal requirements are low in many countries, in particular, the United States. In contrast, the European Union has gone quite far in assuring a legal work-life balance framework, for example pertaining to parental leave and the non-discrimination of part-time workers. According to Stewart Friedman—professor of Management and founding director of the Wharton School's Leadership Program and of its Work/Life Integration Project—a "one size fits all" mentality in human resources management often perpetuates frustration among employees. "[It's not an] uncommon problem in many HR areas where, for the sake of equality, there's a standard policy that is implemented in a way that's universally applicable — [even though] everyone's life is different and everyone needs different things in terms of how to integrate the different pieces. It's got to be customized." Friedman's research indicates that the solution lies in approaching the components of work, home, community, and self as a comprehensive system. Instead of taking a zero-sum approach, Friedman's Total Leadership program teaches professionals how to successfully pursue "four-way wins"—improved performance across all parts of life.

Although employers are offering many opportunities to help their employees balance work and life, these opportunities may be a catch twenty-two for some female employees. Even if the organization offers part-time options, many women will not take advantage of it as this type of arrangement is often seen as "occupational dead end". Even with the more flexible schedule, working mothers opt not to work part-time because these positions typically receive less interesting and challenging assignments; taking these assignments and working part-time may hinder advancement and growth. Even when the option to work part-time is available, some may not take advantage of it because they do not want to be marginalized. This feeling of marginalization could be a result of not fitting into the "ideal worker" framework

Additionally, some mothers, after returning to work, experience what is called the maternal wall. The maternal wall is experienced in the less desirable assignments given to the returning mothers. It is also a sense that because these women are mothers, they cannot perform as "ideal workers". If an organization is providing means for working mothers and fathers to better balance their work-life commitments, the general organizational norm needs to shift so the "ideal worker" includes those who must manage a home, children, elderly parents, etc.

Global Comparisons

United States

According to a new study by Harvard and McGill University researchers, the United States lags far behind nearly all wealthy countries when it comes to family-oriented workplace policies such as maternity leave, paid sick days and support for breast feeding. Jody Heyman, founder of the Harvard-based Project on Global Working Families and director of McGill's Institute for Health and Social Policy, states that, "More countries are providing the workplace protections that millions of Americans can only dream of. The U.S. has been a proud leader in adopting laws that provide for equal opportunity in the workplace, but our work/family protections are among the worst." This observation is being shared by many Americans today and is considered by many experts to be indicative of the current climate. However, the U.S. Labor Department is examining regulations that give workers unpaid leave to deal with family or medical emergencies (a review that supporters of the FMLA worry might be a prelude to scaling back these protections, as requested by some business groups). At the same time, Senator Chris Dodd from Connecticut is proposing new legislation that would enable workers to take six weeks of paid leave. Congress is also expected to reconsider the Healthy Families Act which is a bill that would require employers with at least fifteen employees to provide seven paid sick days per year.

At least 107 countries protect working women's right to breast-feed and, in at least seventy-three of them, women are paid. The U.S. does not have any federal legislation guaranteeing mothers the right to breast-feed their infants at work, but 24 states, the District of Columbia and Puerto Rico have laws related to breastfeeding in the workplace. There is not a federal law requiring paid sick days in the United States. When it comes to sick days, 145 countries provide sick days to their employees; 127 provide a week or more per year.

At least 134 countries have laws setting the maximum length of the work week; the U.S. does not have a maximum work week length and does not place any limits on the amount of overtime that an employee is required to work each week. (survey) Sweden, Denmark and Norway have the highest level of maternity benefits—Sweden provides 68 weeks paid maternity leave, Norway provides 56 weeks paid maternity leave and Denmark provides 52. Even when vacation time is offered in some U.S. companies, some choose not to take advantage of it. A 2003 survey by Management Recruiter International stated that fifty percent of executives surveyed didn't have plans to take a vacation. They decided to stay at work and use their vacation time to get caught up on their increased workloads. American workers average approximately ten paid holidays per year while British workers average twenty-five holidays and German employees thirty. Americans are at "work" twelve weeks more a year in total hours than Europeans though they are no more productive than the average European.

European Union

In Europe, the Working Time Directive has implemented a maximum 48-hour working week. Many countries have opted for fewer hours. France attempted to introduce a thirty-five hour workweek, and Finland experimented with a thirty-hour week in 1996. Contradictory to the Scandinavian countries, there is no evidence of state policies that absolutely encourage men to take on a larger share of domestic work in France, Portugal, or Britain. In a 2007, the European Quality of Life Survey found that countries in south-eastern Europe had the most common problems with work-life balance. In Croatia and Greece, a little over 70% of working citizens say that they are too tired to do household jobs at least several times a month because of work.

In Britain, legislation has been passed allowing parents of children under six to request a more flexible work schedule. Companies must approve this request as long as it does not damage the business. A 2003 Survey of graduates in the UK revealed that graduates value flexibility even more than wages.

In all twenty-five European Union countries, voters "punish" politicians who try to shrink vacations. "Even the twenty-two days Estonians, Lithuanians, Poles and Slovenians count as their own is much more generous than the leave allotted to U.S. workers." According to a report by the Families and Work Institute, the average vacation time that Americans took each year averaged 14.6 days. According to Jeremy Reynolds, unions can lobby for benefits, pay, training, safety measures, and additional factors that impact the costs and benefits of work hours. "Unions can also have a more direct impact on hour mismatches through their efforts to change the length of the workday, work week, and work year, and to increase vacation and leave time." This is why workers in countries where there are strong unions usually work fewer hours and have more generous leave policies than workers who are in countries where there are weaker unions.

It is critical to mention that cultural factors influence why and how much we work. As stated by Jeremy Reynolds, "cultural norms may encourage work as an end in itself or as a means to acquiring other things, including consumer products." This might be why Americans are bound to work more than people in other countries. In general, Americans always want more and more, so Americans need to work more in order to have the money to spend on these consumer products.

TIME LIMIT

A time limit or deadline is a narrow field of time, or particular point in time, by which an objective or task must be accomplished. In project management, deadlines are most often associated with milestone goals.

Origination of the Term Deadline in a Time Limit

The term deadline originated from prison camps during war, and referred to a physical line or boundary. Guards would shoot any prisoner who crossed the deadline. The "deadline" in such prison camps as Confederate Prison Camp Andersonville or Union Prison Camp Douglas Chicago during the Civil War was "Inside (the wall), about 19 feet from the wall," which prisoners were forbidden to cross. The "deadline" was intended to prevent prisoners from climbing over the stockade or from tunneling under it. The term was later adapted in its use to time lines, perhaps to show the seriousness of an end date in a timeline by referring to it as a "deadline."

LIFE EXPECTANCY

Life expectancy is the expected (in the statistical sense) number of years of life remaining at a given age. It is denoted by which means the average number of subsequent years of life for someone now aged according to a particular mortality experience. Because life expectancy is an average, a particular person may well die many years before or many years after their "expected" survival. The term "maximum life span" has a quite different meaning. The "median life span" is also a different concept although fairly similar to life expectancy numerically in most developed countries.

The term that is known as life expectancy is most often used in the context of human populations, but is also used in plant or animal ecology; it is calculated by the analysis of life tables (also known as actuarial tables). The term life expectancy may also be used in the context of manufactured objects although the related term shelf life is used for consumer products and the terms "mean time to breakdown" (MTTB) and "mean time before failures" (MTBF) are used in engineering.

Interpretation of Life Expectancy

It is important to note that life expectancy is an average. In many cultures, particularly before modern medicine was widely available, the combination of high infant mortality and deaths in young adulthood from accidents, epidemics, plagues, wars, and childbirth, significantly lowers the overall life expectancy. But for someone who survived past these early hazards, living into their sixties or seventies would not be uncommon. For example, a society with a life expectancy of 40 may have very few people dying at age 40: most will die before 30 years of age or after 55. In countries with high infant mortality rates, life expectancy at birth is highly sensitive to the rate of death in the first few years of life. Because of this sensitivity to infant mortality, simple life expectancy at age zero can be subject to gross misinterpretation, leading one to believe that a population with a low overall life expectancy will necessarily have a small proportion of older people. For example, in a hypothetical stationary population in which half the population dies before the age of five, but everybody else dies at exactly 70 years old, the life expectancy at age zero will be about 37 years, while about 25% of the population will be between the ages of 50 and 70. Another measure such as life expectancy at age 5 (e5) can be used to exclude the effect of infant mortality to provide a simple measure of overall mortality rates other than in early childhood—in the hypothetical population above, life expectancy at age 5 would be another 64 years. Aggregate population measures such as the proportion of the population in various age classes should also be used alongside individual-based measures like formal life expectancy when analyzing population structure and dynamics.

Human Life Expectancy Patterns

Human beings are expected to live on average 49.42 years in Swaziland and 82.6 years in Japan, although Japan's recorded life expectancy may have been very slightly increased by counting many infant deaths as stillborn. An analysis published in 2011 in *The Lancet* attributes Japanese life expectancy to equal opportunities and public health as well as diet. The oldest confirmed recorded age for any human is 122 years. This is referred to as the "maximum life span", which is the upper boundary of life, the maximum number of years any human is known to have lived.

Life Expectancy Variation Over Time

The following information is derived from *Encyclopædia Britannica*, 1961. and other sources, some with a questionable accuracy. Unless otherwise stated, it represents estimates of the life expectancies of the population as a whole. In many instances life expectancy varied considerably according to class and gender. Life expectancy increases with age as the individual survives the higher mortality rates associated with childhood. For instance, the table above listed life expectancy at birth in Medieval Britain at 30. A male member of the English aristocracy at the same period could expect to live, having survived until the age of 21:

- 1200–1300 A.D.: 43 years (to age 64)
- 1300–1400 A.D.: 34 years (to age 55) (due to the impact of the Black Death)
- 1400–1500 A.D.: 48 years (to age 69)
- 1500–1550 A.D.: 50 years (to age 71).

In general, the available data indicate that longer lifespans became more common recently in human evolution. This increased longevity is attributed by some writers to cultural adaptations rather than genetic evolution, although some research indicates that during the Neolithic

Revolution natural selection favoured increased longevity. Nevertheless, all researchers acknowledge the effect of cultural adaptations upon life expectancy. During the early 1600s in England, life expectancy was only about 35 years, largely because two-thirds of all children died before the age of four. The average life expectancy in Colonial America was under 25 years in the Virginia colony, and in New England about 40% of children failed to reach adulthood. During the Industrial Revolution, the life expectancy of children increased dramatically. The percentage of children born in London who died before the age of five decreased from 74.5% in 1730–1749 to 31.8% in 1810–1829.

Public health measures are credited with much of the recent increase in life expectancy. During the 20th century, the average lifespan in the United States increased by more than 30 years, of which 25 years can be attributed to advances in public health. In order to assess the quality of these additional years of life, 'healthy life expectancies' have been calculated for the last 30 years. Since 2001, the World Health Organization publishes statistics called Healthy life expectancy (HALE), defined as the average number of years that a person can expect to live in "full health", excluding the years lived in less than full health due to disease and/or injury. Since 2004, Eurostat publishes annual statistics called Healthy Life Years (HLY) based on reported activity limitations. The United States of America uses similar indicators in the framework of their nationwide health promotion and disease prevention plan "Healthy People 2010". An increasing number of countries are using health expectancy indicators to monitor the health of their population.

Regional Variations

There are great variations in life expectancy between different parts of the world, mostly caused by differences in public health, medical care, and diet. The impact of AIDS is particularly notable on life expectancy in many African countries. According to predictions made by the United Nations (UN) in 2002, the life expectancy at birth for 2010–2015 (if HIV/AIDS did not exist) would have been:

- 70.7 years instead of 31.6 in Botswana
- 69.9 years instead of 41.5 in South Africa
- 70.5 years instead of 31.8 in Zimbabwe

The UN's predictions were too pessimistic. Actual life expectancy in Botswana declined from 65 in 1990 to 49 in 2000 before increasing to 66 in 2011. In South Africa, life expectancy was 63 in 1990, 57 in 2000, and 58 in 2011. And in Zimbabwe, life expectancy was 60 in 1990, 43 in 2000, and 54 in 2011.Countries in Africa over the last 200 years have generally not had the same improvements in mortality rates that have been enjoyed by countries in Asia, Latin America, and Europe. In the United States, African people have shorter life expectancies than their European counterparts. For example, white Americans born in 2010 are expected to live until age 78.9 but African Americans only until age 75.1. This 3.8-year gap, however, is the lowest it has been since at least 1975. The greatest difference was 7.1 years in 1993. In contrast, Asian-American women live the longest of all ethnic groups in the United States, with a life expectancy of 85.8 years. The life expectancy of Hispanic Americans is 81.2 years.

Economic Circumstances

Economic circumstances also affect life expectancy. For example, in the United Kingdom, life expectancy in the wealthiest areas is several years longer than in the poorest areas. This may reflect factors such as diet and lifestyle as well as access to medical care. It may also reflect a selective effect: people with chronic life-threatening illnesses are less likely to become wealthy or to reside in affluent areas. In Glasgow the disparity is among the highest in the world with life expectancy for males in the heavily deprived Calton standing at 54 – 28 years less than in the affluent area of Lenzie, which is only eight kilometres away.

A 2013 study found a pronounced relationship between economic inequality and life expectancy. However, a study by José A. Tapia Granados and Ana Diez Roux at the University of Michigan found that life expectancy actually increased during the Great Depression, and during recessions and depressions in general. The authors suggest that when people are working extra hard during good economic times, they undergo more stress, exposure to pollution, and likelihood of injury among other longevity-limiting factors. Life expectancy is also likely to be affected by exposure to high levels of highway air pollution or industrial air pollution. This is one way that occupation can have a major effect on life expectancy. Coal miners (and in prior generations, asbestos cutters) often have shorter than average life expectancies. Other factors affecting an individual's life expectancy are genetic disorders, obesity, access to health care, diet, exercise, tobacco smoking, drug use and excessive alcohol use.

Gender Differences

Women tend to have a lower mortality rate at every age. In the womb, male fetuses have a higher mortality rate (babies are conceived in a ratio estimated to be from 107 to 170 males to 100 females, but the ratio at birth in the United States is only 105 males to 100 females). Among the smallest premature babies (those under 2 pounds or 900 g) females again have a higher survival rate. At the other extreme, about 90% of individuals aged 110 are female. The difference in life expectancy between men and women in the United States dropped from 7.8 years in 1979 to 5.3 years in 2005, with women expected to live to age 80.1 in 2005. In the past, mortality rates for females in child-bearing age groups were higher than for males at the same age. This is no longer the case, and female human life expectancy is considerably higher than that of men. The reasons for this are not entirely certain. Traditional arguments tend to favour socio-environmental factors: historically, men have generally consumed more tobacco, alcohol and drugs than females in most societies, and are more likely to die from many associated diseases such as lung cancer, tuberculosis and cirrhosis of the liver. Men are also more likely to die from injuries, whether unintentional (such as occupational or war or car accidents) or intentional (suicide). Men are also more likely to die from most of the leading causes of death (some already stated above) than women. Some of these in the United States include: cancer of the respiratory system, motor vehicle accidents, suicide, cirrhosis of the liver, emphysema, and coronary heart disease. These far outweigh the female mortality rate from breast cancer and cervical cancer etc.

Some argue that shorter male life expectancy is merely another manifestation of the general rule, seen in all mammal species, that larger (size) individuals (within a species) tend on average to have shorter lives. This biological difference occurs because women have more resistance to infections and degenerative diseases. In her extensive review of the existing literature, Kalben concluded that the fact that women live longer than men was observed at least as far back as 1750 and that, with relatively equal treatment, today males in all parts of the world experience greater mortality than females. Of 72 selected causes of death, only 6 yielded greater female than male age-adjusted death rates in 1998 in the United States. With the exception of birds, for almost all of the animal species studied, the males have higher mortality than the females. Evidence suggests that the sex mortality differential in people is due to both biological/genetic and environmental/behavioural risk and protective factors. There is a recent suggestion that mitochondrial mutations that shorten lifespan continue to be expressed in males (but less so in females) because mitochondria are inherited only through the mother. By contrast natural selection weeds out mitochondria that reduce female survival as such mitochondria are less likely to be passed on to the next generation. Therefore it is suggested human females and female animals tend to live longer than males. The authors claim this is a partial explanation.

Centenarians

In developed countries, the number of centenarians is increasing at approximately 5.5% per year, which means doubling the centenarian population every 13 years, pushing it from some 455,000 in 2009 to 4.1 million in 2050. Japan is the country with the highest ratio of centenarians (347 for every 1 million inhabitants in September 2010). Shimane prefecture had an estimated 743 centenarians per million inhabitants. In the United States, the number of centenarians grew from 32,194 in 1980 to 71,944 in November 2010 (232 centenarians per million inhabitants).

Evolution and Aging Rate

Various species of plants and animals, including humans, have different lifespans. There is an evolutionary theory of aging, and general consensus in the academic community of evolutionary theorists; however the theory doesn't work well in practice, and there are many unexplained exceptions. Evolutionary theory states that organisms that, by virtue of their defenses or lifestyle, live for long periods whilst avoiding accidents, disease, predation, etc., are likely to have genes that code for slow aging — which often translates to good cellular repair. This is theorized to be true because if predation or accidental deaths prevent most individuals from living to an old age, then there will be less natural selection to increase intrinsic life span. The finding was supported in a classic study of opossums by Austad, however the opposite relationship was found in an equally prominent study of guppies by Reznick. One prominent and very popular theory attributes aging to a tight budget for food energy called caloric restriction. Caloric restriction observed in many animals (most notably mice and rats), shows a near doubling of life span due to a very limited calorific intake. Support for this theory has been bolstered by several new studies linking lower basal metabolic rate to increased life expectancy. This is the key to why animals like giant tortoises can live so long. Studies of humans with 100+ year life spans have shown a link to decreased thyroid activity, resulting in their lowered metabolic rate.

In a broad survey of zoo animals, no relationship was found between the fertility of the animal and its life span.

Calculating Life Expectancies

The starting point for calculating life expectancies is the age-specific death rates of the population members. In the past, a very simple model of age-specific mortality used the Gompertz function, although these days more sophisticated methods are used. In cases where the amount of data is relatively small, the most common methods are to fit a mathematical formula, such as an extension of the Gompertz function, to the data, or to look at an established mortality table previously derived for a larger population and make a simple adjustment to it (e.g. multiply by a constant factor) to fit the data. With a large amount of data, one looks at the mortality rates actually experienced at each age, and applies smoothing (e.g. by cubic splines) to iron out any apparently random statistical fluctuations from one year of age to the next.

While the data required are easily identified in the case of humans, the computation of life expectancy of industrial products and wild animals involves more indirect techniques. The life expectancy and demography of wild animals are often estimated by capturing, marking and recapturing them. The life of a product, more often termed shelf life is also computed using similar methods. In the case of long-lived components such as those used in critical applications, such as in aircraft methods such as accelerated aging are used to model the life expectancy of a component. Life expectancy is by definition an arithmetic mean. It can also be calculated by integrating the survival curve from ages 0 to positive infinity (or equivalently to the maximum lifespan, sometimes called 'omega'). For an extinct or completed cohort (all people born in year 1850, for example), of course, it can simply be calculated by averaging the ages at death. For cohorts with some survivors, it is estimated by using mortality experience in recent years. These estimates are called period cohort life expectancies.

It is important to note that this statistic is usually based on past mortality experience, and assumes that the same age-specific mortality rates will continue into the future. Thus such life expectancy figures need to be adjusted for temporal trends before calculating how long a currently living individual of a particular age is expected to live. Period life expectancy remains a commonly used statistic to summarize the current health status of a population. However for some purposes, such as pensions calculations, it is usual to adjust the life table used, thus assuming that age-specific death rates will continue to decrease over the years, as they have done in the past. This is often done by simply extrapolating past trends; however some models do exist to account for the evolution of mortality (e.g., the Lee–Carter model). As discussed above, on an individual basis, there are a number of factors that have been shown to correlate with a longer life. Factors that are associated with variations in life expectancy include family history, marital status, economic status, physique, exercise, diet, drug use including smoking and alcohol consumption, disposition, education, environment, sleep, climate, and health care.

Life Expectancy Forecasting

Forecasting life expectancy and mortality forms an important subdivision of demography. Future trends in life expectancy have huge implications for old-age support programs like U.S. Social Security and pension systems, because the cash flow in these systems depends on the number of recipients still living (along with the rate of return on the investments or the tax rate in PAYGO systems). With longer life expectancies, these systems see increased cash outflow; if these systems underestimate increases in life-expectancies, they won't be prepared for the large payments that will inevitably occur as humans live longer and longer.

Life expectancy forecasting usually is based on two different approaches:

- Forecasting the life expectancy directly, generally using ARIMA or other time series extrapolation procedures: This approach has the advantage of simplicity, but it cannot account for changes in mortality at specific ages, and the forecasted number cannot be used to derive other life table results. Analyses and forecasts using this approach can be done with any common statistical/ mathematical software package, like EViews, R, SAS, Stata, Matlab, or SPSS.
- Forecasting age specific death rates and computing the life expectancy from the results with life table methods: This approach is usually more complex than simply forecasting life expectancy because the analyst must deal with correlated age specific mortality rates, but it seems to be more robust than simple one dimensional time series approaches. This approach also yields a set of age specific rates that may be used to derive other measures, like survival curves or life expectancies at different ages. The most important approach within this group is the Lee-Carter model, which uses the singular value decomposition on a set of transformed age-specific mortality rates to reduce their dimensionality to a single time series, forecasts that time series, and then recovers a full set of age-specific mortality rates from that forecasted value. Software for this approach include Professor Rob J. Hyndman's R package called 'demography' and UC Berkeley's LCFIT system.

Policy Uses of Life Expectancy

Life expectancy is one of the factors in measuring the Human Development Index (HDI) of each nation, along with adult literacy, education, and standard of living. Life expectancy is also used in describing the physical quality of life of an area. Disparities in life expectancy are often cited as demonstrating the need for better medical care or increased social support. Life expectancies are also used when determining the value of a life settlement, a life insurance policy sold for a cash asset.

Life Expectancy vs. Life Span

Life expectancy is often confused with life span to the point that they are nearly synonyms; when people hear 'life expectancy was 35 years' they often interpret this as meaning that people of that time or place had short life spans. One such example can be seen in the *In Search of...* episode "The Man Who Would Not Die" (About Count of St. Germain) where it is stated "Evidence recently discovered in the British Museum indicates that St. Germain may have well been the long lost third son of Rákóczi born in Transylvania in 1694. If he died in Germany in 1784, he lived 90 years. The average life expectancy in the 18th century was 35 years. Fifty was a ripe old age. *Ninety...* was forever."

This ignores the fact that the life expectancy generally quoted is the *at birth* number which is an *average* that includes all the babies that die before their first year of life as well as people that die from disease and war. The genetics of humans and rate of aging were no different in preindustrial societies than today, but people frequently died young because of untreatable diseases, accidents, and malnutrition. Many women did not survive childbirth, and individuals who reached old age were likely to succumb quickly to health problems. It can be argued that it is better to compare life expectancies of the period after childhood to get a better handle on life span. Life expectancy can change dramatically after childhood, as is demonstrated by the Roman Life Expectancy table where *at birth* the life expectancy was 25 but at the age of 5 it jumped to 48. Studies like Plymouth Plantation; "Dead at Forty" and Life Expectancy by Age, 1850–2004 similarly show a dramatic increase in life expectancy once adulthood was reached.

GOAL SETTING

Goal setting involves establishing *specific, measurable, achievable, realistic and time-targeted* (S.M.A.R.T.) goals. Work on the theory of goal-setting suggests that an effective tool for making progress is to ensure that participants in a group with a common goal are clearly aware of what is expected from them. On a personal level, setting goals helps people work towards their own objectives. Goal setting features as a major component of personal development literature. It is considered an "open" theory, so as new discoveries are made it is modified. Studies have shown that specific and ambitious goals lead to a higher level of performance than easy or general goals. As long as the individual accepts the goal, has the ability to attain it, and does not have conflicting goals, there is a positive linear relationship between goal difficulty and task performance. Goals are a form of motivation that sets the standard for self-satisfaction with performance. Achieving the goal one has set for oneself is a measure of success, and being able to meet job challenges is a way one measures success in the workplace.

History

The first empirical studies were performed by Cecil Alec Mace in 1935. Edwin A. Locke began to examine goal setting in the mid-1960s and continued researching goal setting for thirty years. Locke derived the idea for goal-setting from Aristotle's form of final causality. Aristotle speculated that purpose can cause action; thus, Locke began researching the impact goals have on individual activity of its time performance. Goal setting theory was developed and refined by Edwin A. Locke in the 1960s. His first article on goal setting theory was "Toward a Theory of Task Motivation and Incentives" which was published in 1968. This article laid the foundation for goal setting theory and established the positive relationship between clearly identified goals and performance.

Concept

Goals that are deemed difficult to achieve and specific tend to increase performance more than goals that are not. A goal can become more specific through quantification or enumeration (should be measurable), such as by demanding "...increase productivity by 50%," or by defining certain tasks that must be completed.

Setting goals affects outcomes in four ways:

1. Choice: goals narrow attention and direct efforts to goal-relevant activities, and away from perceived undesirable and goal-irrelevant actions.
2. Effort: goals can lead to more effort; for example, if one typically produces 4 widgets an hour, and has the goal of producing 6, one may work more intensely towards the goal than one would otherwise.
3. Persistence: someone becomes more prone to work through setbacks if pursuing a goal.

4. Cognition: goals can lead individuals to develop and change their behaviour.

Goal Setting in Business

In business, goal setting encourages participants to put in substantial effort. Also, because every member has defined expectations for their role, little room is left for inadequate, marginal effort to go unnoticed.

Managers cannot constantly drive motivation, or keep track of an employee's work on a continuous basis. Goals are therefore an important tool for managers, since goals have the ability to function as a self-regulatory mechanism that helps employees prioritize tasks. Also Locke and Latham (2002)

The four mechanisms through which goal setting can affect individual performance are:

1. Goals focus attention toward goal-relevant activities and away from goal-irrelevant activities.
2. Goals serve as an energizer: Higher goals induce greater effort, while low goals induce lesser effort.
3. Goals affect persistence; constraints with regard to resources affect work pace.
4. Goals activate cognitive knowledge and strategies that help employees cope with the situation at hand.

Goal Commitment

People perform better when they are committed to achieving certain goals. Through an understanding of the effect of goal setting on individual performance, organizations are able to use goal setting to benefit organizational performance. Locke and Latham have indicated three moderators that indicate goal setting success:

1. The importance of the expected outcomes of goal attainment, and;
2. Self-efficacy – one's belief that they are able to achieve the goals, and;
3. Commitment to others – promises or engagements to others can strongly improve commitment.

Goal–Performance Relationship

Locke et al. (1981) examined the behavioural effects of goal-setting, concluding that 90% of laboratory and field studies involving specific and challenging goals led to higher performance than did easy or no goals.

While some managers believe it is sufficient to urge employees to 'do their best,' Locke and Latham have a contradicting view on this. The authors state that people who are told to 'do their best' don't. 'Doing your best' has no external referent, which makes it useless in eliciting specific behaviour. To elicit some specific form of behaviour from others, it is important that this person has a clear view of what is expected from him/her. A goal is thereby of vital importance because it facilitates an individual in focusing their efforts in a specified direction. In other words, goals canalize behaviour (Cummings & Worley p. 368). However, when goals are established at a management level and thereafter solely promulgated from the top, employee motivation with regard to achieving these goals is rather suppressed (Locke & Latham, 2002 p. 705). To increase motivation, employees not only must be allowed to participate in the goal setting process, but the goals must be challenging as well. (Cummings & Worley p. 369)

Goal Setting and Feedback

Without proper feedback channels it is impossible for employees to adapt or adjust to the required behaviour. Keep track of performance to allow employees to see how effective they have been in attaining their goals. Goal setting and feedback go hand in hand. Without feedback, goal setting is unlikely to work. Providing feedback on short-term objectives helps to sustain motivation and commitment to a goal. Feedback should be provided on the strategies followed to achieve the goals and the final outcomes achieved, as well. Feedback on strategies used to obtain goals is very important, especially for complex work, because challenging goals put focus on outcomes rather than on performance strategies, so they impair performance. Properly-delivered feedback is also very essential, and the following hints may help for providing a good feedback:

- Create a positive context for feedback.
- Use constructive and positive language.
- Focus on behaviours and strategies.
- Tailor feedback to the needs of the individual worker.
- Make feedback a two-way communication process.

Advances in technology can facilitate providing feedback. Systems analysts have designed computer programs that track goals for numerous members of an organization. Such computer systems may maintain every employee's goals, as well as their deadlines. Separate methods may check the employee's progress on a regular basis, and other systems may require perceived slackers to explain how they intend to improve. More difficult goals require more cognitive strategies and well-developed skills.

The more difficult the tasks, the smaller the group of people who possess the necessary skills and strategies. From an organizational perspective, it is thereby more difficult to successfully attain more difficult goals, since resources become more scarce.

Honing Goal Setting Using Temporal Motivation Theory

Locke and Latham (2004) note that goal setting theory lacks "the issue of time perspective". Taking this into consideration, Steel and Konig (2006) utilize their Temporal Motivation Theory (TMT) to account for goal setting's effects, and suggest new hypotheses regarding a pair of its moderators: goal difficulty and proximity. The effectiveness of goal setting can be explained by two aspects of TMT: the principle of diminishing returns and temporal discounting. Similar to the expression "the sum of the parts can be greater than the whole", a division of a project into several, immediate, subgoals appears to take advantage of these two elements.

Employee Motivation

The more employees are motivated, the more they are stimulated and interested in accepting goals. These success factors are interdependent. For example, the expected outcomes of goals are positively influenced when employees are involved in the goal setting process. Not only does participation increase commitment in attaining the goals that are set, participation influences self-efficacy as well. Additionally, feedback is necessary to monitor one's progress. When feedback is not present, an employee might think (s)he is not making enough progress. This can reduce self-efficacy and thereby harm the performance outcomes in the long run.

- Goal-commitment, the most influential moderator, becomes especially important when dealing with difficult or complex goals. If people lack commitment to goals, they lack motivation to reach them. To commit to a goal, one must believe in its importance or significance.
- Attainability: individuals must also believe that they can attain — or at least partially reach — a defined goal. If they think no chance exists of reaching a goal, they may not even try.
- Self-efficacy: the higher someone's self-efficacy regarding a certain task, the more likely they will set higher goals, and the more persistence they will show in achieving them.

Limitations

Goal-setting theory has limitations. In an organization, a goal of a manager may not align with the goals of the organization as a whole. In such cases, the goals of an individual may come into direct conflict with the employing organization. Without aligning goals between the organization and the individual, performance may suffer. For complex tasks, goal-setting may actually impair performance. In these situations, an individual may become preoccupied with meeting the goals, rather than performing tasks. Some evidence suggests that goal-setting can foster unethical behaviour when people do not achieve specified goals. Some people feel that goal setting may have the drawback of inhibiting implicit learning: goal setting may encourage simple focus on an outcome without openness to exploration, understanding, or growth.

Developments in Goal-Setting Theory

Goal Choice

Self-efficacy, past performance and various other social factors influence goal setting. Failure to meet previous goals often leads to setting lower (and more likely achievable) goals.

Learning Goals

There are times when having specific goals is not a best option; this is the case when the goal requires new skills or knowledge. "Tunnel vision" is a consequence of specific goals; if one is too focused on attaining a specific goal they ignore the need to learn new skills or acquire new information. In situations like this, the best option is to set a learning goal. A learning goal is a generalized goal to achieve knowledge in a certain topic or field, but it can ultimately lead to better performance in specific goals related to the learning goals. Locke and Latham attribute this response to metacognition. They believe that "a learning goal facilitates or enhances metacognition—namely, planning, monitoring, and evaluating progress toward goal attainment". This is necessary in environments with little or no guidance and structure. Although jobs typically have set goals, individual goals and achievement can benefit from metacognition.

Framing

How goals are viewed influences performance. When one feels threatened and or intimidated by a high goal they perform poorer than those who view the goal as a challenge. The framing of a goal as a gain or a loss influences one's eventual performance.

Affect

Realization of goals has an effect on feelings of success and satisfaction. Achieving goals has a positive effect, and failing to meet goals has negative consequences. However, the affect of goals is not exclusive to one realm. Success in one's job can compensate for feelings of failure in one's personal life.

Group Goals

The relationship between group goals and individual goals influences group performance; when goals are compatible there is a positive effect, but when goals are incompatible the effects can be detrimental to the group's performance. There is another factor at work in groups, and that is the sharing factor; a positive correlation exists between sharing information within the group and group performance. In the case of group goals, feedback needs to be related to the group, not individuals, in order for it to improve the group's performance.

Goals and Traits

On a basic level the two types of goals are learning goals and performance goals. Each possesses different traits associated with the kind of goal that is selected.

1. Learning goals
   - Tasks where skills and knowledge can be acquired
2. Performance goals
   - Avoid tasks where error and judgment are possible
   - Select tasks that are easy to accomplish and will make one appear successful

A more complex trait-mediation study is the one conducted by Lee, Sheldon, and Turban, which yielded the following results:

> "Amotivated orientation" (low confidence in one's capabilities) is associated with goal-avoidance motivation, and more generally, associated with lower goals levels and lower performance.
>
> "Control orientation" (extrinsic motivation) is associated with both avoidance and approach goals. Approach goals are associated with higher goal levels and higher performance.
>
> "Autonomy goals" (intrinsic motivation) leads to mastery goals, enhanced focus, and therefore enhanced performance.

Macro-Level Goals

This is goal setting applied to the company as a whole. Cooperative goals reduce the negative feelings that occur as a result of alliances and the formation of groups. The most common parties involved are the company and its suppliers. The three motivators for macro-level goals are: self-efficacy, growth goals, and organizational vision.

Goals and Subconscious Priming

The effects of subconscious priming and conscious goals are independent, although a conscious goal has a larger effect. The interaction effect is that priming can enhance the effects of difficult goals, but it has no effect on easy goals. There is also the situation in which priming and conscious goals conflict with one another, and in this situation the conscious goals have a greater effect on performance.

REQUIREMENT PRIORITIZATION

Requirement prioritization is used in Software product management for determining which candidate requirements of a software product should be included in a certain release. Requirements are also prioritized to minimize risk during development so that the most important or high risk requirements are implemented first. Several methods for assessing a prioritization of software requirements exist.

Introduction

In Software product management there exist several sub processes. First of all there is portfolio management where a product development strategy is defined based on information from the market and partner companies. In product roadmapping (or technology roadmapping), themes and core assets of products in the portfolio are identified and roadmap constructions are created. In requirements management candidate software requirements for a product are gathered and organized. Finally, in the release planning activity, these requirements are prioritized and selected for a release, after which the launch of the software product can be prepared. Thus, one of the key steps in release planning is requirements prioritization.

Cost-Value Approach

Cost Value Approach is like Cost Estimation for .... A good and relatively easy to use method for prioritizing software product requirements is the cost-value approach. This approach was created by Joachim Karlsson and Kevin Ryan. The approach was then further developed and commercialized in the company Focal Point (that was acquired by Telelogic in 2005). Their basic idea was to determine for each individual candidate requirement what the cost of implementing the requirement would be and how much value the requirement has. The assessment of values and costs for the requirements was performed using the Analytic Hierarchy Process (AHP). This method was created by Thomas Saaty. Its basic idea is that for all pairs of (candidate) requirements a person assesses a value or a cost comparing the one requirement of a pair with the other. For example, a value of 3 for (Req1, Req2) indicates that requirement 1 is valued three times as high as requirement 2. Trivially, this indicates that (Req2, Req1) has value S!. In the approach of Karlsson and Ryan, five steps for reviewing candidate requirements and determining a priority among them are identified. These are summed up below.

1. Requirement engineers carefully review candidate requirements for completeness and to ensure that they are stated in an unambiguous way.
2. Customers and users (or suitable substitutes) apply AHP's pairwise comparison method to assess the relative value of the candidate requirements.
3. Experienced software engineers use AHP's pairwise comparison to estimate the relative cost of implementing each candidate requirement.
4. A software engineer uses AHP to calculate each candidate requirement's relative value and implementation cost, and plots these on a cost-value diagram. Value is depicted on the y axis of this diagram and estimated cost on the x-axis.
5. The stakeholders use the cost-value diagram as a conceptual map for analyzing and discussing the candidate requirements. Now software managers prioritize the requirements and decide which will be implemented.

Now, the cost-value approach and the prioritizing of requirements in general can be placed in its context of Software product management. As mentioned earlier, release planning is part of this process. Prioritization of software requirements is a sub process of the release planning process.

The release planning process consists of the sub processes:

1. Prioritize requirements
2. Select requirements
3. Define release requirements
4. Validate release requirements
5. Prepare launch

Other Prioritization Techniques

- Quality Function Deployment (QFD)
- Binary Search Tree (BST)
- Planning game (PG)
- PROMETHEE
- 100-point method (100P) also known as Cumulative voting
- Planning Game combined with AHP (PGcAHP)

- MoSCoW Method
- Software Engineering Risk: Understanding and Management (SERUM)
- EVOLVE
- Value Oriented Prioritation Method (VOP)
- Minimal Spanning Tree (MST),
- Bubble Sort (BS),
- Numeral Assignment

PERSONAL ORGANIZER

A personal organizer, day planner, personal analog assistant, personal planner, year planner, or agenda (from Latin *agenda* - things to do), is a small book or binder that is designed to be portable. It usually contains a diary, calendar, address book, blank paper, and other sections. A personal organizer may also include pages with useful information, such as maps and telephone codes. It is related to the separate desktop stationery items that have one or more of the same functions, such as appointment calendars, rolodexes, notebooks, and almanacs. By the end of the 20th century, paper-and-binder personal organizers started to be replaced by electronic devices like personal digital assistants (PDAs), personal information manager software, and online organizers. This process has accelerated in the beginning of the 21st century with the advent of smartphones and tablet computers and a variety of mobile apps.

PROFESSIONAL ORGANIZING

Professional organizing is an industry that has been developed in order to help individuals and businesses design systems and processes using organizing principles and through transferring skills. Professional organizers aim to help individuals and businesses take control of their surroundings, their time, their paper, and their systems for life. Professional organizers help redirect paradigms into more useful cross-applications that ensure properly co-sustainable futures for their clients' spaces and processes.

Types of Organizing

There are several categories and specializations of professional organizing: Ergonomice, Feng Shui, Office-Commercial, Office-Home, Storage/Warehouse,Closets, Garages,Attics,Basements, Kitchens, Office and Filing Rooms,Inventory/Storage Areas,Paper Organization Photographs, Memorabilia,Collecting,Time Management,Moving Techniques and Labeling, People w/ Physical Disabilities, Seniors Citizens

College Students and Dorm Rooms,Downsizing, Home Staging, Clutter Control, Retirement Organizing,Paper and Document Organizing, Attention Deficit Disorder Organizing Workflow,Space Planning.

Organizing Process

Organizing is a multi-step process by which a person decides on a way to store items so they can be easily placed, found, retrieved, and maintained. Everything should have its own 'home'.

The first step, requires sorting through items to determine which are most needed, which can be thrown away (or recycled), and which can be given away. The second step is deciding how the freed space can best be used, what storage items and sizes will be needed and how to label those containers. Decisions made are based upon personal priorities.

The third step involves putting in place any additional needed storage systems for items, such as shelving.

The fourth step involves placing items in the space, giving priority to items that are most often used by making them the most accessible. Items that are used most often should be on the bottom shelves and items used seasonally are stored on the higher shelves. The fifth step involves disposing of items that were previously selected for the trash or for giving away. Junk should be eliminated right away and thrown in the refuse containers. Items donated should be added to a container depicting the donation place; Goodwill, Salvation Army etc. You may also have a container that you will want to donate to your church or that you will save for a rummage sale. The organizer's primary skill is in helping the client decide what should be done with their items, educating the client on organizational techniques, developing strategies and installing systems so the client can maintain the organized space for the long-term.

Growth of the Industry

There are approximately 5,200 professional organizers in the U.S. and 8 foreign countries who are members of the trade association NAPO. Another well known International Organizing Association is 'Faithful Organizers'. There have been a number of several popular television programs, starting with Life Laundry in 2002, and followed by others such as Clean Sweep, Neat, Mission: Organization, Hoarders, Clean House, and NeatTV as well as magazines like Real Simple, and many articles that appear on a regular basis in a wide range of media.

Hiring a Professional Organizer

Hiring the right professional organizer is key to the success of your project. Make sure the organizer is willing to listen, to be creative, patient and non-judgmental. Let the organizer know if you are willing to think 'outside the box' for creative storage ideas. Set your goals and a budget you want to stay in, talk this over with the organizer to make sure that you both are in agreement on the goal to achieve. The cost of a Professional Organizer will very depending on project and location. Cost will normally range from $50–$150 an hour.

MANAGING OF TIME IN CRISIS MANAGEMENT

Crisis management is the process by which an organization deals with a major event that threatens to harm the organization, its stakeholders, or the general public. The study of crisis management originated with the large scale industrial and environmental disasters in the 1980s. Three elements are common to a crisis: (a) a threat to the organization, (b) the element of surprise, and (c) a short decision time. Venette argues that "crisis is a process of transformation where the old system can no longer be maintained." Therefore the fourth defining quality is the need for change. If change is not needed, the event could more accurately be described as a failure or incident. In contrast to risk management, which involves assessing potential threats and finding the best ways to avoid those threats, crisis management involves dealing with threats before, during, and after they have occurred. It is a discipline within the broader context of management consisting of skills and techniques required to identify, assess, understand, and cope with a serious situation, especially from the moment it first occurs to the point that recovery procedures start.

Introduction

Crisis management consists of different aspects including;

- Methods used to respond to both the reality and perception of crises.
- Establishing metrics to define what scenarios constitute a crisis and should consequently trigger the necessary response mechanisms.
- Communication that occurs within the response phase of emergency-management scenarios.

Crisis-management methods of a business or an organization are called a crisis-management plan. Crisis management is occasionally referred to as incident management, although several industry specialists such as Peter Power argue that the term "crisis management" is more accurate. A crisis mindset requires the ability to think of the worst-case scenario while simultaneously suggesting numerous solutions. Trial and error is an accepted discipline, as the first line of defense might not work. It is necessary to maintain a list of contingency plans and to be always on alert. Organizations and individuals should always be prepared with a rapid response plan to emergencies which would require analysis, drills and exercises. The credibility and reputation of organizations is heavily influenced by the perception of their responses during crisis situations. The organization and communication involved in responding to a crisis in a timely fashion makes for a challenge in businesses. There must be open and consistent communication throughout the hierarchy to contribute to a successful crisis-communication process. The related terms emergency management and business-continuity management focus respectively on the prompt but short lived "first aid" type of response (e.g. putting the fire out) and the longer-term recovery and restoration phases (e.g. moving operations to another site). Crisis is also a facet of risk management, although it is probably untrue to say that crisis management represents a failure of risk management, since it will never be possible to totally mitigate the chances of catastrophes' occurring.

Types of Crisis

During the crisis management process, it is important to identify types of crises in that different crises necessitate the use of different crisis management strategies. Potential crises are enormous, but crises can be clustered.

Lerbinger categorized eight types of crises

1. Natural disaster
2. Technological crises
3. Confrontation
4. Malevolence
5. Organizational Misdeeds
6. Workplace Violence
7. Rumours
8. Terrorist attacks/man-made disasters

Natural Crisis

Natural crises, typically natural disasters considered as 'acts of God,' are such environmental phenomena as earthquakes, volcanic eruptions, tornadoes and hurricanes, floods, landslides, tsunamis, storms, and droughts that threaten life, property, and the environment itself.

Technological Crisis

Technological crises are caused by human application of science and technology. Technological accidents inevitably occur when technology becomes complex and coupled and something goes wrong in the system as a whole (Technological breakdowns). Some technological crises occur when human error causes disruptions (Human breakdowns). People tend to assign blame for a technological disaster because technology is subject to human manipulation whereas they do not hold anyone responsible for natural disaster. When an accident creates significant environmental damage, the crisis is categorized as *megadamage*. Samples include software failures, industrial accidents, and oil spills.

Confrontation Crisis

Confrontation crisis occur when discontented individuals and/or groups fight businesses, government, and various interest groups to win acceptance of their demands and expectations. The common type of confrontation crisis is boycotts, and other types are picketing, sit-ins, ultimatums to those in authority, blockade or occupation of buildings, and resisting or disobeying police.

Crisis of Malevolence

An organization faces a crisis of malevolence when opponents or miscreant individuals use criminal means or other extreme tactics for the purpose of expressing hostility or anger toward, or seeking gain from, a company, country, or economic system, perhaps with the aim of destabilizing or destroying it. Sample crisis include product tampering, kidnapping, malicious rumors,terrorism, and espionage.

Crisis of Organizational Misdeeds

Crisis occur when management takes actions it knows will harm or place stakeholders at risk for harm without adequate precautions. Lerbinger specified three different types of crises of organizational misdeeds: crises of skewed management values, crises of deception, and crises of management misconduct.

Crises of Skewed Management Values

Crises of skewed management values are caused when managers favour short-term economic gain and neglect broader social values and stakeholders other than investors. This state of lopsided values is rooted in the classical business creed that focuses on the interests of stockholders and tends to disregard the interests of its other stakeholders such as customers, employees, and the community

Crisis of Deception

Crisis of deception occur when management conceals or misrepresents information about itself and its products in its dealing with consumers and others.

Crises of Management Misconduct

Some crises are caused not only by skewed values and deception but deliberate amorality and illegality.

Workplace Violence

Crises occur when an employee or former employee commits violence against other employees on organizational grounds.

Rumors

False information about an organization or its products creates crises hurting the organization's reputation. Sample is linking the organization to radical groups or stories that their products are contaminated.

Crisis Leadership

Erika Hayes James, an organizational psychologist at the University of Virginia's Darden Graduate School of Business, identifies two primary types of organizational crisis. James defines organizational crisis as "any emotionally charged situation that, once it becomes public, invites negative stakeholder reaction and thereby has the potential to threaten the financial well-being, reputation, or survival of the firm or some portion thereof."

1. Sudden crisis
2. Smoldering crises

Sudden Crisis

Sudden crises are circumstances that occur without warning and beyond an institution's control. Consequently, sudden crises are most often situations for which the institution and its leadership are not blamed.

Smoldering Crisis

Smoldering crises differ from sudden crises in that they begin as minor internal issues that, due to manager's negligence, develop to crisis status. These are situations when leaders are blamed for the crisis and its subsequent effect on the institution in question.

James categorises five phases of crisis that require specific crisis leadership competencies. Each phase contains an obstacle that a leader must overcome to improve the structure and operations of an organization. James's case study on crisis in the financial services sector, for example, explores why crisis events erode public trust in leadership. James's research demonstrates how leadership competencies of integrity, positive intent, capability, mutual respect, and transparency impact the trust-building process.

1. Signal detection
2. Preparation and prevention
3. Containment and damage control
4. Business recovery
5. Learning

Signal Detection

Si Sense-making: represents an attempt to create order and make sense, retrospectively, of what occurs. Perspective-taking: the ability to consider another person's or group's point of view.

Preparation and Prevention

It is during this stage that crisis handlers begin preparing for or averting the crisis that had been foreshadowed in the signal detection stage. Organizations such as the Red Cross's primary mission is to prepare for and prevent the escalation of crisis events. Walmart has been described as an emergency-relief standard bearer after having witnessed the incredibly speedy and well-coordinated effort to get supplies to the Gulf Coast of the United States in anticipation of Hurricane Katrina.

Containment and Damage Control

Usually the most vivid stage, the goal of crisis containment and damage control is to limit the reputational, financial, safety, and other threats to firm survival. Crisis handlers work diligently during this stage to bring the crisis to an end as quickly as possible to limit the negative publicity to the organization, and move into the business recovery phase.

Business Recovery

When crisis hits, organizations must be able to carry on with their business in the midst of the crisis while simultaneously planning for how they will recover from the damage the crisis caused. Crisis handlers not only engage in continuity planning (determining the people, financial, and technology resources needed to keep the organization running), but will also actively pursue organizational resilience.

Learning

In the wake of a crisis, organizational decision makers adopt a learning orientation and use prior experience to develop new routines and behaviours that ultimately change the way the organization operates. The best leaders recognize this and are purposeful and skillful in finding the learning opportunities inherent in every crisis situation.

Crisis Communication

The effort taken by an organization to communicate with the public and stakeholders when an unexpected event occurs that could have a negative impact on the organization's reputation. This can also refer to the efforts to inform employees or the public of a potential hazard which could have a catastrophic impact. The Crisis Communication usually consists of three elements: 1. A holding statement (a passive prepared press statement which has been approved by the Crisis Communicators and Legal Advisors), 2. Questions & answers (Q&A) with prepared and agreed answers for foreseeable questions if asked and, 3. Internal communication.

Models and Theories Associated with Crisis Management

Crisis Management Model

Successfully defusing a crisis requires an understanding of how to handle a crisis – before they occur. Gonzalez-Herrero and Pratt found the different phases of Crisis Management.

There are 3 phases in any Crisis Management as shown below

1. The diagnosis of the impending trouble or the danger signals.
2. Choosing appropriate Turnaround Strategy.
3. Implementation of the change process and its monitoring.

Crisis Management Planning

No corporation looks forward to facing a situation that causes a significant disruption to their business, especially one that stimulates extensive media coverage. Public scrutiny can result in a negative financial, political, legal and government impact. Crisis management planning deals with providing the best response to a crisis.

Contingency Planning

Preparing contingency plans in advance, as part of a crisis-management plan, is the first step to ensuring an organization is appropriately prepared for a crisis. Crisis-management teams can rehearse a crisis plan by developing a simulated scenario to use as a drill. The plan should clearly stipulate that the only people to speak publicly about the crisis are the designated persons, such as the company spokesperson or crisis team members. The first hours after a crisis breaks are the most crucial, so working with speed and efficiency is important, and the plan should indicate how quickly each function should be performed. When preparing to offer a statement externally as well as internally, information should be accurate. Providing incorrect or manipulated information has a tendency to backfire and will greatly exacerbate the situation. The contingency plan should contain information and guidance that will help decision makers to consider not only the short-term consequences, but the long-term effects of every decision.

Business Continuity Planning

When a crisis will undoubtedly cause a significant disruption to an organization, a business continuity plan can help minimize the disruption. First, one must identify the critical functions and processes that are necessary to keep the organization running. Then each critical function and or/process must have its own contingency plan in the event that one of the functions/processes ceases or fails. Testing these contingency plans by rehearsing the required actions in a simulation will allow for all involved to become more sensitive and aware of the possibility of a crisis. As a result, in the event of an actual crisis, the team members will act more quickly and effectively.

Structural-Functional Systems Theory

Providing information to an organization in a time of crisis is critical to effective crisis management. Structural-functional systems theory addresses the intricacies of information networks and levels of command making up organizational communication. The structural-functional theory identifies information flow in organizations as "networks" made up of members and "links". Information in organizations flow in patterns called networks.

Diffusion of Innovation Theory

Another theory that can be applied to the sharing of information is Diffusion of Innovation Theory. Developed by Everett Rogers, the theory describes how innovation is disseminated and communicated through certain channels over a period of time. Diffusion of innovation in communication occurs when an individual communicates a new idea to one or several others. At its most elementary form, the process involves: (1) an innovation, (2) an individual or other unit of adoption that has knowledge of or experience with using the innovation, (3) another individual or other unit that does not yet have knowledge of the innovation, and (4) a communication channel connecting the two units. A communication channel is the means by which messages get from one individual to another.

Role of Apologies in Crisis Management

There has been debate about the role of apologies in crisis management, and some argue that apology opens an organization up for possible legal consequences. "However some evidence indicates that compensation and sympathy, two less expensive strategies, are as effective as an apology in shaping people's perceptions of the organization taking responsibility for the crisis because these strategies focus on the victims' needs. The sympathy response expresses concern for victims while compensation offers victims something to offset the suffering."

Crisis Leadership

James identifies five leadership competencies which facilitate organizational restructuring during and after a crisis.

1. Building an environment of trust
2. Reforming the organization's mindset
3. Identifying obvious and obscure vulnerabilities of the organization
4. Making wise and rapid decisions as well as taking courageous action
5. Learning from crisis to effect change.

Crisis leadership research concludes that leadership action in crisis reflects the competency of an organization, because the test of crisis demonstrates how well the institution's leadership structure serves the organization's goals and withstands crisis. Developing effective human resources is vital when building organizational capabilities through crisis management executive leadership.

Unequal Human Capital Theory

James postulates that organizational crisis can result from discrimination lawsuits. James's theory of unequal human capital and social position derives from economic theories of human and social capital concluding that minority employees receive fewer organizational rewards than those with access to executive management. In a recent study of managers in a *Fortune* 500 company, race was found to be a predictor of promotion opportunity or lack thereof. Thus, discrimination lawsuits can invite negative stakeholder reaction, damage the company's reputation, and threaten corporate survival.

Social Media and Crisis Management

Social media has accelerated the speed that information about a crisis can spread. The viral affect of social networks such as Twitter means that stakeholders can break news faster than traditional media - making managing a crisis harder. This can be mitigated by having the right training and policy in place as well as the right social media monitoring tools to detect signs of a crisis breaking. Social media also gives crisis management teams access to real-time information about how a crisis is impacting stakeholder sentiment and the issues that are of most concern to them. The crisis management mantra of Lanny Davis, former counsellor to Bill Clinton is to "Tell it Early, Tell it All, Tell it Yourself". A strategy employed at the Clinton White House 1996 – 1998, to any breaking Organizations should have a planned approach to releasing information to the media in the event of a crisis. A media reaction plan should include a company media representative as part of the Crisis Management Team (CMT). Since there is always a degree of unpredictability during a crisis, it is best that all CMT members understand how to deal with the media and be prepared to do so, should they be thrust into such a situation. In 2010 Procter & Gamble Co called reports that its new Pampers with Dry Max caused rashes and other skin irritations "completely false" as it aimed to contain a public relations threat to its biggest diaper innovation in 25 years. A Facebook group called "Pampers bring back the OLD CRUISERS/SWADDLERS" rose to over 4,500 members. Pampers denied the allegation and stated that only two complaints had been received for every one million diapers sold. Pampers quickly reached out to people expressing their concerns via social media, Pampers even held a summit with four influential "mommy bloggers," to help dispel the rumour. Pampers acted quickly and decisively to an emerging crisis, before competitors and critics alike could fuel the fire further. There is no truth. There is only perception.

Examples of Successful Crisis Management

Tylenol (Johnson and Johnson)

In the fall of 1982, a murderer added 65 milligrams of cyanide to some Tylenol capsules on store shelves, killing seven people, including three in one family. Johnson & Johnson recalled and destroyed 31 million capsules at a cost of $100 million. The affable CEO, James Burke, appeared in television ads and at news conferences informing consumers of the company's actions. Tamper-resistant packaging was rapidly introduced, and Tylenol sales swiftly bounced back to near pre-crisis levels. When another bottle of tainted Tylenol was discovered in a store, it took only a matter of minutes for the manufacturer to issue a nationwide warning that people should not use the medication in its capsule form.

Odwalla Foods

When Odwalla's apple juice was thought to be the cause of an outbreak of E. coli infection, the company lost a third of its market value. In October 1996, an outbreak of E. coli bacteria in Washington state, California, Colorado and British Columbia was traced to unpasteurized apple juice manufactured by natural juice maker Odwalla Inc. Forty-nine cases were reported, including the death of a small child. Within 24 hours, Odwalla conferred with the FDA and Washington state health officials; established a schedule of daily press briefings; sent out press releases which announced the recall; expressed remorse, concern and apology, and took responsibility for anyone harmed by their products; detailed symptoms of E. coli poisoning; and explained what consumers should do with any affected products. Odwalla then developed - through the help of consultants - effective thermal processes that would not harm the products' flavors when production resumed. All of these steps were communicated through close relations with the media and through full-page newspaper ads.

Mattel

Mattel Inc., the toy maker, has been plagued with more than 28 product recalls and in Summer of 2007, amongst problems with exports from China, faced two product recalls in two weeks. The company "did everything it could to get its message out, earning high marks from consumers and retailers. Though upset by the situation, they were appreciative of the company's response. At Mattel, just after the 7 a.m. recall announcement by federal officials, a public relations staff of 16 was set to call reporters at the 40 biggest media outlets. They told each to check their e-mail for a news release outlining the recalls, invited them to a teleconference call with executives and scheduled TV appearances or phone conversations with Mattel's chief executive. The Mattel CEO Robert Eckert did 14 TV interviews on a Tuesday in August and about 20 calls with individual reporters. By the week's end, Mattel had responded to more than 300 media inquiries in the U.S. alone."

Pepsi

The Pepsi Corporation faced a crisis in 1993 which started with claims of syringes being found in cans of diet Pepsi. Pepsi urged stores not to remove the product from shelves while it had the cans and the situation investigated. This led to an arrest, which Pepsi made public and then followed with their first video news release, showing the production process to demonstrate that such tampering was impossible within their factories. A second video news release displayed the man arrested. A third video news release showed surveillance from a convenience store where a woman was caught replicating the tampering incident. The company simultaneously publicly worked with the FDA during the crisis. The corporation was completely open with the public throughout, and every employee of Pepsi was kept aware of the details. This made public communications effective throughout the crisis. After the crisis had been resolved, the corporation ran a series of special campaigns designed to thank the public for standing by the corporation, along with coupons for further compensation. This case served as a design for how to handle other crisis situations.

Examples of Unsuccessful Crisis Management

Bhopal

The Bhopal disaster in which poor communication before, during, and after the crisis cost thousands of lives, illustrates the importance of incorporating cross-cultural communication in crisis management plans. According to American University's Trade Environmental Database Case Studies (1997), local residents were not sure how to react to warnings of potential threats from the Union Carbide plant. Operating manuals printed only in English is an extreme example of mismanagement but indicative of systemic barriers to information diffusion. According to Union Carbide's own chronology of the incident (2006), a day after the crisis Union Carbide's upper management arrived in India but was unable to assist in the relief efforts because they were placed under house arrest by the Indian government. Symbolic intervention can be counter productive; a crisis management strategy can help upper management make more calculated decisions in how they should respond to disaster scenarios. The Bhopal incident illustrates the difficulty in consistently applying management standards to multi-national operations and the blame shifting that often results from the lack of a clear management plan.

Ford and Firestone Tire and Rubber Company

The Ford-Firestone Tire and Rubber Company dispute transpired in August 2000. In response to claims that their 15-inch Wilderness AT, radial ATX and ATX II tire treads were separating from the tire core—leading to grisly, spectacular crashes—Bridgestone/Firestone recalled 6.5 million tires. These tires were mostly used on the Ford Explorer, the world's top-selling sport utility vehicle (SUV). The two companies committed three major blunders early on, say crisis experts. First, they blamed consumers for not inflating their tires properly. Then they blamed each other for faulty tires and faulty vehicle design. Then they said very little about what they were doing to solve a problem that had caused more than 100 deaths—until they got called to Washington to testify before Congress.

Exxon

On March 24, 1989, a tanker belonging to the Exxon Corporation ran aground in the Prince William Sound in Alaska. The Exxon Valdez spilled millions of gallons of crude oil into the waters off Valdez, killing thousands of fish, fowl, and sea otters. Hundreds of miles of coastline were polluted and salmon spawning runs disrupted; numerous fishermen, especially Native Americans, lost their livelihoods. Exxon, by contrast, did not react quickly in terms of dealing with the media and the public; the CEO, Lawrence Rawl, did not become an active part of the public relations effort and actually shunned public involvement; the company had neither a communication plan nor a communication team in place to handle the event—in fact, the company did not appoint a public relations manager to its management team until 1993, 4 years after the incident; Exxon established its media center in Valdez, a location too small and too remote to handle the onslaught of media attention; and the company acted defensively in its response to its publics, even laying blame, at times, on other groups such as the Coast Guard. These responses also happened within days of the incident.

Lessons Learned in Crisis Management

Impact of Catastrophes on Shareholder Value

One of the foremost recognized studies conducted on the impact of a catastrophe on the stock value of an organization was completed by Dr Rory Knight and Dr Deborah Pretty (1996, Templeton College, University of Oxford - commissioned by the Sedgewick Group). This study undertook a detailed analysis of the stock price (post impact) of organizations that had experienced catastrophes. The study identified organizations that recovered and even exceeded pre-catastrophe stock price, (*Recoverers*), and those that did not recover on stock price, (*Non-recoverers*). The average cumulative impact on shareholder value for the recoverers was 5% plus on their original stock value. So the net impact on shareholder value by this stage was actually positive. The non-recoverers remained more or less unchanged between days 5 and 50 after the catastrophe, but suffered a net negative cumulative impact of almost 15% on their stock price up to one year afterwards. One of the key conclusions of this study is that "Effective management of the consequences of catastrophes would appear to be a more significant factor than whether catastrophe insurance hedges the economic impact of the catastrophe". While there are technical elements to this report it is highly recommended to those who wish to engage their senior management in the value of crisis management.

Crisis as Opportunity

To address such shareholder impact, management must move from a mindset that manages crisis to one that generates crisis leadership. Research shows that organizational contributory factors affect the tendency of executives to adopt an effective "crisis as opportunity" mindset. Since pressure is both a precipitator and consequence of crisis, leaders who perform well under pressure can effectively guide the organization through such crisis. James contends that most executives focus on communications and public relations as a reactive strategy. While the company's reputation with shareholders, financial well-being, and survival are all at stake, potential damage to reputation can result from the actual management of the crisis issue. Additionally, companies may stagnate as their risk management group identifies whether a crisis is sufficiently "statistically significant". Crisis leadership, on the other hand, immediately addresses both the damage and implications for the company's present and future conditions, as well as opportunities for improvement.

Public-Sector Crisis Management

Corporate America is not the only community that is vulnerable to the perils of a crisis. Whether a school shooting, a public health crisis or a terrorist attack that leaves the public seeking comfort in the calm, steady leadership of an elected official, no sector of society is immune to crisis. In response to that reality, crisis management policies, strategies and practices have been developed and adapted across multiple disciplines.

Schools and Crisis Management

In the wake of the Columbine High School Massacre, the September 11 attacks in 2001, and shootings on college campuses including the Virginia Tech massacre, educational institutions at all levels are now focused on crisis management.

A national study conducted by the University of Arkansas for Medical Sciences (UAMS) and Arkansas Children's Hospital Research Institute (ACHRI) has shown that many public school districts have important deficiencies in their emergency and disaster plans (The School Violence Resource Center, 2003). In response the Resource Center has organized a comprehensive set of resources to aid schools is the development of crisis management plans. Crisis-management plans cover a wide variety of incidents including bomb threats, child abuse, natural disasters, suicide, drug abuse and gang activities – just to list a few. In a similar fashion the plans aim to address all audiences in need of information including parents, the media and law enforcement officials.

Government and Crisis Management

Historically, government at all levels—local, state, and national—has played a large role in crisis management. Indeed, many political philosophers have considered this to be one of the primary roles of government. Emergency services, such as fire and police departments at the local level, and the United States National Guard at the federal level, often play integral roles in crisis situations. To help coordinate communication during the response phase of a crisis, the U.S. Federal Emergency Management Agency (FEMA) within the Department of Homeland Security administers the National Response Plan (NRP). This plan is intended to integrate public and private response by providing a common language and outlining a chain-of-command when multiple parties are mobilized. It is based on the premise that incidences should be handled at the lowest organizational level possible. The NRP recognizes the private sector as a key partner in domestic incident management, particularly in the area of critical infrastructure protection and restoration. The NRP is a companion to the National Incidence Management System, which acts as a more general template for incident management regardless of cause, size, or complexity. FEMA offers free web-based training on the National Response Plan through the Emergency Management Institute. Common Alerting Protocol (CAP) is a relatively recent mechanism that facilitates crisis communication across different mediums and systems. CAP helps create a consistent emergency alert format to reach geographically and linguistically diverse audiences through both audio and visual mediums.

Elected Officials and Crisis Management

Historically, politics and crisis go hand in hand. In describing crisis, President Abraham Lincoln said, "We live in the midst of alarms, anxiety beclouds the future; we expect some new disaster with each newspaper we read." Crisis management has become a defining feature of contemporary governance. In times of crisis, communities and members of organizations expect their public leaders to minimize the impact of the crisis at hand, while critics and bureaucratic competitors try to seize the moment to blame incumbent rulers and their policies. In this extreme environment, policymakers must somehow establish a sense of normality, and foster collective learning from the crisis experience. In the face of crisis, leaders must deal with the strategic challenges they face, the political risks and opportunities they encounter, the errors they make, the pitfalls they need to avoid, and the paths away from crisis they may pursue. The necessity for management is even more significant with the advent of a 24-hour news cycle and an increasingly internet-savvy audience with ever-changing technology at its fingertips. Public leaders have a special responsibility to help safeguard society from the adverse consequences of crisis. Experts in crisis management note that leaders who take this responsibility seriously would have to concern themselves with all crisis phases: the incubation stage, the onset, and the aftermath. Crisis leadership then involves five critical tasks: sense making, decision making, meaning making, terminating, and learning.

A brief description of the five facets of crisis leadership includes:

1. Sense making may be considered as the classical situation assessment step in decision making.
2. Decision making is both the act of coming to a decision as the implementation of that decision.
3. Meaning making refers to crisis management as political communication.
4. Terminating a crisis is only possible if the public leader correctly handles the accountability question.
5. Learning, refers to the actual learning from a crisis is limited. The authors note, a crisis often opens a window of opportunity for reform for better or for worse.

Professional Organizations

There are a number of professional industry associations that provide advice, literature and contacts to turnaround professionals and academics. Some are:

1. Turnaround Management Society (International / Focus on Europe)
2. Institute for Turnaround (England)
3. Turnaround Management Association (International)
4. Institut für die Standardisierung von Unternehmenssanierungen (Germany)

FRANKLIN PLANNER

The Franklin Planner, a paper-based time management system created by Hyrum W. Smith and marketed from 1997 by the FranklinCovey company, consists physically of a ring binder holding specially designed loose-leaf pages. Divided by monthly tabs between the pages and accepting a wide variety of specialized accessories and inserts, the system aims to consolidate tasks and appointments along with personal records in one place for improved personal information management by eliminating "floating pieces of paper". Smith named his planning system after Benjamin Franklin (1706-1790), who famously kept a small private book as detailed in his autobiography. A core technique of the Franklin Planner system involves beginning each day with fifteen minutes of "solitude and planning".

Versions

The planner comes in five sizes:

1. Monarch (8.5x11", 216x280 mm)
2. Classic (5.5x8.5", 140x216 mm)
3. Compact (4.5x6.75",108x172 mm)
4. Pocket (3.5x6", 89x153 mm)
5. Micro

The standard daily section of the planner has two pages per day and has areas for a prioritized task list, an agenda of appointments and a daily record of events (diary) page. A key section at the rear of the book contains addresses. Other inserts include ledger sheets for tracking finances or vehicle mileage, exercise logs and other individualized reference materials.

Functions

Because of its overall design, the Franklin-Covey system lends itself to use as a tickler file, as well as a long-range planner. Most annual versions of the page inserts for the Franklin system include yearly calendars for at least five years; future monthly calendars for at least three years; and then the current year's pages and associated monthly calendars for planning. When used as a total package, the system provides a means of tracking minute details; storage of signed agreements (especially if pages are archived in the archival binders); and tracking of business and personal expenses for taxes.

Marketing

FranklinCovey markets the planner heavily to government and corporate workers in the United States, with a business strategy that creates revenue from sales of seminars, books, stationery and luxury-grade accessories. Marketing channels also exist outside the United States of America.

History

The Franklin Day Planner was first produced in 1984. There followed a time-management workshop, which emphasized clarification of personal values, priorities and mission. In August 1989 Simon and Schuster published *The Seven Habits of Highly Effective People* by Stephen Covey, and training and consulting based on its concepts were developed for this and for the 1994 book by Covey, Merrill, and Merrill, *First Things First*, in 1994. Ancillary software products were also created for Palm OS and Microsoft Windows in the late 1990s, promoted at specialized Franklin Covey retail stores. Although FranklinCovey (founded in 1997) operated 125 such stores in January 1999, many have closed in favour of retail sales through Office Depot, Staples, Office Max and licensed variants such as the "DayOne" line at Wal-Mart.

COMPUTER MULTITASKING

In computing, multitasking is a method where multiple tasks, also known as processes, are performed during the same period of time. The tasks share common processing resources, such as a CPU and main memory. In the case of a computer with a single CPU, only one task is said to be *running* at any point in time, meaning that the CPU is actively executing instructions for that task. Multitasking solves the problem by scheduling which task may be the one running at any given time, and when another waiting task gets a turn. The act of reassigning a CPU from one task to another one is called a context switch. When context switches occur frequently enough the illusion of parallelism is achieved. Even on computers with more than one CPU (called multiprocessor machines), multitasking allows many more tasks to be run than there are CPUs. The term "multitasking" has become an international term, as the same word is used in many other languages such as German, Italian, Dutch, Danish and Norwegian. Operating systems may adopt one of many different scheduling strategies, which generally fall into the following categories:

- In *multiprogramming* systems, the running task keeps running until it performs an operation that requires waiting for an external event (e.g. reading from a tape) or until the computer's scheduler forcibly swaps the running task out of the CPU. Multiprogramming systems are designed to maximize CPU usage.
- In *time-sharing* systems, the running task is required to relinquish the CPU, either voluntarily or by an external event such as a hardware interrupt. Time sharing systems are designed to allow several programs to execute apparently simultaneously.
- In *real-time* systems, some waiting tasks are guaranteed to be given the CPU when an external event occurs. Real time systems are designed to control mechanical devices such as industrial robots, which require timely processing.

Multiprogramming

In the early days of computing, CPU time was expensive, and peripherals were very slow. When the computer ran a program that needed access to a peripheral, the Central processing unit (CPU) would have to stop executing program instructions while the peripheral processed the data. This was deemed very inefficient. The first computer using a multiprogramming system was the British *Leo III* owned by J. Lyons and Co. Several different programs in batch were loaded in the computer memory, and the first one began to run. When the first program reached an instruction waiting for a peripheral, the context of this program was stored away, and the second program in memory was given a chance to run. The process continued until all programs finished running. The use of multiprogramming was enhanced by the arrival of virtual memory and virtual machine technology, which enabled individual programs to make use of memory and operating system resources as if other concurrently running programs were, for all practical purposes, non-existent and invisible to them. Multiprogramming doesn't give any guarantee that a program will run in a timely manner. Indeed, the very first program may very well run for hours without needing access to a peripheral. As there were no users waiting at an interactive terminal, this was no problem: users handed in a deck of punched cards to an operator, and came back a few hours later for printed results. Multiprogramming greatly reduced wait times when multiple batches were being processed.

Cooperative Multitasking/time-Sharing

The expression 'time sharing' was usually used to designate computers shared by interactive users at terminals, such as IBM's TSO, and VM/CMS. The term *time-sharing* is no longer commonly used, having been replaced by simply *multitasking*, and by the advent of personal computers and workstations rather than shared interactive systems. When computer usage evolved from batch mode to interactive mode, multiprogramming was no longer a suitable approach. Each user wanted to see their program running as if it were the only program in the computer. The use of time sharing made this possible, with the qualification that the computer would not seem as fast to any one user as it really would be if it were running only that user's program. Early multitasking systems used applications that voluntarily ceded time to one another. This approach, which was eventually supported by many computer operating systems, is known today as cooperative multitasking. Although it is now rarely used in larger systems, cooperative multitasking was once the scheduling scheme employed by Microsoft Windows (prior to Windows 95 and Windows NT) and Mac OS (prior to Mac OS X) in order to enable multiple applications to be run simultaneously. Windows 9x also used cooperative multitasking, but only for 16-bit legacy applications, much the same way as pre-

Leopard PowerPC versions of Mac OS X used it for Classic applications. The network operating system NetWare used cooperative multitasking up to NetWare 6.5. Cooperative multitasking is still used today on RISC OS systems. Because a cooperatively multitasked system relies on each process regularly giving up time to other processes on the system, one poorly designed program can consume all of the CPU time for itself or cause the whole system to hang. In a server environment, this is a hazard that makes the entire network brittle and fragile. All software must be evaluated and cleared for use in a test environment before being installed on the main server, or a misbehaving program on the server slows down or freezes the entire network. Despite the difficulty of designing and implementing cooperatively multitasked systems, time-constrained, real-time embedded systems (such as spacecraft) are often implemented using this paradigm. This allows highly reliable, deterministic control of complex real time sequences, for instance, the firing of thrusters for deep space course corrections.

Preemptive Multitasking/Time-Sharing

Preemptive multitasking allows the computer system to guarantee more reliably each process a regular "slice" of operating time. It also allows the system to deal rapidly with important external events like incoming data, which might require the immediate attention of one or another process. Operating systems were developed to take advantage of these hardware capabilities and run multiple processes preemptively. Digital Equipment Corporation was a leader in this. For example, preemptive multitasking was implemented in the earliest version of Unix in 1969, and is standard in Unix and Unix-like operating systems, including Linux, Solaris and BSD with its derivatives.

At any specific time, processes can be grouped into two categories: those that are waiting for input or output (called "I/O bound"), and those that are fully utilizing the CPU ("CPU bound"). In primitive systems, the software would often "poll", or "busywait" while waiting for requested input (such as disk, keyboard or network input). During this time, the system was not performing useful work. With the advent of interrupts and preemptive multitasking, I/O bound processes could be "blocked", or put on hold, pending the arrival of the necessary data, allowing other processes to utilize the CPU. As the arrival of the requested data would generate an interrupt, blocked processes could be guaranteed a timely return to execution. The earliest preemptive multitasking OS available to home users was Sinclair QDOS on the Sinclair QL, released in 1984, but very few people bought the machine. Commodore's powerful Amiga, released the following year, was the first commercially successful home computer to use the technology, and its multimedia abilities make it a clear ancestor of contemporary multitasking personal computers. Microsoft made preemptive multitasking a core feature of their flagship operating system in the early 1990s when developing Windows NT 3.1 and then Windows 95. It was later adopted on the Apple Macintosh by Mac OS 9.x as an additional API, i.e. the application could be programmed to use the preemptive or cooperative model, and all legacy applications were multitasked cooperatively within a single process. Mac OS X, being a Unix-like system, uses preemptive multitasking for all native applications, although Classic applications are multitasked cooperatively in a Mac OS 9 environment that itself is running as an OS X process (and is subject to preemption like any other OS X process).

Real Time

Another reason for multitasking was in the design of real-time computing systems, where there are a number of possibly unrelated external activities needed to be controlled by a single processor system. In such systems a hierarchical interrupt system is coupled with process prioritization to ensure that key activities were given a greater share of available process time.

Multithreading

As multitasking greatly improved the throughput of computers, programmers started to implement applications as sets of cooperating processes (e. g., one process gathering input data, one process processing input data, one process writing out results on disk). This, however, required some tools to allow processes to efficiently exchange data. Threads were born from the idea that the most efficient way for cooperating processes to exchange data would be to share their entire memory space. Thus, threads are basically processes that run in the same memory context. Threads are described as *lightweight* because switching between threads does not involve changing the memory context. While threads are scheduled preemptively, some operating systems provide a variant to threads, named *fibers*, that are scheduled cooperatively. On operating systems that do not provide fibers, an application may implement its own fibers using repeated calls to worker functions. Fibers are even more lightweight than threads, and somewhat easier to program with, although they tend to lose some or all of the benefits of threads on machines with multiple processors.

Memory Protection

When multiple programs are present in memory, an ill-behaved program may (inadvertently or deliberately) overwrite memory belonging to another program, or even to the operating system itself. The operating system therefore restricts the memory accessible to the running program. A program trying to access memory outside its allowed range is immediately stopped before it can change memory belonging to another process. Another key innovation was the idea of privilege levels. Low privilege tasks are not allowed some kinds of memory access and are not allowed to perform certain instructions. When a task tries to perform a privileged operation a trap occurs and a supervisory program running at a higher level is allowed to decide how to respond.

Memory Swapping

Use of a swap file or swap partition is a way for the operating system to provide more memory than is physically available by keeping portions of the primary memory in secondary storage. While multitasking and memory swapping are two completely unrelated techniques, they are very often used together, as swapping memory allows more tasks to be loaded at the same time. Typically, a multitasking system allows another process to run when the running process hits a point where it has to wait for some portion of memory to be reloaded from secondary storage.

Programming in a Multitasking Environment

Processes that are entirely independent are not much trouble to program. Most of the complexity in multitasking systems comes from the need to share computer resources between tasks and to synchronize the operation of co-operating tasks. Various concurrent computing techniques are used to avoid potential problems caused by multiple tasks attempting to access the same resource. Bigger systems were sometimes built with a central processor(s) and some number of I/O processors, a kind of asymmetric multiprocessing. Over the years, multitasking systems have been refined. Modern operating systems generally include detailed mechanisms for prioritizing processes, while symmetric multiprocessing has introduced new complexities and capabilities.

HUMAN MULTITASKING

Human multitasking is the apparent performance by an individual of handling more than one task at the same time. The term is derived from computer multitasking. An example of multitasking is taking phone calls while typing an email. Multitasking can result in time wasted due to human context switching and apparently causing more errors due to insufficient attention.

Etymology

The term "multitasking" originated in the computer engineering industry. It refers to the ability of a microprocessor to apparently process several tasks simultaneously. Computer multitasking in single core microprocessors actually involves time-sharing the processor; only one task can actually be active at a time, but tasks are rotated through many times a second. With multi-core computers, each core can perform a separate task simultaneously.

The first published use of the word "multitask" appeared in an IBM paper describing the capabilities of the IBM System/360 in 1965.

Research

Since the 1990s, experimental psychologists have started experiments on the nature and limits of human multitasking. It has been shown multitasking is not as workable as concentrated times. In general, these studies have disclosed that people show severe interference when even very simple tasks are performed at the same time, if both tasks require selecting and producing action (e.g., (Gladstones, Regan & Lee 1989) (Pashler 1994)). Many researchers believe that action planning represents a "bottleneck", which the human brain can only perform one task at a time. Psychiatrist Edward M. Hallowell has gone so far as to describe multitasking as a "mythical activity in which people believe they can perform two or more tasks simultaneously as effectively as one."

Others have researched multitasking in specific domains, such as learning. Mayer and Moreno have studied the phenomenon of cognitive load in multimedia learning extensively and have concluded that it is difficult, and possibly impossible to learn new information while engaging in multitasking. Junco and Cotten examined how multitasking affects academic success and found that students who engaged in more multitasking reported more problems with their academic work. A more recent study on the effects of multitasking on academic performance found that using Facebook and text messaging while studying were negatively related to student grades, while online searching and emailing were not.

The Brain's Role

Because the brain cannot fully focus when multitasking, people take longer to complete tasks and are predisposed to error. When people attempt to complete many tasks at one time, "or [alternate] rapidly between them, errors go way up and it takes far longer—often double the time or more—to get the jobs done than if they were done sequentially," states Meyer. This is largely because "the brain is compelled to restart and refocus". A study by Meyer and David Kieras found that in the interim between each exchange, the brain makes no progress whatsoever. Therefore, multitasking people not only perform each task less suitably, but lose time in the process. When presented with much information, the brain is forced to pause and refocus continuously as one switches between tasks. Realistically, this is "a rapid toggling among tasks rather than simultaneous processing." According to a study done by Jordan Grafman, chief of the cognitive neuroscience section at the National Institute of Neurological Disorders and Stroke, "the most anterior part [of the brain] allows [a person] to leave something when it's incomplete and return to the same place and continue from there," while Broadman's Area 10, a part of the brain's frontal lobes, is important for establishing and attaining long term goals. Focusing on multiple dissimilar tasks at once forces the brain to process all activity in its anterior. Though the brain is complex and can perform a myriad of tasks, it cannot multitask well.

Another study by René Marois, a psychologist of Vanderbilt University, discovered that the brain exhibits a "response selection bottleneck" when asked to perform several tasks at once. The brain must then decide which activity is most important, thereby taking more time. Psychologist David Meyer of the University of Michigan claims that, instead of a "bottleneck," the brain experiences "adaptive executive control" which places priorities on each activity. These viewpoints differ in that, while bottlenecking attempts to force many thoughts through the brain at once, adaptive executive control prioritizes tasks to maintain a semblance of order. The brain better understands this order and, as psychologists such as Dr. Meyer believe, can therefore be trained to multitask. It is not known exactly how the brain processes input and reacts to overstimulation.

Some research suggests that the human brain can be trained to multitask. A study published in Child Development by Monica Luciana, associate professor of psychology at the University of Minnesota, discovered that the brain's capability of categorizing competing information continues to develop until ages sixteen and seventeen. A study by Vanderbilt University found that multitasking is largely limited by "the speed with which our prefrontal cortex processes information." Paul E. Dux, co-author of the study, believes that this process can become faster through proper training. The study trained seven people to perform two simple tasks, either separately or together, and conducted brain scans of the participants. The individuals multitasked poorly at first but, with training, were able to adeptly perform the tasks simultaneously. Brain scans of the participants indicate that the prefrontal cortex quickened its ability to process the information, enabling the individuals to multitask more efficiently. However, the study also suggests that the brain is incapable of performing multiple tasks at one time, even after extensive training. This study further indicates that, while the brain can become adept at processing and responding to certain information, it cannot truly multitask.

People have a limited ability to retain information, which worsens when the amount of information increases. For this reason people alter information to make it more memorable, such as separating a ten-digit phone number into three smaller groups or dividing the alphabet into sets of three to five letters. George Miller, former psychologist at Harvard University, believes the limits to the human brain's capacity centers around "the number seven, plus or minus two." An illustrative example of this is a test in which a person must repeat numbers read aloud. While two or three numbers are easily repeated, shown in the beginning straight line, fifteen numbers becomes more difficult, as the line curves. The person would, on average, repeat seven correctly. Brains are only capable of storing a limited amount of information in their short term memories.

This ineffectiveness of the human brain for multitasking has been demonstrated in different studies. Laboratory based studies of multi-tasking indicate that one motivation for switching between tasks is to increase the time spent on the task that produces the most reward (Payne, Duggan & Neth, 2007). This reward could be progress towards an overall task goal or it could simply be the opportunity to pursue a more interesting or fun activity. Payne, Duggan and Neth (2007) found that decisions to switch task reflected either the reward provided by the current task or the availability of a suitable opportunity to switch (i.e. the completion of a subgoal). A French fMRI study published in 2010 indicated preliminary support for the hypothesis that the brain can pursue at most two goals simultaneously, one for each frontal lobe (which has a goal-oriented area).

Continuous Partial Attention

Author Steven Berlin Johnson describes one kind of multitasking: "It usually involves skimming the surface of the incoming data, picking out the relevant details, and moving on to the next stream. You're paying attention, but only partially. That lets you cast a wider net, but it also runs the risk of keeping you from really studying the fish." Multimedia pioneer Linda Stone coined the phrase "continuous partial attention" for this kind of processing. Continuous partial attention is multitasking where things do not get studied in depth.

Rapidly increasing technology fosters multitasking because it promotes multiple sources of input at a given time. Instead of exchanging old equipment like TV, print, and music, for new equipment such as computers, the Internet, and video games, children and teens combine forms of media and continually increase sources of input. According to studies by the Kaiser Family Foundation, in 1999 only 16 percent of time spent using media such as internet, television, video games, telephones, text-messaging, or e-mail was combined. In 2005, 26 percent of the time this media was used together. This increase in simultaneous media usage decreases the amount of attention paid to each device. In 2005 it was found that 82 percent of American youth use the Internet by the seventh grade. A 2005 survey by the Kaiser Family Foundation found that, while their usage of media continued at a constant 6.5 hours per day, Americans ages 8 to 18 were crowding roughly 8.5 hours' worth of media into their days due to multitasking.

The survey showed that one quarter to one third of the participants have more than one input "most of the time" while watching television, listening to music, or reading. The 2007 Harvard Business Review featured Linda Stone's idea of "continuous partial attention," or, "constantly scanning for opportunities and staying on top of contacts, events, and activities in an effort to miss nothing". As technology provides more distractions, attention is spread among tasks more thinly. A prevalent example of this inattention to detail due to multitasking is apparent when people talk on cell phones while driving. One study found that having an accident is four times more likely when using a cell phone while driving. Another study compared reaction times for experienced drivers during a number of tasks, and found that the subjects reacted more slowly to brake lights and stop signs during phone conversations than during other simultaneous tasks.

A 2006 study published in the Human Factors journal showed that drivers talking on cell phones were more involved in rear-end collisions and sped up slower than drivers intoxicated over the .08% legal limit. When talking, people must withdraw their attention from the road in order to formulate responses. Because the brain cannot focus on two sources of input at one time, driving and listening or talking, constantly changing input provided by cell phones distracts the brain and increases the likelihood of accidents.

Gender Differences

Although the idea that women are better multitaskers than men has been popular in the media as well in conventional thought, there is very little data available to support claims of a real gender difference. Most studies that do show any gender differences tend to find that the differences are small and inconsistent. A study by psychologist Keith Laws was widely reported in the press to have provided the first evidence of female multitasking superiority. In another study, females were found to perform slightly better at coordinating a primary test with a secondary test, supporting the notion that females are better at multitasking. However, the authors concluded their tests may not reflect real life multitasking and that further research was required. Conversely, a Swedish study found that men actually outperformed women at handling multiple tasks simultaneously, with the performance gap being correlated to the female menstrual cycle.

Popular Commentary on Practical Multitasking

Multitasking has been criticized as a hindrance to completing tasks or feeling happiness. Barry Schwartz has noted that, given the media-rich landscape of the Internet era, it is tempting to get into a habit of dwelling in a constant sea of information with too many choices, which has been noted to have a negative effect on human happiness. Observers of youth in modern society often comment upon the apparently advanced multitasking capabilities of the youngest generations of humans (Generation Y and Generation Z). While it is true that contemporary researchers find that youths in today's world exhibit high levels of multitasking, most experts believe that members of the Net Generation are not any better at multitasking than members of older generations. However, recent studies by Bardhi, Rohm, and Sultan argue that Generation Y is becoming better at media multitasking. This is evidenced by the fact that they are gaining control over deciding which messages they pay attention to or not. Furthermore, while there is a great deal of evidence showing the negative effects of multitasking on cognitive tasks, there is no evidence showing that multitasking has a positive or neutral effect on these tasks.

PARKINSON'S LAW

Parkinson's law is the adage which states that "work expands so as to fill the time available for its completion".

History

First articulated by Cyril Northcote Parkinson as part of the first sentence of a humorous essay published in *The Economist* in 1955, it was later reprinted together with other essays in the book *Parkinson's Law: The Pursuit of Progress* (London, John Murray, 1958). He derived the dictum from his extensive experience in the British Civil Service.

The current form of the law is not that which Parkinson refers to by that name in the article. Rather, he assigns to the term a mathematical equation describing the rate at which bureaucracies expand over time. Much of the essay is dedicated to a summary of purportedly scientific observations supporting his law, such as the increase in the number of employees at the Colonial Office while Great Britain's overseas empire declined (indeed, he shows that the Colonial Office had its greatest number of staff at the point when it was folded into the Foreign Office because of a lack of colonies to administer). He explains this growth by two forces: (1) "An official wants to multiply subordinates, not rivals" and

(2) "Officials make work for each other." He notes in particular that the total of those employed inside a bureaucracy rose by 5–7% per year "irrespective of any variation in the amount of work (if any) to be done". In 1986, Alessandro Natta complained about the swelling bureaucracy in Italy. Mikhail Gorbachev responded that "Parkinson's Law works everywhere".

Corollaries

In time, however, the first-referenced meaning of the phrase has dominated, and sprouted several corollaries, the most well known being the Stock-Sanford Corollary to Parkinson's Law:

> If you wait until the last minute, it only takes a minute to do.

Other corollaries include (relating to computers):

> Data expands to fill the space available for storage.
>
> or
>
> Storage requirements will increase to meet storage capacity.

Generalization

"Parkinson's Law" could be generalized further still as:

> The demand upon a resource tends to expand to match the supply of the resource.

An extension is often added to this, stating that:

> The reverse is not true.
>
> This generalization has become very similar to the economic law of demand; that the lower the price of a service or commodity, the greater the quantity demanded.

Some define Parkinson's Law in regard to time as:

> The amount of time which one has to perform a task is the amount of time it will take to complete the task.

Related Efficiency

Parkinson also proposed a rule about the efficiency of administrative councils. He defined a "coefficient of inefficiency" with the number of members as the main determining variable. The coefficient of inefficiency is a semi-humorous attempt of Parkinson to define the size of a committee or other decision-making body at which it becomes completely inefficient. In *Parkinson's Law: The Pursuit of Progress*, London: John Murray, 1958 one of the chapters is devoted to the basic question of comitology: how committees, government cabinets, and other such bodies are created and eventually grow irrelevant (or are initially designed as such).

Empirical evidence is drawn from historical and contemporary government cabinets. Most often, the minimal size of a state's most powerful and prestigious body is five members. From English history, Parkinson notes a number of bodies that lost power as they grew:

- The first cabinet was the Council of the Crown, now the House of Lords, which grew from an unknown initial number of members, to 29, to 50 before 1600, by which time it had lost much of its power.
- A new body was appointed in 1257, the "Lords of the King's Council", numbering fewer than 10. The body grew, and eventually ceased to meet when it numbered 172 members.
- The third incarnation of the English cabinet was the Privy Council, initially also numbering fewer than 10 members, rising to 47 in 1679.
- In 1615, the Privy Council lost power to the Cabinet Council, initially with 8 members, rising to 20 by 1725.
- Around 1740, the Cabinet Council was superseded by an inner group, called the Cabinet, initially with 5 members.

At the time of Parkinson's study (the 1950s), the Cabinet was still the official governing body. Parkinson observed that, from 1939 on, there was an effort to save the Cabinet as an institution. The membership had been fluctuating from a high of 23 members in 1939, down to 18 in 1954. A detailed mathematical expression is proposed by Parkinson for the coefficient of inefficiency, featuring many possible influences. In 2008, an attempt was made to empirically verify the proposed model. Parkinson's conjecture that membership exceeding a number "between 19.9 and 22.4" makes a committee manifestly inefficient seems well justified by the evidence proposed. Less certain is the optimal number of members, which must lie between three (a logical minimum) and 20. That it may be eight seems both justified and ruled out by observation: no contemporary government in Parkinson's data set had eight members, and only the unfortunate king Charles I of England had a Committee of State with that membership. He also wrote the book *Mrs. Parkinson's Law: and Other Studies in Domestic Science*.

In Popular Culture

A "generalization" of Parkinson's law, is mentioned in an episode of British comedy series Yes Minister, The Skeleton in the Cupboard, originally aired on November 25, 1982. In that episode, an undersecretary of the

Department, played by Ian Lavender, explains to the Minister that a certain county "has the smallest establishment of social workers in the U.K." Answering the Minister's question "Is that supposed to be a good thing?", he replies, "Oh yes, sign of efficiency. Parkinson's law of social work you see; it's well known that social problems increase to occupy the total number of social workers to deal with them".

REFERENCES

Adam Gorlick (2009). Media multitaskers pay mental price, Stanford study shows, Stanford Report, August 24, 2009.

Alan B. Bernstein and Cindy Rakowitz (2012). *Emergency Public Relations: Crisis Management In a 3.0 World*. p. 5.

Anders Hayden – Common Dreams (2012-06-11). "Working Less for a Sustainable Future". CommonDreams.com.

Ansley J. Coale; Judith Banister (December 1996). "Five decades of missing females in China". *Proceedings of the American Philosophical Society* 140 (4): 421–450.

Barker, James. "Tightening the Iron Cage: Concertive Control in Self-Managing Teams." *Administrative Science Quarterly* 38 (1993): 408-37.

Bechler, J.G (1984). *The Productivity Management Process*. American Productivity Center.

Boswell, Wendy, and Julie Olson-Buchanan. "The Use of Communication Technologies After Hours: The Role of Work Attitudes and Work-Life Conflict." *Journal of Management* 33.4 (2007): 592-608.

Caspari, Rachel & Lee, Sang-Hee (July 27, 2004). "Older age becomes common late in human evolution". *Proceedings of the National Academy of Sciences* 101 (20): 10895–10900.

Cecil Alec Mace: The man who discovered goal-setting, by Paula Phillips Carsona; Kerry D. Carsona; Ronald B. Headya;

Cohen, Yehudi (1974). *Man in Adaptation: the cultural present*. Aldine Transaction. pp. 94–95.

Conrad, Lawrence I. (2006). *The Western Medical Tradition*. Cambridge University Press. p. 137.

Coombs, W. T. (2007). *Ongoing Crisis Communication: Planning, Managing, and Responding* (2nd ed.). Thousand Oaks, CA: Sage.

Coote, A. *et al.* (2012) *21 Hours: Why a Shorter Working Week Can Help Us All to Flourish in the 21st Century* (London: New Economics Foundation)

Courbois, R.; Temple, P. (1975). *La methode des "Comptes de surplus" et ses applications macroeconomiques*. 160 des Collect,INSEE,Serie C (35). p. 100.

Craig, C.; Harris, R. (1973). "Total Productivity Measurement at the Firm Level". *Sloan Management Review* (Spring 1973): 13–28.

Eliahu Zahavi,Vladimir Torbilo & Solomon Press (1996) Fatigue Design: Life Expectancy of Machine Parts. CRC Press.

Farb, Peter (1968). *Man's Rise to Civilization As Shown by the Indians of North America from Primeval Times to the Coming of the Industrial State.*

Fowler, Elizabeth M (May 5, 1957). *It's a 'Law' now: Payrolls grow.* The New York Times.

Frier, Bruce W. (2001). "More is worse: some observations on the population of the Roman empire". In Scheidel, Walter. *Debating Roman Demography.* Leiden: Brill. pp. 144–145.

Galor, Oded & Moav, Omer (2007). "The Neolithic Revolution and Contemporary Variations in Life Expectancy". *Brown University Working Paper.* Retrieved 12 September 2010.

Genesca, G.E.; Grifell, T. E. (1992). "Profits and Total Factor Productivity: A Comparative Analysis". *Omega. the International Journal of Management Science* 20 (5/6): 553–568.

Gollop, F.M. (1979). "Accounting for Intermediate Input: The Link Between Sectoral and Aggregate Measures of Productivity Growth". *Measurement and Interpretation of Productivity,* (National Academy of Sciences).

Hans-Joachim Voth (2000) *Time and work in England 1750–1830, Chapter 5,* Comparisons and conclusions *pp. 242–5*

Horowitz, C.F. (August 30, 2004) "The Wrong Way to Shorten the Work Week" *Mises Daily* (The Ludwig von Mises Institute)

Iyengar, S; Kinder, D (1987). *News that mattes: Television and American opinion.* Chicago, IL: University of Chicago Press.

Janice Peterson – DAILY HERALD (2008-06-09). "Study finds four-day work week optimal". Heraldextra.com.

Junco, R. & Cotten, S. (2012). No A 4 U: The relationship between multitasking and academic performance. Computers & Education, 59(2), 505–514.

Klingberg, Torkel (2009). *The Overflowing Brain: Information Overload and the Limits of Working Memory.* Oxford: Oxford UP. pp. 7, 8.

Latham, Gary P.; Budworth, Marie-Hélène (2006), "The Study of Work Motivation in the 20th Century", in Koppes, Laura L., *Historical Perspectives in Industrial and Organizational Psychology,* Lawrence Erlbaum Associates, p. 366.

Lin, Lin (Sep 11). "Multitasking in Today's Learning Environment:Does Technology Make a Difference? University of North Texas.".

Lombardo, C.N. (February 4, 2010) "Shorter Workweek in a Tough Economy" *Wisconsin Employment Law Letter* (hrhero.com)

Reynolds, J. (2005). In the face of conflict: Work-life conflict and desired work hour adjustments. In *Journal of Marriage and Family* 67 (pp. 1313-1331).

Rogers, E (1993). "The anatomy of agenda-setting research". *Journal of Communication* 43 (2): 68–84.

Santrock, John (2007). Life Expectancy. A Topical Approach to: Life-Span Development(pp. 128-132). New York, New York: The McGraw-Hill Companies, Inc.

Shrivastava, P. Mitroff, I.I., Miller, D. and A. Miglani, " Understanding industrial crises".*Journal of Management Studies*, 1988, 25, 4, 285-304.

3

Time Perception, Allocation and Time Discipline: An Overview

"Everything requires time. It is the only truly universal condition. All work takes place in time and uses up time. Yet most people take for granted this unique, irreplaceable, and necessary resource. Nothing else, perhaps, distinguishes effective executives as much as their tender loving care of time."

—Peter F. Drucker

UNDERSTANDING TIME PERCEPTION

Time perception is a field of study within psychology and neuroscience. It refers to the sense of time, which differs from other senses since time cannot be directly perceived but must be reconstructed by the brain. Humans can perceive relatively short periods of time, in the order of milliseconds, and also durations that are a significant fraction of a lifetime. Human perception of duration is subjective and variable. Some researchers attempt to categorise people by how they differ in their perception of time. Pioneering work, emphasizing species-specific differences, was done by Karl Ernst von Baer. Experimental work began under the influence of the psycho-physical notions of Gustav Theodor Fechner with studies of the relationship between perceived and measured time. Work with animals conducted by Jakob von Uexküll included measurement of length of momentum in snails.

Theories

William J. Friedman also contrasted two theories for a sense of time:

- The strength model of time memory. This posits a *memory*

trace that persists over time, by which one might judge the age of a memory (and therefore how long ago the event remembered occurred) from the strength of the trace. This conflicts with the fact that memories of recent events may fade more quickly than more distant memories.

- The inference model suggests the time of an event is inferred from information about relations between the event in question and other events whose date or time is known.

Short-Term

Although the sense of time is not associated with a specific sensory system the work of psychologists and neuroscientists indicates that human brains do have a system governing the perception of time, composed of a highly distributed system involving the cerebral cortex, cerebellum and basal ganglia. One particular component, the suprachiasmatic nucleus, is responsible for the circadian (or daily) rhythm, while other cell clusters appear to be capable of shorter-range (ultradian) timekeeping. Experiments have shown that rats can successfully estimate intervals of time around 40 seconds despite having their cortex entirely removed, which suggests it is a low level (subcortical) process.

Specious Present

The specious present is the time duration wherein a state of consciousness is experienced as being in the present. The term was first introduced by the philosopher E. R. Clay. and developed by William James. A version of the concept was used by Edmund Husserl in his works and discussed further by Francisco Varela based on the writings of Husserl, Heidegger, and Merleau-Ponty. The experienced present is an interval; it's not a momentary instant except 'speciously'. The concept was further developed by Harvard professor of philosophy William James. James defined the specious present to be "the prototype of all conceived times... the short duration of which we are immediately and incessantly sensible". C.D. Broad in "Scientific Thought" (1930) further elaborated on the concept of the specious present, and considered that the Specious Present may be considered as the temporal equivalent of a sensory datum.

Long-Term

Psychologists assert that time seems to go faster with age, but the literature on this age-related perception of time remains controversial. One day to an eleven-year-old would be approximately 1/4,000 of their life, while one day to a 55-year-old would be approximately 1/20,000 of their life. This is perhaps why a day would appear much longer to a young child than to an adult. In an experiment comparing a group of subjects aged between 19 and 24 and a group between 60 and 80 asked to estimate when they thought 3 minutes had passed, it was found that the younger group's estimate was on average 3 minutes and 3 seconds, while the older group averaged 3 minutes and 40 seconds, indicating a change in the perception of time with age. People tend to recall recent events as occurring further back in time (backward telescoping) and distant events occurring more recently (forward telescoping). It has been proposed that the subjective experience of time changes with age due to changes in the individual's biological makeup.

Illusions of Time

A temporal illusion is a distortion in sensory perception caused when the time between the occurrence of two or more events is very short (typically less than a second). In such cases a person may misperceive the temporal order of the events. The kappa effect is a form of temporal illusion verifiable by experiment whereby time intervals between visual events are perceived as relatively longer or shorter depending on the relative spatial positions of the events. In other words: the perception of temporal intervals appears to be directly affected, in these cases, by the perception of spatial intervals. The Kappa effect can be displayed when considering a journey made in two parts that take an equal amount of time. Between these two parts, the journey that covers more distance will appear to take longer than the journey covering less distance, even though they take an equal amount of time.

Psychoactive Substances

Psychoactive drugs can alter the judgement of time. Some – such as entheogens – may also dramatically alter a person's temporal judgement. Substances as LSD, psilocybin, and peyote may affect our time perception. At higher doses time may appear to slow down, stop, speed up, go backwards or even seem out of sequence. In 1955, British MP Christopher Mayhew took mescaline hydrochloride in an experiment under the guidance of his friend, Dr Humphry Osmond. On the BBC documentary *The Beyond Within*, he described that half a dozen times during the experiment, he had "a period of time that didn't end for me". Stimulants can lead both humans and rats to overestimate time intervals. while depressants can have the opposite effect. The level of activity in the brain of neurotransmitters such as dopamine and norepinephrine may be the reason for this.

Altered States

Hypnosis can affect the perception of time.

Clinical Disorders

The sense of time is altered in some people with neurological diseases such as Parkinson's disease and attention deficit disorder.

Personality Characteristics

Some researchers aim to explain the differences between people in the way they relate to the time they have to perform different tasks. They claim that time perception is influenced by both internal-personal characteristics and by external-environmental factors. Some theorists suggest that time perception is categorized by two axes: "time perspective" and "time urgency" and these ideas have been used in occupational psychology settings. These axes typically create four personalities that differ in their personal characteristics and the way they deal with tasks. Time perspective can be affected by genetics, culture, religion, arise from education, family, past employment, and so on. As it is well known, the timeline axis moves between past, present and future, which is also the way the time perspective axis is organized. People with a present perspective of time have a tendency to believe that the actions in the present do not significantly affect the future. That is, these people do not think that an action taken place in the present will increase the probability of a future outcome.

People with this perspective tend to use the term "why do today what can be done tomorrow?" Individuals with personality characteristics of present time perspective tend to think that it is unnecessary to make future plans. These individuals also tend to take risks and act impulsively. People with future perspective tend to believe that an action taken place in the present increases the probability of a future outcome. These people are very goal-oriented, with high capacity to infer future results, usually prepare task lists, use a calendar, and tend to wear a watch. When a team is assembled from the majority of future time perspective people, the team tends to be more "flexible" and tends to make more changes in strategic thinking than teams with more present time perception individuals. Such an individual will delay his or her performances to the very last moment, which can at times lead to inability to meet deadlines. When such a person belongs to a work team, he/she makes the team less focused strategically, being late in submitting tasks and acting impulsively. Time urgency relates to the need for quick response or action, to achieve a particular goal (or non existence of this feeling). It can be described as an axis ranging from high to low.

The two dimensions described above, produce four types of personalities, that can be described as follows: Organizers have high time urgency and future time perspective and are characterized by high awareness of time, scheduling tasks and activities and high achievement striving. Crammers have high time urgency and present time perspective and are characterized by high awareness of time, needing to exert control over deadlines, competitiveness, high achievement striving and impatience. Relators have low time urgency and present time perspective and are characterized by attending little to deadlines or passage of time, taking risks, acting impulsively, focusing on present tasks and focusing on relations with others. Visioners have low time urgency and future time perspective and are characterized by attending little to deadlines or passage of time, taking risks, acting impulsively and focusing on future goals.

UNDERSTANDING TIME ALLOCATION

Time allocation is the allocation of time to different tasks and activities. The measurement of such allocations may be used analytically in studies of human behaviour. Scheduling and time management may be used to plan and control the amount of time allocated to various activities, so as to improve productivity and satisfy multiple goals and targets.

USING TIME TRACKING SOFTWARE

Time tracking software is a category of computer software that allows its users to record time spent on tasks. This software is typically used by professionals who bill their customers by the hour, including lawyers and accountants. It represents an electronic version of the traditional paper timesheet. Many such packages allow the automatic generation of invoices to the professional's clients or customers based on the time spent and the hourly fee, and allow for the additional billing of related costs to each client or file.

Types of Time Tracking Software

Timesheet software software - allows to enter time spent performing different tasks while working. Time tracking/recording software - automatically records activities performed on a computer. Time tracking software can be:

- Standalone - used only to record timesheets, and generate reports
- Integrated into accounting system - where timesheet data is directly fed into company accounts
- Integrated into billing system - used to generate invoices, especially used by contractors and professionals such as lawyers
- Integrated into project management systems - timesheet data is used in project management software to graph the effort being spent on each project or task.

- Integrated into payroll system - timesheet data is used in payroll software to pay employees based on their time worked.

Timesheet Software

Timesheet software is an accounting software used to maintain timesheets. This was the very first wave of the time tracking software when computers came to many offices. The idea is to replace all heavy paperwork and get more organized. Timesheet software allows entering time spent performing different tasks while working. When used within companies, employees enter their time into an electronic timesheet, which can then be approved or rejected by supervisors or project managers. When used by freelancers, this software allows creating reports for clients to explain how their time was spent. Increasingly, timesheet software is web-based, making deployment much easier.

Time Tracking/Recording Software

Time tracking/recording software automates time tracking process by recording what activities, when and for how long are performed on a computer. This was the second wave of the time tracking software. The idea is to get the actual picture about computer usage. Automatic time tracking/recording software shows applications, documents, games, websites usage. When used within companies, this software allows monitoring employees' productivity by recording computer and Internet usage. Also, it can be used to help to complete timesheets. When used by freelancers, this software helps to create reports for clients (like timesheets and invoices) or to prove work.

Note: information in this article is based on the current time tracking market research.

UNDERSTANDING TIMESHEET

A timesheet (or time sheet) is a method for recording the amount of a worker's time spent on each job.

Use

Originally developed for an employer to determine payroll, timesheets are not just for payroll any more. Timesheets may record the start and end time of tasks, or just the duration. It may contain a detailed breakdown of tasks accomplished throughout the project or program. This information may be used for payroll, client billing, and increasingly for project costing, estimation, tracking and management. Some companies provide web-based timesheet software or services that provide a means to track time for payroll, billing and project management.

One of the major uses of timesheets in a project management environment is comparing planned costs versus actual costs, as well as measuring employee performance, and identifying problematic tasks. This knowledge can drive corporate strategy as users stop performing or reassign unprofitable work.

Time Cards

Factory workers often have a "time card" and "punch in" by inserting their card into an automatic timestamp machine (sometimes known as a bundy clock) when starting and ending their work shift.

Advantages

Time tracking can lower costs in 3 ways: by making payroll processing more efficient, by making costs visible so you can lower them, and by automating billing & invoicing. Time tracking can increase revenue through automating billing, which tends to make it easier for a company to get correct invoices out for all hours worked by consulting staff. This speeds up payment and eliminates the hassles of 'dropping' bills. By lowering costs in 3 ways, and increasing revenue in one way, timesheet management technologies that are web-based can improve the health of companies. In the project management world, timesheets can also be used to build a body of knowledge about how much effort tasks take to develop. For example if developing a training plan has historically taken a month, then it can be assumed that creating a new one will take a month. Also most timesheet software has the ability to track resource costs and project expenses to allow for better future budgeting. For the HR function, the time spent on activities by individuals can be analyzed over a period of time and categorized into broad types. Based on the outcome roles could be realigned.

Disadvantages

- Based on Karl Marx's Labor Theory of Value.
- Prone to human error.

- Repetitive.
- Stressful to employees when used inflexibly.
- Rounding errors (12:27:34 is not the same as 12:30) Although Federal law in the USA requires that if employers round up when you clock in, they must round up when you clock out. So in this case it is not a disadvantage to the employee's pay calculation. It is only a disadvantage for accuracy

UNDERSTANDING TIMEBOXING

Timeboxing is a planning technique common in planning projects (typically for software development), where the schedule is divided into a number of separate time periods (timeboxes, normally two to six weeks long), with each part having its own deliverables, deadline and budget. Timeboxing is a core aspect of rapid application development (RAD) software development processes such as dynamic systems development method (DSDM) and agile software development. Timeboxes are used as a form of risk management, especially for tasks that may easily extend past their deadlines.

The end date (deadline) is one of the primary drivers in the planning and should not be changed as it is usually linked to a delivery date of the product. If the team exceeds the deadline, the team failed in proper planning and / or effective execution of the plan. This can be the result of: the wrong people on the wrong job (lack of communication between teams, lack of experience, lack of commitment / drive / motivation, lack of speed) or underestimation of the (complexity of the) requirements. When the team exceeds the deadline, the following actions might be taken after conferring with the Client:

1. Dropping requirements of lower impact (the ones that will not be directly missed by the user)
2. Working overtime to compensate for the time lost

Triple Constraint Management

There are three main constraints to managing projects: time, cost, and scope (often extended to four including quality). Without timeboxing, projects usually work to a fixed scope, such that when it is clear that some deliverables cannot be completed, either the deadline slips (to allow more time) or more people are involved (to do more in the same time). Usually both happen, delivery is late, costs go up, and often quality suffers (if only that requirements had changed by the time the project delivered). With timeboxing, the deadline is fixed, but the scope may be reduced. This focuses work on the most important deliverables. For this reason, timeboxing depends on the prioritization (with the MoSCoW Method for example) of deliverables, to ensure that it is the project stakeholders who determine the important deliverables rather than software developers. A lack of detailed specifications typically is the result of a lack of time, or the lack of knowledge of the desired end result (solution). In many types of projects, and especially in software engineering, analyzing and defining *all* requirements and specifications before the start of the realization phase is impossible. Timeboxing can be a favourable type of contracting for projects in which the deadline is *the* most critical aspect and when not all requirements are completely specified up front. The advantages of timeboxing over working with more traditional methods - in which there is a need to specify all details and features upfront - are that work can be started on the actual solution, or product, sooner, because less requirements and specifications gathering is necessary upfront. There is also a better structure for allowing for new insights that are developed during the project to be reflected in the end result.

Personal Timeboxing

Individuals can use timeboxing for personal tasks, as well. This technique utilizes a reduced scale of time (e.g., thirty minutes instead of a week) and deliverables (e.g., chores instead of a component of a business project). Personal timeboxing also works to curb perfectionist tendencies by setting a firm time and not overcommitting to a task. This method can also be used to overcome procrastination.

UNDERSTANDING OPPORTUNITY COST

Opportunity cost is the cost of any activity measured in terms of the best alternative forgone. It is the sacrifice related to the second best choice available to someone who has picked among several mutually exclusive choices. It is a key concept in economics. It has been described as expressing "the basic relationship between scarcity and choice." The notion of opportunity cost plays a crucial part in ensuring that scarce resources are used efficiently. Thus, opportunity costs are not restricted to monetary or financial costs: the real cost of output forgone, lost time, pleasure or any other benefit that provides utility should also be considered opportunity costs. The concept of an opportunity cost was first developed by John Stuart Mill.

Opportunity Costs in Consumption

Opportunity cost is assessed in not only monetary or material terms, but also in terms of anything which is of value. For example, a person who desires to watch each of two television programs being broadcast simultaneously, and does not have the means to make a recording of one, can watch only one of the desired programs. Therefore, the opportunity cost of watching *Dallas* could be not enjoying the other program (e.g. *Dynasty*). Of course, if an individual records one program while watching the other, the opportunity cost will be the time that the individual spends watching one program versus the other. In a restaurant situation, the opportunity cost of eating steak could be trying the salmon. For the diner, the opportunity cost of ordering both meals could be twofold - the extra $20 to buy the second meal, and his reputation with his peers, as he may be thought gluttonous or extravagant for ordering two meals. A family might decide to use a short period of vacation time to visit Disneyland rather than doing household improvements.

The opportunity cost of having happier children could therefore be a remodeled bathroom. In environmental protection, the opportunity cost is also applicable. This has been demonstrated in the legislation that required the carcinogenic aromatics (mainly reformate) to be largely eliminated from gasoline. Unfortunately, this required refineries to install equipment at a cost of hundreds of millions of dollars - and pass the cost to the consumer. The absolute number of cancer cases following from exposure to gasoline, however, is low, estimated a few cases per year in the U.S. Thus, the decision to legally require less aromatics has been criticized on the grounds of opportunity cost: the hundreds of millions spent on process redesign could have been spent on other, more fruitful ways of reducing deaths caused by cancer or automobiles. These actions (or strictly, the best one of them) are the opportunity cost of reduction of aromatics in gasoline.

Opportunity Costs in Production

Opportunity costs may be assessed in decision-making process of production. If the workers on a farm can produce either 1 million pounds of wheat or 2 million pounds of barley, then the opportunity cost of producing 1 pound of wheat is the 2 pounds of barley forgone. Firms would make rational decisions by weighing the sacrifices involved.

Explicit Costs

Explicit costs are opportunity costs that involve direct monetary payment by producers. The opportunity cost of the factors of production not already owned by a producer is the price that the producer has to pay for them. For instance, a firm spends $100 on electrical power consumed, the opportunity cost is $100. The firm has sacrificed $100, which could have been spent on other factors of production.

Implicit Costs

Implicit costs are by contrast, the opportunity costs that involve only factors of production that a producer already owns. They are equivalent to what the factors could earn for the firm in alternative uses, either operated within the firm or rent out to other firms.

Evaluation

The consideration of opportunity costs is one of the key differences between the concepts of economic cost and accounting cost. Assessing opportunity costs is fundamental to assessing the true cost of any course of action. In the case where there is no explicit accounting or monetary cost (price) attached to a course of action, or the explicit accounting or monetary cost is low, then, ignoring opportunity costs may produce the illusion that its benefits cost nothing at all. The unseen opportunity costs then become the implicit hidden costs of that course of action. Note that opportunity cost is not the sum of the available alternatives when those alternatives are, in turn, mutually exclusive to each other. The opportunity cost of the city's decision to build the hospital on its vacant land is the loss of the land for a sporting center, or the inability to use the land for a parking lot, or the money which could have been made from selling the land, as use for any one of those purposes would preclude the possibility to implement any of the other. It is also the cost of the forgone products after making a choice. However, most opportunities are difficult to compare. Opportunity cost has been seen as the foundation of the marginal theory of value as well as the theory of time and money. In some cases it may be possible to have more of everything by making different choices; for instance, when an economy is within its production possibility frontier. In microeconomic models this is unusual, because individuals are assumed to maximise utility, but it is a feature of Keynesian macroeconomics. In these circumstances opportunity cost is a less useful concept. In a 2005 survey at the annual meeting of American Economic Association, 21.6% of professional economists surveyed chose the correct answer to a question on opportunity cost. The researchers later asked a similar but differently phrased question, to which a majority of the economists surveyed gave an incorrect answer. When the researchers posed the original question to a larger group of college students, 7.4% of those who had taken a course in economics answered correctly, compared to 17.2% of those who had never taken one. The researchers, Paul J. Ferraro and Laura O. Taylor of Georgia State University, labeled the results "a dismal performance from the dismal science."

RELEVANCE OF AFRICAN TIME

African time (or Africa time) is a colloquial term used to describe a perceived cultural tendency, in some parts of Africa, toward a more relaxed attitude to time. This is sometimes used in a pejorative sense, about tardiness in appointments, meetings and events. The term is also sometimes used to describe the more leisurely, relaxed and less rigorously scheduled lifestyle found in African countries, especially as opposed to the more clock-bound pace of daily life in Western countries. As such it is similar to time orientations in some other non-Western culture regions.

Aspects of African Time

African cultures are often described as "polychronic," which means basically that people tend to manage more than one thing at a time rather than in a strict sequence. Personal interactions and relationships are also managed in this way (such that it is not uncommon, for instance, to have more than one simultaneous conversation). Perhaps for this reason, an African "emotional time consciousness" has been suggested in contrast with Western "mechanical time consciousness" as a way of understanding African time. Therefore, what appears to be a simple lack of punctuality or a lax attitude about time in Africa, may actually reflect (at least in large part) a different approach and set of priorities in managing tasks, events, and interactions. Being kept waiting, which may be perceived by an outsider as another example of African time, may, depending on the context, actually be a statement of relative status by the person keeping others waiting (which is not uncommon in various cultures).

Reactions to Time Orientation in Africa

Self-Criticism

The concept of African time has become a key topic of self-criticism in modern Africa. According to one Ghanaian writer,

> One of the main reasons for the continuing underdevelopment of our country is our nonchalant attitude to time and the need for punctuality in all aspects of life. The problem of punctuality has become so endemic that lateness to any function is accepted and explained off as 'African time.'

In October 2007, an Ivorian campaign against African time, backed by President Laurent Gbagbo, received international media attention when an event called "Punctuality Night" was held in Abidjan to recognize business people and government workers for regularly being on time. The slogan of the campaign is "'African time' is killing Africa - let's fight it." Reuters reported that "organizers hope to heighten awareness of how missed appointments, meetings or even late buses cut productivity in a region where languid tardiness is the norm." It was remarked that this year's winner, legal adviser Narcisse Aka—who received a $60,000 villa in recognition of his punctuality—"is so unusually good at being punctual that his colleagues call him 'Mr White Man's Time'".

Popular Culture

The contrast between African time and Western time is illustrated in the award-winning short film *Binta and the Great Idea*. The protagonist of the film, a fisherman in a small village in Senegal, can't understand the new ideas brought back from Europe by his friend; these are symbolized by a Swiss wristwatch, which rings at various times to the delight of the friend, but for no apparent reason. The fisherman is shown making his way through the various ranks of officials with his idea, which in the end is a sharp criticism of Western culture's obsession with efficiency and progress.

UNDERSTANDING PUNCTUALITY

Punctuality is the characteristic of being able to complete a required task or fulfill an obligation before or at a previously-designated time. "Punctual" is often used synonymously with "on time." Punctual can also, when talking about grammar, mean to be accurate. According to each culture, there is often an understanding about what is considered an acceptable degree of punctuality. Usually, a small amount of lateness is acceptable; this is commonly about ten or fifteen minutes in Western cultures. In some cultures, such as Japanese society, or in the military there basically is no allowance. Some cultures have an unspoken understanding that actual deadlines are different from stated deadlines; for example, it may be understood in a particular culture that people will turn up an hour later than advertised. In this case, since everyone understands that a 9 am meeting will actually start around 10 am, no one is inconvenienced when everyone turns up at 10 am. In cultures which value punctuality, being late is tantamount to showing disrespect for another's time and may be considered insulting. In such cases, punctuality may be enforced by social penalties, for example by excluding low-status latecomers from meetings entirely. Such considerations can lead on to considering the value of punctuality in econometrics and to considering the effects of non-punctuality on others in queueing theory.

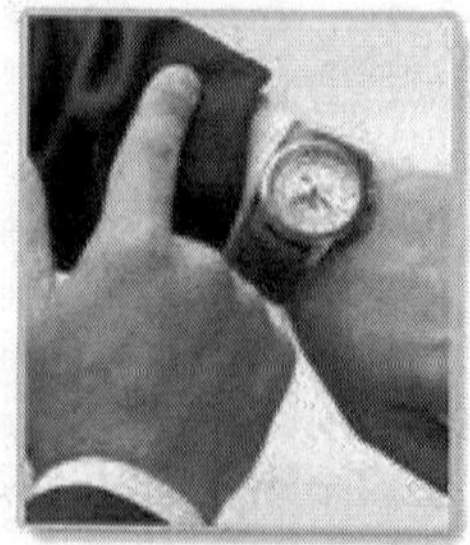

Punctuality, Time Value and Queuing Theory

In many situations the requirement for punctuality is asymmetric. For example, in a doctor's clinic or airport, customers are expected to turn up on time for their appointment or lose it, yet may be kept waiting for an unspecified time before they can see the doctor or board the plane. This can be regarded as an assessment of the relative value of the provider's time and that of the customer, the exact value of which can be determined by a combination of queuing theory and game theory. If the relative value was different, it would be easy to reduce waiting times by providing extra planes or doctors, and under-utilizing them, at the cost of increasing the price of travel or medical treatment proportionately. This can be seen in the behaviour of the wealthy, who can afford to hire private planes and have doctors who visit them, rather than vice versa, and in the extreme case of the ultra-rich, to have their own personal physicians and dedicated private planes and flight crews who wait on their needs exclusively. This expression of punctuality as a relative valuation of personal time value may be the reason for the description, often attributed to Louis XVIII, of punctuality as "the politeness of kings."

UNDERSTANDING VALUE OF TIME

In transport economics, the value of time is the opportunity cost of the time that a traveller spends on his/her journey. In essence, this makes it the amount that a traveller would be willing to pay in order to save time, or the amount they would accept as compensation for lost time. One of the main justifications for transport improvements is the amount of time that travellers will save. Using a set of values of time, the economic benefits of a transport project can be quantified in order to compare them to the costs In particular, savings (or, for that matter, increases) in travel time form part of the change in consumer surplus for a transport project. Values of time are used to calculate the non-monetary costs incurred as part of a journey, so that the generalised cost of the journey (a combination of both monetary and non-monetary costs) can be calculated. The value of time varies considerably from person to person and depends upon the purpose of the journey, but can generally be divided into two sets of valuations: working time and non-working time. This division is appropriate because the value of working time (i.e. time spent travelling in the course of work) is calculated differently from the value of non-working time (i.e. time spent travelling outside work).

Working Time

Working time is subject to the forces of the labour market, and can thus be valued in a relatively straightforward manner. The value of working time is the opportunity cost of that time to the employer, which is generally equivalent to the wages of the worker. For example, if a worker on a salary of £20 per hour travels to a meeting, the value of time in that case is £20 per hour, because that is the amount the employer would be willing to pay to reduce travel time (as travel time can be considered to be "wasted", i.e. not spent working). In practice, time spent travelling on certain modes (e.g. train) can sometimes be used to carry out some work, whereas time spent using other modes (e.g. car) may not be available at all, so the value of time may not exactly match up with the salary of the traveller - for example, if the £15/hour employee could carry on doing some work on a train journey to the meeting, but couldn't do so if they drove there, then the value of time on the train journey might be lower, as the employer is less willing to pay to save time on that mode. The UK Department for Transport calculates average values of time for travel on various modes of transport so that these values can be used to appraise transport projects as part of its New Approach to Appraisal [1]. Some examples are given below in 2002 prices:

- Car drivers: £26.43 per hour
- Car passengers: £18.94 per hour
- Bus passengers: £20.22 per hour
- Rail passengers: £36.96 per hour*
- Underground passengers: £35.95 per hour
- Walkers: £29.64 per hour
- Cyclists: £17.00 per hour

Non Working Time

This is time spent outside work, which might include journeys to and from work and leisure journeys. Since this time is not valued in a market, it can only be estimated from revealed preference or stated preference analysis techniques, where the real or hypothetical choices of travellers between faster, more expensive modes and slower, cheaper modes can be examined. For example, if a traveller has a choice between a coach which takes six hours and costs £10, or a train which takes four hours and costs £30, we can deduce that if the traveller chooses the train, their value of time is £10 per hour or more (because they are willing to spend *at least* £20 to save two hours' travel time). The difficulty in narrowing down the *actual* value of time from a pair of choices means that hypothetical situations are generally used (the stated preference technique) to deduce values of time. The value of non-working time is linked strongly to utility theory.

UNDERSTANDING TIME DISCIPLINE

In sociology and anthropology, time discipline is the general name given to social and economic rules, conventions, customs, and expectations governing the measurement of time, the social currency and awareness of time measurements, and people's expectations concerning the observance of these customs by others. The concept of "time discipline" as a field of special attention in sociology and anthropology was pioneered by E. P. Thompson in *Time, Work-Discipline, and Industrial Capitalism*, published in 1967. Coming from a Marxist viewpoint, Thompson argued that observance of clock-time is a consequence of the European industrial revolution, and that neither industrial capitalism nor the creation of the modern state would have been possible without the imposition of synchronic forms of time and work discipline.

The new clock time imposed by government and capitalist interests replaced earlier, collective perceptions of time that Thompson believed flowed from the collective wisdom of human societies. While, in fact, it appears likely that earlier views of time were imposed instead by religious and other social authorities prior to the industrial revolution, Thompson's work identified time discipline as an important concept for study within the social sciences.

Time Discipline and the Natural World

In societies based around agriculture, hunting, and other pursuits that involve human interaction with a natural world, time discipline is a matter governed by astronomical and biological factors. Specific times of day or seasons of the year are defined by reference to these factors, and measured, to the extent that they need measuring, by observation. Different peoples' needs with respect to these things mean sharply differing cultural perceptions of time. For example, it surprises many non-Muslims that the Islamic calendar is entirely lunar and makes no reference at all to the seasons; the desert-dwelling Arabs who devised it were nomads rather than agriculturalists, and a calendar that made no reference to the seasons was no inconvenience for most of thems.

Time Discipline in Western Societies

In more urban societies, some of these natural phenomena were no longer at hand, and most were of much less consequence to the inhabitants. Artificial means of dividing and measuring time were needed. Plautus complained of the social effect of the invention of such divisions in his lines complaining of the sundial:

> The gods confound the man who first found out
> How to distinguish hours! Confound him, too,
> Who in this place set up a sun-dial,
> To cut and hack my days so wretchedly
> Into small portions. When I was a boy
> My belly was my sun-dial; one more sure,
> Truer, and more exact than any of them.
> This dial told me when 'twas proper time
> To go to dinner, when I had aught to eat.
> But now-a-days, why, even when I have,
> I can't fall-to, unless the sun give leave.
> The town's so full of these confounded dials,
> The greatest part of its inhabitants,
> Shrunk up with hunger, creep along the streets.

Plautus's protagonist here complains about the social discipline and expectations that arose when these measurements of time were introduced. The invention of artificial units of time measurement made the introduction of time management possible, and time management was not universally appreciated by those whose time was managed.

Religious Influences on Western Time Discipline

In western Europe, the practice of Christian monasticism introduced new factors into the time discipline observed by members of religious communities. The rule of Saint Benedict introduced canonical hours; these were religious observances that were held on a daily basis, and based on factors again mostly unrelated to natural phenomena. It is no surprise, then, that religious communities were likely the inventors, and certainly the major consumers, of early clocks. The invention of the mechanical clock in western Europe, and its subsequent technical developments, enabled a public time discipline even less related to natural phenomena. (Highly sophisticated clepsydras existed in China, where they were used by astrologers connected with the imperial court; these water clocks were quite large, and their use limited to those who were professionally interested in precise timekeeping.)

The Invention of the Clock

The English word *clock* comes from an Old French word for "bell"; for the striking feature of early clocks was a greater concern than their dials. Shakespeare's Sonnet XII begins, "When I do count the clock that tells the time." Even after the introduction of the clock face, clocks were costly, and found mostly in the homes of aristocrats. The vast majority of urban dwellers had to rely on clock towers, and outside the sight of their dials or the sound of their bells, clock time held no sway. Clock towers, at least, defined the time of day for those who could hear and see them. As the saying goes, "a person with a clock always knows what time it is; a person with two clocks is never sure."

Improvements of the Clock

The discipline imposed by these public clocks still remained lax by contemporary standards. A clock that only strikes the hours can only record the nearest hour that has passed; most early clocks had only hour hands in any case. Minute hands did not come into widespread use until the pendulum made a large leap in the accuracy of clocks; for watches, a similar leap in accuracy was not made possible before the invention of the balance spring. Before these improvements, the equation of time, the difference between apparent and mean solar time, was not even noticed. During the 17th and 18th centuries, private ownership of clocks and watches became more common, as their improved manufacture made them available for purchase by at least the bourgeoisie of the cities. Their proliferation had many social and even religious consequences for those who could afford and use them.

Religious Consequences of Improved Clocks

Religious texts of the period make many more references to the irreversible passage of time, and artistic themes appeared at this time such as *Vanitas*, a reminder of death in the form of a still life, which always included a watch, clock, or some other timepiece. The relentless ticking of a clock or watch, and the slow but certain movement of its hands, functioned as a visible and audible *memento mori*. Clocks and sundials would be decorated with mottos such as *ultima forsan* ("perhaps the last" [hour]) or *vulnerant omnes, ultima necat* ("they all wound, and the last kills"). Even today, clocks often carry the motto *tempus fugit*, "time flies." Mary, Queen of Scots was said to have owned a large watch made in the shape of a silver skull.

Economic Consequences of Improved Clocks

Economically, their impact was even greater; an awareness that *time is money*, a limited commodity not to be wasted, also appears during this period. Because Protestantism was at this time chiefly a religion of literate city dwellers, the so-called "Protestant work ethic" came to be associated with this newly fashion time discipline; production of clocks and watches during this period shifted from Italy and Bavaria to Protestant areas such as Geneva, the Netherlands, and England; the names of French clockmakers during this time disclose a large number of Huguenot-fashion names from the Old Testament.

Standard, Synchronous, Public Time

In the nineteenth century, the introduction of standard time and time zones divorced the "time of day" from local mean solar time and any links to astronomy. Time signals, like the bells and dials of public clocks, once were relatively local affairs; the ball that is dropped in Times Square on New Year's Eve in New York City once served as a time signal whose original purpose was for navigators to check their marine chronometers. However, when the railroads began running trains on complex schedules, keeping a schedule that could be followed over hundreds of miles away required synchronization on a scale not attempted before. Telegraphy, and later, shortwave radio were used to broadcast time signals from the most accurate clocks available. Radio and television broadcasting schedules created a further impetus to regiment everyone's clock so that they all told the same time within a very small tolerance; the broadcasting of time announcements over radio and television enabled all the households in their audience to get in synch with the clocks at the network.

The mass production of clocks and watches further tightened time discipline in the Western world; before these machines were made, and made to be more accurate, it would be idle to complain about someone's being fifteen, or five, minutes late. For many employees, the time clock was the clock that told the time that mattered: it was the clock that recorded their hours of work. By the time that time clocks became commonplace, public, synchronized clock time was considered a fact of life. Uniform, synchronized, public clock time did not exist until the nineteenth century. When one speaks about the intellectual history of time, one essentially is stating that changes have occurred in the way humans experience and measure time. Our conceived abstract notions of time have presumably developed in accordance with our art, our science, and our social infrastructure.

Towards Time-Keeping

The units of time first developed by humans would likely have been days and months (moons). In some parts of the world the cycle of seasons are apparent enough to lead to people speaking about years & seasons (e.g. 4 summers ago, or 4 floods ago). With the invention of agriculture in the 3rd millennium BC, people relied heavily on the cycles of the season for planting and harvesting crops. Most humans came to live in settled societies and the whole community relied upon accurate predictions of the seasonal cycle. This led to the development of calendars. Over time, some people came to recognize patterns of the stars with the seasons. Learning astronomy became an assigned duty for certain people so they could coordinate the lunar and solar calendars by adding days or months to the year. At about the same time, sundials were developed, likely marked first at noon, sunrise and sunset. In ancient Sumer and Egypt, numbers were soon used to divide the day into 12 hours, as was the night. In Egypt there is not as much seasonal variation in the length of the day, but those further from the equator would need to make many more modifications in calibrating their sundials to deal with these differences. Ancient traditions did *not* begin the day at midnight, but rather some at dawn, others at dusk (both being more obvious). Since a sundial has only one "hand", a minute probably only meant "a short time". It took centuries for technology to make measurements precise enough for minutes (and later seconds) to become fixed meaningful units—longer still for milliseconds, nanoseconds, and further subdivisions. When the water clock was invented, time could also be measured at night – though there was significant variation in flow rate and less accuracy and precision.

With water clocks, and also candle clocks, modifications were made to have them make sounds on a regular basis. (The English word *clock* actually comes from French, Latin, and German words that mean *bell*.) With the invention of the hourglass (perhaps as early as the 11th Century) hours and units of time smaller than an hour could be measured much more reliably than with water clocks and candle clocks. The earliest reasonably accurate mechanical clocks are the 13th century tower clocks probably developed for (and perhaps by) monks in Northern Italy. Using gears and gradually falling weights, these were adjusted to conform with canonical hours—which varied with the length of the day. As these were used primarily to ring bells for prayer, the clock dial likely only came later. When dials were eventually incorporated into clocks, they were analogous to the dials on sundials, and, like a sundial, the clocks themselves had only one hand. A possible explanation for the shift from having the first hour being the one after dawn, to having the hour after noon being designated as 1 p.m. (post meridiem), is that these clocks would likely regularly be reset at local high noon each day. This, of course, results in midnight becoming 12 o'clock. Peter Henlein, a locksmith and burgher of Nuremberg, Germany, invented a spring-powered clock around 1510. It had only one hand, had no glass cover, and was rather imprecise because it slowed down as the spring unwound. In fact, Henlein went so far as to develop the first portable watch; it was six inches high. People usually carried it by hand, or wore it around their necks or in large pockets. The first reported person to actually wear a watch on the wrist was the French mathematician and philosopher, Blaise Pascal (1623–1662). With a piece of string, he attached his pocket watch to his wrist. In 1577, the minute hand was added by a Swiss clock maker, Jost Burgi (who also is a contender for the invention of logarithms), and was incorporated into a clock Burgi made for astronomer Tycho Brahe who had a need for more accuracy as he charted the heavens.

Isochronous Time

With invention of the pendulum clock in 1656 by Christiaan Huygens, came isochronous time, with a fixed pace of 3600 seconds per hour. By 1680, both a minute hand and then a second hand were added. Some of the first of these had a separate dial for the minute hand (turning counter-clockwise), and a *second* hand that took 5 minutes per cycle. Even as late as 1773, towns were content to order clocks without minute hands. But the clocks were still aligned with the local noonday sun. Following the invention of the locomotive in 1830, time had to be synchronized across vast distances in order to organize the train schedules. This eventually led to the development of time zones, and, thus, global isochronous time. These time changes were not accepted everywhere right away, because many people's lives were still tied closely to the length of the daytime. With the invention in 1879 of the light bulb, that changed too. The isochronous clock changed lives. Appointments are rarely "within the hour", but at quarter hours (and being five minutes late is often considered being tardy). People often eat, drink, sleep, and even go to the bathroom in adherence to some time-dependent schedule.

RELEVANCE OF TIME LIMIT

A time limit or deadline is a narrow field of time, or particular point in time, by which an objective or task must be accomplished. In project management, deadlines are most often associated with milestone goals.

RELEVANCE OF LEISURE

Leisure, or free time, is time spent away from business, work, and domestic chores. It is also the periods of time before or after necessary activities such as eating, sleeping and, where it is compulsory, education. The distinction between leisure and unavoidable activities is loosely applied, i.e. people sometimes do work-oriented tasks for pleasure as well as for long-term utility. A distinction may also be drawn between free time and leisure. For example, Situationist International maintains that free time is illusory and rarely free; economic and social forces appropriate free time from the individual and sell it back to them as the commodity known as "leisure". Leisure studies is the academic discipline concerned with the study and analysis of leisure.

Cultural Differences

Time for leisure varies from one society to the next, although anthropologists have found that hunter-gatherers tend to have significantly more leisure time than people in more complex societies. As a result, band societies such as the Shoshone of the Great Basin came across as extraordinarily lazy to European colonialists. Workaholics are those who work compulsively at the expense of other activities. They prefer to work rather than spend time socializing and engaging in other leisure activities.

Gender Gap

Men generally have more leisure time than women. In Europe and the United States, adult men usually have between one and nine hours more leisure time than women do each week.

Adolescents

Free time has potential for youth development, which is influenced by parental attitudes of interest and control, mediated by adolescent motivational style.

REFERENCES

Anonymous (E. Robert Kelly), *The Alternative: A Study in Psychology*. London: Macmillan and Co., 1882.

Aveni, Anthony: *Empires of Time: Calendars, Clocks, and Cultures*: (Basic Books, 1989).

Erin Hiley Sharp, Linda L. Caldwell, John W. Graham and Ty A. Ridenour: *Individual Motivation and Parental Influence on Adolescents' Experiences of Interest in Free Time: A Longitudinal Examination*, Journal of Youth and Adolescence, Volume 35, Number 3, pp. 340-353, 2006.

Farb, Peter (1968). *Man's Rise to Civilization As Shown by the Indians of North America from Primeval Times to the Coming of the Industrial State*. New York City: E.P. Dutton. pp. 28. LCC E77.F36.

G Underwood, RA Swain (1973). "Selectivity of attention and the perception of duration". *Perception* 2 (1): 101.

George Stigler (November 1955). "The Nature and Role of Originality in Scientific Progress". *Economica* XXII.

Goodin, Robert E.; Rice, James Mahmud; Bittman, Michael; & Saunders, Peter. (2005). "The time-pressure illusion: Discretionary time vs free time". *Social Indicators Research* 73(1), 43–70. (JamesMahmudRice.info, "Time pressure" (PDF)).

Gruber, Ronald P.; Wagner, Lawrence F.; Block, Richard A. (2000). "Subjective Time

Versus Proper (Clock) Time". In Buccheri, R.; Di Gesù, V.; Saniga, Metod. *Studies on the structure of time: from physics to psycho(patho)logy*. Springer. p. 54.

Hamminga, Bert "The Western versus the African Time Concept," accessed 2010-1-30 (this webpage article appears to be the author's synopsis of a discussion of the subject of time in John S. Mbiti's *African Religions and Philosophy*, London: Heinemann 1969).

Harold A. Wittcoff, Bryan G. Reuben, Jeffery S. Plotkin. Industrial Organic Chemicals. Wiley 2004.

Jaldow, Eli J.; Oakley, David A.; Davey, Graham C. L. (1989). "Performance of Decorticated Rats on Fixed Interval and Fixed Time Schedules". *European Journal of Neuroscience* (European Journal of Neuroscience) 1 (5): 461.

James M. Buchanan (2008). "Opportunity cost". *Second Edition*. The New Palgrave Dictionary of Economics Online.

James, W. (1893). The principles of psychology. New York: H. Holt and Company. Page 609.

John Davidson (August 1, 2010), *Time Management that Doesn't Suck*, http://www.tmtds.com/time-management-that-doesnt-suck-sample-chapter.pdf </ref>

Landes, David: *Revolution in Time: Clocks and the Making of the Modern World*: (Belknap/Harvard, 1983).

Linda L. Edwards, J. Stanley Edwards, *Introduction to paralegal studies and the law: a practical approach* (Cengage Learning, 2001.

OECD Organization for Economic Co-operation and Development (2009). *Society at a Glance 2009: OECD Social Indicators*. oecd publishing. p. 31.

"Progress and punctuality". *Ghanaian Chronicle* (Asia Africa Intelligence Wire). May 17, 2004.

RM Schmidt (1983), "Who maximizes what? A study in student time allocation", *The American Economic Review*.

Robert H Frank (2005-09-01). "The Opportunity Cost of Economics Education". *New York Times*.

Snedaker, Susan; Nels Hoenig (2005). *How to Cheat at IT Project Management*. Syngress.

Solomon, Charlene, and Michael S. Schellalse. 2009. *Managing Across Cultures: The 7 Keys to Doing Business with a Global Mindset*, p. 174, accessed 2010-1-30.

Svetlana V. Ukraintseva (2001). "Aging and the subjective sense of time". *Current Concepts in Experimental Gerontology*.

4

Information Management and Time Management: Analyzing the Interrelationship

"The time you enjoy wasting is not wasted time."

—*Bertrand Russell*

RELEVANCE OF PERSONAL INFORMATION MANAGEMENT

Personal information management (PIM) refers to the practice and the study of the activities people perform in order to acquire, organize, maintain, retrieve and use information items such as documents (paper-based and digital), web pages and email messages for everyday use to complete tasks (work-related or not) and fulfill a person's various roles (as parent, employee, friend, member of community, etc.). One ideal of PIM is that we always have the right information in the right place, in the right form, and of sufficient completeness and quality to meet our current need. Technologies and tools such as personal information managers help us spend less time with time-consuming and error-prone activities of PIM (such as looking for information). We then have more time to make creative, intelligent use of the information at hand in order to get things done, or to simply enjoy the information itself.

History and Background

Knowledge acquisition/elicitation has been an important area of study in its own right receiving special prominence in the 1980s as a way to define rules to drive expert systems. A seminal paper in personal information management research is "Finding and Reminding" by Barreau and Nardi in 1995. It shows how ethographic field studies can be used to derive testable theories for improving personal information management practices and tools. Many publications by others followed, until a workshop series was initiated with the first NSF-sponsored workshop on PIM held in Seattle, Washington, on January 27-29, 2005. The group gathered at this workshop started defining the field in a published report.

This report formed the basis of the book *Personal Information Management* and follow-up workshops. Research in the area of PIM also relates to work done under the term personal knowledge management. Whereas the focus there is on philosophy and integration with the theories created within knowledge management – a holistic approach – the focus of PIM research is on collecting statistically relevant data to support the core hypothesis of PIM, and on creating and validating tools for PIM.

Tools

There are a number of tools available for managing personal information, but these tools can become a part of the problem leading to "information fragmentation". Different devices and applications often come with their separate ways of storing and organizing information. Many people confuse PIM tools with the study and practice of personal information management itself. See personal information manager for information about tools for personal information management.

Study

Interest in the study of PIM has increased in recent years. One goal in the study of PIM is to identify ways to introduce new tool support without inadvertently increasing the complexity of a person's information management challenge. The study of PIM means understanding better how people manage information across tools and over time. It is not enough simply to study, for example, e-mail use in isolation. A related point is that the value of a new tool must be assessed over time and in a broader context of a person's various PIM activities.

Related Activities and Areas

PIM shares considerable, potentially synergistic overlap with disciplines such as cognitive science, human-computer interaction, information science, artificial intelligence, database management and information retrieval. PIM relates to but differs from other fields of inquiry that study the interactions between people, information and technology.

Cognitive Psychology and Cognitive Science

Cognitive psychology, as the study of how people learn and remember, problem solve, and make decisions, necessarily also includes the study of how people make smart use of available information. The related field of cognitive science, in its efforts to apply these questions more broadly to the study and simulation of intelligent behaviour, is also related to PIM. Cognitive science has strong connections to, some would say subsumes, the field of artificial intelligence. There is great potential for a mutually beneficial interplay between cognitive science and PIM. Sub-areas of cognitive science of clear relevance to PIM include problem solving and decision making. For example, folders created to hold information for a big project such as "plan my wedding" may sometimes resemble a problem-decomposition. To take another example, signal detection task has long been used to frame and explain human behaviour and has recently been used as a basis for analyzing our choices concerning what information to keep and how – a key activity of PIM. Or consider categorization and concept formation. How are categories and concepts learned and used? Categories and concepts can be seen directly but may be reflected in the tags and folders people use to organize their information. Or consider the activities of reading and writing. Both are areas of study in cognitive psychology with clear relevance to the study of PIM.

Now large portions of a document may be the product of "copy-and-paste" operations (from our previous writings) rather than a product of original writing. Certainly, management of text pieces pasted for re-use is a PIM activity, and this raises several interesting questions. How do we go about deciding when to re-use and when to write from scratch? We may sometimes spend more time chasing down a paragraph we have previously written than it would have taken to simply write a new paragraph expressing the same thoughts. Beyond this, we can wonder at what point a reliance on an increasing (and increasingly available) supply of previously written material begins to impact our creativity. As people do PIM they work in an external environment that includes other people, available technology and organizational setting. This means that situated cognition, distributed cognition, and social cognition all relate to the study of PIM.

Human-Computer and Human-Information Interaction

The study of PIM is also related to the field of human-computer interaction (HCI). But PIM research puts emphasis on the broader study of how people manage their information over time using a variety of tools – some computer-based, some not. The User-Subjective Approach is the first approach dedicated specifically to PIM systems design. Its theoretical foundations were first published in a Journal of the American Society for Information Science and Technology paper in 2003. Another JASIST paper with evidence and implementation for the approach was published in 2008. The paper had won the Best JASIST Paper award in 2009. The first user-subjective design scheme was developed and positively evaluated in a Conference on Human Factors in Computing Systems paper published in 2009.

Management of Data, Information, Knowledge, Time and Tasks

The study of information management and knowledge management in organizations relates to the study of PIM. Jones notes that issues seen first at an organizational level often migrate to the PIM domain. PIM can help to motivate and will also benefit from work in information retrieval and database management. For example, data mining techniques might be applied to mine and structure personal information.

Relation to Time Management and Productivity

By similar argument, a discussion of time management or task management on a personal level quickly takes us back to a discussion of PIM. Both time and task management make heavy use of information tools and external forms of information such as to-do lists, calendars, timelines, Gantt charts, etc. This information, to be managed like other information.

RELEVANCE OF PERSONAL ORGANIZER

A personal organizer, day planner, personal analog assistant, or personal planner is a small book/binder, designed to be portable, usually containing a diary, calendar, address book, and other sections usually including blank paper. It may also include pages with useful information, such as maps, telephone codes. It is related to the separate desktop stationery items that have one or more of the same functions, such as appointment calendars, rolodexes, notebooks, and almanacs.. For some the function of paper-and-binder personal organizers, a 20th century innovation, is being assumed by electronic personal digital assistants (PDAs) and personal information manager software on personal computers. Some personal organizers attempt to bridge the gap by featuring holders for PDAs.

ROLE OF INFORMATION MANAGEMENT

Information management (IM) is the collection and management of information from one or more sources and the distribution of that information to one or more audiences. This sometimes involves those who have a stake in, or a right to that information. Management means the organization of and control over the structure, processing and delivery of information. Throughout the 1970s this was largely limited to files, file maintenance, and the life cycle management of paper-based files, other media and records. With the proliferation of information technology starting in the 1970s, the job of information management took on a new light, and also began to include the field of Data maintenance. No longer was information management a simple job that could be performed by almost anyone.

An understanding of the technology involved, and the theory behind it became necessary. As information storage shifted to electronic means, this became more and more difficult. By the late 1990s when information was regularly disseminated across computer networks and by other electronic means, network managers, in a sense, became information managers. Those individuals found themselves tasked with increasingly complex tasks, hardware and software. With the latest tools available, information management has become a powerful resource and a large expense for many organizations. In short, information management entails organizing, retrieving, acquiring and maintaining information. It is closely related to and overlapping with the practice of Data Management.

Information Management Concepts

Following the behavioural science theory of management, mainly developed at Carnegie Mellon University and prominently represented by Barnard, Richard M. Cyert, March and Simon, most of what goes on in service organizations is actually decision making and information processes. The crucial factor in the information and decision process analysis is thus individuals' limited ability to process information and to make decisions under these limitations. According to March and Simon, organizations have to be considered as cooperative systems with a high level of information processing and a vast need for decision making at various levels. They also claimed that there are factors that would prevent individuals from acting strictly rational, in opposite to what has been proposed and advocated by classic theorists Instead of using the model of the economic man, as advocated in classic theory, they proposed the administrative man as an alternative based on their argumentation about the cognitive limits of rationality.

While the theories developed at Carnegie Mellon clearly filled some theoretical gaps in the discipline, March and Simon did not propose a certain organizational form that they considered especially feasible for coping with cognitive limitations and bounded rationality of decision-makers. Through their own argumentation against normative decision-making models, i.e., models that prescribe people how they ought to choose, they also abandoned the idea of an ideal organizational form. In addition to the factors mentioned by March and Simon, there are two other considerable aspects, stemming from environmental and organizational dynamics. Firstly, it is not possible to access, collect and evaluate all environmental information being relevant for taking a certain decision at a reasonable price, i.e., time and effort. In other words, following a national economic framework, the transaction cost associated with the information process is too high.

Secondly, established organizational rules and procedures can prevent the taking of the most appropriate decision, i.e., that a sub-optimum solution is chosen in accordance to organizational rank structure or institutional rules, guidelines and procedures, an issue that also has been brought forward as a major critique against the principles of bureaucratic organizations. According to the Carnegie Mellon School and its followers, information management, i.e., the organization's ability to process information, is at the core of organizational and managerial competencies.

Consequently, strategies for organization design must be aiming at improved information processing capability. Jay Galbraith has identified five main organization design strategies within two categories — increased information processing capacity and reduced need for information processing.

1. Reduction of information processing needs
   (a) Environmental management
   (b) Creation of slack resources
   (c) Creation of self-contained tasks
2. Increasing the organizational information processing capacity
   (a) Creation of lateral relations
   (b) Vertical information systems

Environmental management. Instead of adapting to changing environmental circumstances, the organization can seek to modify its environment. Vertical and horizontal collaboration, i.e. cooperation or integration with other organizations in the industry value system are typical means of reducing uncertainty. An example of reducing uncertainty in relation to the prior or demanding stage of the industry system is the concept of Supplier-Retailer collaboration or Efficient Customer Response. Creation of slack resources. In order to reduce exceptions, performance levels can be reduced, thus decreasing the information load on the hierarchy. These additional slack resources, required to reduce information processing in the hierarchy, represent an additional cost to the organization. The choice of this method clearly depends on the alternative costs of other strategies. Creation of self-contained tasks. Achieving a conceptual closure of tasks is another way of reducing information processing. In this case, the task-performing unit has all the resources required to perform the task. This approach is concerned with task (de-)composition and interaction between different organizational units, i.e. organizational and information interfaces.

Creation of lateral relations. In this case, lateral decision processes are established that cut across functional organizational units. The aim is to apply a system of decision subsidiarity, i.e. to move decision power to the process, instead of moving information from the process into the hierarchy for decision-making. Investment in vertical information systems. Instead of processing information through the existing hierarchical channels, the organization can establish vertical information systems. In this case, the information flow for a specific task (or set of tasks) is routed in accordance to the applied business logic, rather than the hierarchical organization.

Following the lateral relations concept, it also becomes possible to employ an organizational form that is different from the simple hierarchical information. The Matrix organization is aiming at bringing together the functional and product departmental bases and achieving a balance in information processing and decision making between the vertical (hierarchical) and the horizontal (product or project) structure. The creation of a matrix organization can also be considered as management's response to a persistent or permanent demand for adaptation to environmental dynamics, instead of the response to episodic demands.

UNDERSTANDING THE GROUP INFORMATION MANAGEMENT

Erickson (2006) uses the phrase group information management or GIM, for short, to refer to personal information management (PIM) "as it functions in more public spheres." People acquire, organize, maintain, retrieve and use information items to support individual needs. But these PIM activities are usually embedded in group or organizational contexts (Lutters, Ackerman & Zhou, 2007) and people usually perform these activities with sharing in mind (Erickson, 2006). The act of sharing moves personal information into spheres of group activity and also creates tensions that shape what and how the information is shared. The practice and the study of GIM focuses on this interaction between personal information and group contexts.

Issues in the Study and Practice of GIM

- formerly private calendar entries could be used for ends other than scheduling meetings
- what users choose to reveal or conceal
- how their disclosure of personal information is related to the ends that they hope to achieve

- the ethics of 'counterfeiting' links or conspiring to garner 'inauthentic' recommendations to increase their stature in the system.
- complex questions of privacy and access and ownership. (user control, privacy and trust)
- user reliance on system defaults

Tool Support for GIM

- Group calendaring
- Social networking
- Patient medical records
- Collaborative filtering and recommendations
- Collaborative tagging
- File sharing and presentation

UNDERSTANDING POLYCHRONICITY

Polychronicity is a term that describes people who prefer to work on multiple activities at the same time. Examples of polychronic behaviours include talking on the phone while driving a car and browsing the internet while sitting in meetings. Polychronicity is in contrast to those who prefer monochronicity (doing one thing at a time). The polychronic-monochronic concept was first developed by Edward Hall in 1959 in his anthropological studies of time use in different cultures.

Measuring Polychronicity

Researchers have developed the following questionnaires to measure polychronicity:

- Inventory of Polychronic Values (IPV) developed by Bluedorn et al. (1997) which is a 10-item scale designed to assess "the extent to which people in a culture prefer to be engaged in two or more tasks or events simultaneously and believe their preference is the best way to do things."
- Polychronic Attitude Index (PAI) developed by Kaufman-Scarborough & Lindquist in 1991 which is a 4-item scale measuring individual preference for polychronicity:
    1. I do not like to juggle several activities at the same time.
    2. People should not try to do many things at once.
    3. When I sit down at my desk, I work on one project at a time.
    4. I am comfortable doing several things at the same time.

UNDERSTANDING HIPSTER PDA

The Hipster PDA is a paper-based personal organizer, popularized by Merlin Mann. Originally a tongue-in-cheek reaction to the increasing expense and complexity of personal digital assistants, the Hipster PDA (said to stand for "Parietal Disgorgement Aid" and often abbreviated to "hPDA") simply comprises a sheaf of index cards held together with a binder clip. Following widespread coverage in the media and blogs, the hPDA has become a popular personal management tool particularly with followers of David Allen's Getting Things Done methodology. Although it began as a joke, or perhaps a statement about technology fetishism, the Hipster PDA has rapidly gained popularity with serious users, with hundreds posting pictures of their customized hPDAs on photo sharing sites and exchanging tips on Internet mailing lists. Advocates of the hPDA claim that it is a cheap, lightweight, freeform organizer that doesn't need batteries and is unlikely to be stolen. Enthusiasts also design and share index-card-size printable templates for storing contacts, to-do lists, calendars, notes, project plans, and so on. A Hipster Nano PDA utilizes business cards with blank backs and one that has a calendar on the back.

UNDERSTANDING INDEX CARD

An index card (or System card in Australian English) consists of heavy paper stock cut to a standard size, used for recording and storing small amounts of discrete data. It was invented by Carl Linnaeus. The most common size for index cards in North America and Russia is 3 by 5 inches (76.2 by 127.0 mm), hence the common name 3-by-5 card. Other sizes widely available include 4 by 6 inches (101.6 by 152.4 mm), 5 by 8 inches (127.0 by 203.2 mm) and ISO-size A7 (74 by 105 mm/2.9 by 4.1 in). Cards are available in blank, ruled and grid styles in a variety of colours. Special divider cards with protruding tabs and a variety of cases and trays to hold the cards are also sold by stationers and office product companies. They are part of standard stationary and office supplies in the United States, but in other countries, such as China, are not. Index cards are used for a wide range of applications and environments: in the home to record and store recipes, shopping lists, contact information and other organizational data; in business to record presentation notes, project research and notes and contact information; in schools as flash cards or other visual aids; and in academic research to hold data such as bibliographical citations or notes. An often-suggested organization method is to use the smaller 3-inch by 5-inch cards to record the title and citation information of works cited, while using larger cards for recording quotes or other data. Index cards are used for many events and are very helpful for planning.

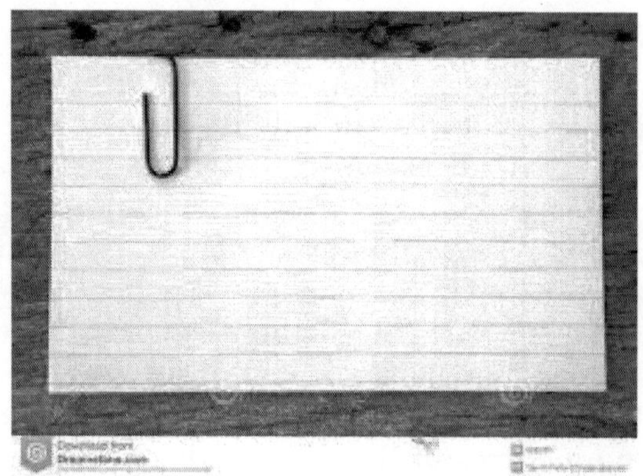

Until the conversion of library catalogs beginning in the 1980s, the primary tool used to locate books was the card catalog in which every book was filed with three cards, filed alphabetically under its title, author and subject (if non-fiction.) Similar catalogs were used by law firms and other organizations to organize large quantities of stored documents. However, the adoption of standard cataloging protocols throughout nations with international agreements, along with the rise of the Internet and the conversion of cataloging systems to digital storage and retrieval, have made widespread use of index cards for cataloging purposes obsolete.

UNDERSTANDING TASKWARRIOR

Taskwarrior is an open-source, cross platform time and task management tool. It has a command-line interface rather than a graphical user interface. Taskwarrior uses concepts and techniques described in *Getting Things Done* by David Allen, but is paradigm-agnostic in that it does not require users to adhere to any given life-management philosophy. According to its author, Taskwarrior was created "to address layout and feature issues" in the Todo.txt applications popularized by Gina Trapani.

Availability

Taskwarrior's source code is freely available and can be compiled and run on a variety of architectures and operating systems, or installed using binaries obtained with common package management tools: (apt, Fink, yum, etc.)

Typical Workflow

Taskwarrior comprises three main commands: *add*, *list*, and *done*. All other functionality – recurrences, tags, priorities, etc. – are optional.

Adding a Task

$ task add Pick up keys to the new apartment

Created task 1.

Listing Tasks

$ task list

ID Project Pri Due Active Age 1

1 task

Description:

4 secs Pick up keys to the new apartment

Marking a Task as Completed

$ task 1 done

Completed 1 'Pick up keys to the new apartment'.

Marked 1 task as done.

Creating a Task with Due Dates, Recurrences, and Tags

$ task add Mow the lawn project:Lawnwork due:tomorrow recur:biweekly +home

Created task 1.

Accolades

Issue 124 of the UK Linux Format magazine (November 2009) featured Taskwarrior in its Hot Picks section.

RELEVANCE OF GETTING THINGS DONE

Getting Things Done (GTD) is an organizational method created by productivity consultant David Allen, described in a book of the same name. The Getting Things Done method rests on the principle that a person needs to move tasks out of the mind by recording them externally. That way, the mind is freed from the job of remembering everything that needs to be done, and can concentrate on actually performing those tasks.

Methodology

In traditional time management, priorities usually play a central role. In contrast, Allen's approach uses two key elements — *control* and *perspective*. He proposes a workflow process to gain control over all the tasks and commitments that one needs or wants to get done, and "6 different levels of focus" to provide them with useful perspective. The author advocates a weekly review focused on different levels, and suggests that the perspective gained from these reviews should drive one's priorities, which can in turn determine the priority of the individual tasks and commitments gathered during the workflow process. During a weekly review, the user determines the context for the tasks and puts them on the appropriate lists. An example of grouping together similar tasks would be making a list of outstanding telephone calls, or errands to perform while downtown.

Context lists can be defined by the set of tools available or by the presence of individuals or groups for whom one has items to discuss or present. GTD is based on making it easy to store, track and retrieve all information related to the things that need to get done. Allen suggests that many of the mental blocks we encounter are caused by insufficient 'front-end' planning. It is most practical, according to Allen, to do this thinking in advance, generating a series of actions which we can later undertake without any further planning. The human brain's "reminder system" is inefficient and seldom reminds us of what we need to do at the time and place when we can do it. Consequently, the "next actions" stored by context in the "trusted system" act as an external support which ensures that we are presented with the right reminders at the right time. Since GTD relies on external memories, it can be seen as an application of the scientific theories of distributed cognition or the extended mind.

Reception

In 2005, *Wired* called GTD "A new cult for the info age", describing the enthusiasm for this methodology among information technology and knowledge workers as a kind of cult following. Allen's ideas have also been popularized through the Internet, especially via blogs such as Lifehacker, 43 Folders, and The Simple Dollar. In 2005, Ben Hammersley interviewed David Allen for *The Guardian*, with an article called "Meet the man who can bring order to your universe", saying "For me, as with the hundreds of thousands around the world who press the book into their friends' hands with fire in their eyes, Allen's ideas are nothing short of life-changing". In 2007, *Time Magazine* called *Getting Things Done* the self-help business book of its time. In 2007, *Wired* ran another article about GTD and Allen, quoting him as saying "the workings of an automatic transmission are more complicated than a manual transmission... to simplify a complex event, you need a complex system".

Software Implementations

Although GTD material is careful to remain "tool agnostic" and in fact advises people to start with a paper-based system, many task management tools claim to be GTD compliant. A wide spectrum of software exists, from commercial packages like Remember The Milk, OmniFocus, Things and ThinkingRock to open source applications such as Getting Things Gnome to command-line implementations such as Taskwarrior. TiddlyWiki has long been used as a personal productivity tool geared towards Allen's GTD methodology.

RELEVANCE OF POMODORO TECHNIQUE

The Pomodoro Technique is a time management method developed by Francesco Cirillo in the late 1980s. The technique uses a timer to break down periods of work into 25-minute intervals called 'pomodori' (from the Italian word for 'tomato') separated by breaks. Closely related to concepts such as timeboxing and iterative and incremental development used in software design, the method has been adopted in pair programming contexts. The method is based on the idea that frequent breaks can improve mental agility. There are five basic steps to implementing the technique:

1. decide on the task to be done
2. set the pomodoro (timer) to 25 minutes
3. work on the task until the timer rings; record with an x
4. take a short break (5 minutes)
5. every four "pomodori" take a longer break (15–20 minutes)

Underlying Principles

The stages of planning, tracking, recording, processing and visualizing are fundamental to the technique. In the planning phase tasks are prioritized by recording them in a "To Do Today" list. This enables users to estimate the effort tasks require. As "pomodori" are completed, they are recorded, adding to a sense of accomplishment and providing raw data for subsequent self-observation and improvement. For the purposes of the technique 'pomodoro' refers to an indivisible 25-minute period of time. An essential aim of the technique is to cut down on interruptions, both internal and external. This is done by recording and postponing other activities that interrupt the "pomodoro".

Tools

The technique's author encourages a low-tech approach using a mechanical timer, paper and pencil. In his view the physical act of winding up the timer confirms the user's determination to start the task, and the ticking and ringing sounds are related to how the relationship to time will be conditioned by the technique. Nonetheless, the technique has inspired a large number of software applications and timers for a variety of platforms, perhaps because of the technique's following amongst software developers.

Name

The Pomodoro Technique is named after the tomato-shaped kitchen timer that was first used by technique creator Francesco Cirillo when he was a university student (Pomodoro is Italian for tomato).

REFERENCES

Erickson, T. (2006). From PIM to GIM: personal information management in group contexts. *Commun. ACM* 49, 1 (Jan. 2006), 74-75.

Francis Heylighen & Clement Vidal (2008): *Getting Things Done: The Science behind Stress-Free Productivity"*, Long Range Planning 41, no. 6: 585-605.

Galbraith, Jay R. p. 49 ff. (1977), *Organization Design*, Addison-Wesley.

Hedberg, Bo (1981), "How organizations learn and unlearn", in: Nyström, P.C. & Starbuck, W.H., *Handbook of Organizational Design*, Oxford University Press.

Jones, W. (2004).Finders, keepers? The present and future perfect in support of personal information management. First Monday.

Jones, W., Phuwanartnurak, A. J., Gill, R., & Bruce, H. (2005, April 2-7). Don't take my folders away! Organizing personal information to get things done. Paper presented at the ACM SIGCHI Conference on Human Factors in Computing Systems (CHI 2005), Portland, OR.

Jones, William; Bruce, Harry, *A Report on the NSF-Sponsored Workshop on Personal Information Management, Seattle, WA, 2005*, The Information School, University of Washington.

Lutters, W.G., Ackerman, M.S. & Zhou, X. (2007). "Group Information Management." In William Jones and Jaime Teevan (Eds.), *Personal Information Management* (pp. 236-248), Seattle: University of Washington Press.

Mackenzie K.D. (1978), *Organizational Structures*, AHM Publishing Corporation.

March, James G. and Simon, Herbert A. (1958),Pradeep praduman wg (2008) *Organizations*, John Wiley & Sons.

"Meet the man who can bring order to your universe". London: Technology.guardian.co.uk. 2005-09-29. http://technology.guardian.co.uk/businesssense/story/0,,1580180,00.html. Retrieved 2010-03-05.

Mullins, L.J (1993), *Management and Organizational Behaviours*, 3 ed., Pitman Publishing.

Peterson, W. W., Birdsall, T. G., & Fox, W. C. (1954). The theory of signal detectability. Institute of Radio Engineers Transactions, PGIT-4, 171-212.

5

Knowing Modern Time Management Tips and Skills

> "Managing your time without setting priorities is like shooting randomly and calling whatever you hit the target."
>
> —*Peter Turla*

Effective time management is a primary means to a less stressful life. These practices can help you reduce your stress and reclaim your personal life. Do you find yourself overwhelmed by the number and complexity of projects you have that need to be completed at work each day? Do you often feel the day flies by without your devoting the necessary attention to each assignment because other tasks keep landing on your desk, co-workers interrupt you with questions or you can't get it all organized? You probably know that effective time management will help you get more done each day. It has important health benefits, too. By managing your time more wisely, you can minimize stress and improve your quality of life. But how do you get back on track when organizational skills don't come naturally? To get started, choose one of these strategies, try it for two to four weeks and see if it helps. If it does, consider adding another one. If not, try a different one.

- Plan each day. Planning your day can help you accomplish more and feel more in control of your life. Write a to-do list, putting the most important tasks at the top. Keep a schedule of your daily activities to minimize conflicts and last-minute rushes.
- Prioritize your tasks. Time-consuming but relatively unimportant tasks can consume a lot of your day. Prioritizing tasks will ensure that you spend your time and energy on those that are truly important to you.

- Say no to nonessential tasks. Consider your goals and schedule before agreeing to take on additional work.
- Delegate. Take a look at your to-do list and consider what you can pass on to someone else.
- Take the time you need to do a quality job. Doing work right the first time may take more time upfront, but errors usually result in time spent making corrections, which takes more time overall.
- Break large, time-consuming tasks into smaller tasks. Work on them a few minutes at a time until you get them all done.
- Practice the 10-minute rule. Work on a dreaded task for 10 minutes each day. Once you get started, you may find you can finish it.
- Evaluate how you're spending your time. Keep a diary of everything you do for three days to determine how you're spending your time. Look for time that can be used more wisely. For example, could you take a bus or train to work and use the commute to catch up on reading? If so, you could free up some time to exercise or spend with family or friends.
- Limit distractions. Block out time on your calendar for big projects. During that time, close your door and turn off your phone, pager and e-mail.
- Get plenty of sleep, have a healthy diet and exercise regularly. A healthy lifestyle can improve your focus and concentration, which will help improve your efficiency so that you can complete your work in less time.
- Take a time management course. If your employer offers continuing education, take a time management class. If your workplace doesn't have one, find out if a local community college, university or community education program does.
- Take a break when needed. Too much stress can derail your attempts at getting organized. When you need a break, take one. Take a walk. Do some quick stretches at your workstation. Take a day of vacation to rest and re-energize.

TIME MANAGEMENT TIPS I

Do you feel the need to be more organized and/or more productive? Do you spend your day in a frenzy of activity and then wonder why you haven't accomplished much? Time management skills are especially important for small business people, who often find themselves performing many different jobs during the course of a single day. These time management tips will help you increase your productivity and stay cool and collected.

Time Management Tips

1) Realize that time management is a myth: No matter how organized we are, there are always only 24 hours in a day. Time doesn't change. All we can actually manage is ourselves and what we do with the time that we have.

2) Find out where you're wasting time: Many of us are prey to time-wasters that steal time we could be using much more productively. What are your time-bandits? Do you spend too much time 'Net surfing, reading email, or making personal calls? Tracking Daily Activities explains how to track your activities so you can form a accurate picture of what you actually do, the first step to effective time management.

3) Create time management goals: Remember, the focus of time management is actually changing your behaviours, not changing time. A good place to start is by eliminating your personal time-wasters. For one week, for example, set a goal that you're not going to take personal phone calls while you're working. For a fun look at behaviours that can interfere with successful time management, see my article Time Management Personality Types. Find out if you're a Fireman, an Aquarian or a Chatty Kathy!

4) Implement a Time Management Plan: Think of this as an extension of time management tip # 3. The objective is to change your behaviours over time to achieve whatever general goal you've set for yourself, such as increasing your productivity or decreasing your stress. So you need to not only set your specific goals, but track them over time to see whether or not you're accomplishing them.

5) Use time management tools: Whether it's a Day-Timer or a software program, the first step to physically managing your time is to know where it's going now and planning how you're going to spend your time in the future. A software program such as Outlook, for instance, lets you schedule events easily and can be set to remind you of events in advance, making your time management easier.

6) Prioritize ruthlessly: You should start each day with a time management session prioritizing the tasks for that day and setting your performance benchmark. If you have 20 tasks for a given day, how many of them do you truly need to accomplish? For more on daily planning and prioritizing daily tasks, see Start The Day Right With Daily Planning.

7) Learn to delegate and/or outsource: No matter how small your business is, there's no need for you to be a one-person show. For effective time management, you need to let other people carry some of the load. Determining Your Personal ROI explains two ways to pinpoint which tasks you'd be better off delegating or outsourcing, while Decide To Delegate provides tips for actually getting on with the job of delegating.

8) Establish routines and stick to them as much as possible: While crises will arise, you'll be much more productive if you can follow routines most of the time.

9) Get in the habit of setting time limits for tasks: For instance, reading and answering email can consume your whole day if you let it. Instead, set a limit of one hour a day for this task and stick to it.

10) Be sure your systems are organized: Are you wasting a lot of time looking for files on your computer? Take the time to organize a file management system. Is your filing system slowing you down? Redo it, so it's organized to the point that you can quickly lay your hands on what you need. You'll find more information about setting up filing systems and handling data efficiently in my Data Management library.

11) Don't waste time waiting: From client meetings to dentist appointments, it's impossible to avoid waiting for someone or something. But you don't need to just sit there and twiddle your thumbs. Always take something to do with you, such as a report you need to read, a checkbook that needs to be balanced, or just a blank pad of paper that you can use to plan your next marketing campaign. Technology makes it easy to work wherever you are; your PDA and/or cell phone will help you stay connected. You can be in control and accomplish what you want to accomplish - once you've come to grips with the time management myth and taken control of your time.

OTHER TIME MANAGEMENT TIPS II

Time management starts with the commitment to change. Time management is easy as long as you commit to action. The key to successful time management is planning and then protecting the planned time, which often involves re-conditioning your environment, and particularly the re-conditioning the expectations of others. In terms of time management, you are at your most efficient the day before you start your annual leave. Your time management and efficiency on this day is probably awesome. If you really want to, you can be that well-organized every day... Time management enables each of us to improve and be more productive and fulfilled individually, so logically the effects across whole organizations of good or poor time management are enormous. The collective implications of wasted time, and happily also the benefits of increasing personal productivity, are immense.

Some Interesting Time Management Statistics

Emphasising the huge significance and opportunities in time management, a 2007 survey by the Proudfoot Consulting (Guardian 22 Oct 07) covering 2,500 businesses over four years and 38 countries, indicated that wasted time costs UK businesses £80bn per year, equivalent to 7% of GDP. The causes of wasted time - labour inefficiency in other words - were:

- inadequate workforce supervision (31%)
- poor management planning (30%)
- poor communication (18%)
- IT problems, low morale, and lack or mismatch of skills (21%)

Clearly organizations are vastly under-utilising their people, and could be doing a lot more to enable more efficient working. These failings of organization and leadership make it all the more important for individual people to think creatively about time management, and particularly to start making changes to improve time management at a personal individual level.

Time Management Tips - and Ideas for Time Management Skills Training

Be prepared to make drastic changes. Be creative to find and introduce different ways of doing things. If you need a starting point see the 'Pareto Principle' (80:20 Rule), to assess what efforts and activities are most productive, and which are not. Manage your emails and phone calls - don't let them manage you. Ideally check at planned times, and avoid continuous notification of incoming emails. The more senior you are the more selective you need to be about when to be available to receive phone calls. Try to minimise the time that you are available to take unplanned phone calls, unless you are in a customer-facing, reactive role (customers can be internal too), and even if you are customer-facing, you must plan some time-slots when you are not available, or you'll never get anything important and pro-active done.

Challenge your own tendency to say 'yes' without scrutinising the request - start asking and probing what's involved - find out what the real expectations and needs are. Really think about how you currently spend your time. If you don't know, keep a time log for a few days to find out there's a free time management time-log template tool here. Knowing exactly what's wrong is the first step to improving it. Challenge anything that could be wasting time and effort, particularly habitual tasks, meetings and reports where responsibility is inherited or handed down from above. Don't be a slave to a daft process or system. Download and use the free time management assessment tool at the free online resources section, which will help you or another person to objectively judge your time management, and underlying issues. Review your activities in terms of your own personal short-term and long-term life and career goals, and prioritise your activities accordingly. Plan preparation and creative thinking time in your diary for the long-term jobs, because they need it. The short-term urgent tasks will always use up all your time unless you plan to spend it otherwise. Use a diary, and an activity planner to schedule when to do things, and time-slots for things you know will need doing or responding to. There's a sample time management activity schedule template with examples on the new time management section. Re-condition the expectations of others as to your availability and their claim on your time - use an activity planner to help you justify why you and not others should be prioritising your activities and time. Manage your environment as a whole - especially at the proposed or actual introduction of new systems, tools, technology, people, or processes, which might threaten to generate new demands on your time. If you accept changes without question - particularly new technology that helps others but not you - then you will open the way for new increasing demands on your time, or new interruptions, or new tasks and obligations. Instead consider new technology and other changes from the point of view of your time and efficiency. Ask yourself - is this going to save my time or add to my burden? Managing your environment - which includes managing, redefining, or reconditioning the expectations of others - is a critical aspect of effective time management. You must plan time slots for unplanned activities - you may not know exactly what you'll need to do, but if you plan the time to do it, then other important things will not get pushed out of the way when the demand arises.

Use the 'urgent-important' system of assessing activities and deciding priorities. See more at the new time management section. When you're faced with a pile of things to do, go through them quickly and make a list of what needs doing and when. After this handle each piece of paper only once. Do not under any circumstances pick up a job, do a bit of it, then put it back on the pile. Do not start lots of jobs at the same time - even if you can handle different tasks at the same time it's not the most efficient way of dealing with them, so don't kid yourself that this sort of multi-tasking is good - it's not. Be firm and diplomatic in dealing with time allocated for meetings, paperwork, telephone, and visitors, etc. When you keep your time log you will see how much time is wasted. Take control. Provided you explain why you are managing your time in this way, people will generally understand and respect you for it. Keep a clean desk and well-organized systems. Don't be obsessive about tidiness - busy people often make a mess - but ensure your mess doesn't undermine your effectiveness. Delegate as much as possible to others. If you have one, give 25% of your responsibility to your successor. You don't need to be a manager to delegate. Just asking nicely is sometimes all that's required to turn one of your difficult tasks into an easy one for somebody else better able to do it. If you can't stop interruptions when you need a quiet space for planned concentration time-slots, then find somewhere else in the building to work, and if necessary work at home or another site, and fight for the right to do this - it's important for you and the organization that you be able to work uninterrupted when you need to. Set up an acceptable template for the regular weekly or monthly reports you write, so you only need to slot in the updated figures and narrative, each time. If you can, get a good assistant, secretary or pa.

Sharpen Up Your Decision-Making

Always probe deadlines to establish the true situation - people asking you to do things will often say 'now' when 'later today' would be perfectly acceptable. Appeal to the other person's own sense of time management: it's impossible for anyone to do a good job without the opportunity to plan and prioritise. Break big tasks down into stages and plan time-slots for them. Use project management methods. Now read the time management systems, techniques and training section. Choose some of the above time management tips and commit to putting them into effect. The priest and the politician (a story about time management and being late) After twenty-five years in the same parish, Father O'Shaunessey was saying his farewells at his retirement dinner.

An eminent member of the congregation - a leading politician - had been asked to make a presentation and a short speech, but was late arriving. So the priest took it upon himself to fill the time, and stood up to the microphone:

> "I remember the first confession I heard here twenty-five years ago and it worried me as to what sort of place I'd come to... That first confession remains the worst I've ever heard. The chap confessed that he'd stolen a TV set from a neighbour and lied to the police when questioned, successfully blaming it on a local scallywag. He said that he'd stolen money from his parents and from his employer; that he'd had affairs with several of his friends' wives; that he'd taken hard drugs, and had slept with his sister and given her VD. You can imagine what I thought... However I'm pleased to say that as the days passed I soon realised that this sad fellow was a frightful exception and that this parish was indeed a wonderful place full of kind and decent people..."

At this point the politician arrived and apologised for being late, and keen to take the stage, he immediately stepped up to the microphone and pulled his speech from his pocket:

> "I'll always remember when Father O'Shaunessey first came to our parish," said the politician, "In fact, I'm pretty certain that I was the first person in the parish that he heard in confession..."

TIME MANAGEMENT TIPS III

TIPS TO REDUCE STRESS AND IMPROVE PRODUCTIVITY

Time is the one commodity we all have in common. No matter how hard we try, we really can't "save" time or "buy" time. Yet, we can learn to "spend" our time wisely to avoid "losing" time. Here's a baker's dozen of time management tips to help you "find" and keep track of your 24 hours today!

- Use a To Do List — It's not only a good reminder, but also a time management tool to help you see what you accomplish and how long it takes.
- Get set in your ways — Good time management is synonymous with good organization. Put your daily routines into detail. While you don't need to schedule every move you make, listing routine tasks helps you to remember each step you need to take to meet your goal, whether it's getting to work or school on time or doing Saturday morning chores.
- Break it up — Divide large tasks into small ones to get a better sense of accomplishment as you complete each step. In addition, when you're interrupted in the middle of a task, it's much easier to get back on track and regain your focus.
- Be realistic — Don't under or over estimate time. Over estimating time makes it difficult to fit all your tasks into your daily schedule, while under estimating "cuts your day short" and makes it impossible to complete your schedule. However, do be generous with your time allotments. It's much easier to fit a small task into "extra" time than it is to try to make up for "lost" time.
- Pick up a good habit — Try to keep something in hand going both to and from a destination. If you need to run copies, pick up some office supplies while you wait for the copy machine to finish.
- Big messes start with little piles — Completely finish your

circles. Put things away as you finish using them. Aside from keeping you out of clutter and giving you a big clean up at the end of a project, you'll know where things are the next time you need to use them.

- Start tomorrow tonight! — Get in the habit of preparing for the next day at the end of your day. Write out a "to do" list for tomorrow's tasks. Leave keys, wallet (or purse), and your To Do List all in the same place. For optimum time management, you can even lay out tomorrow's clothing before you go to bed.
- Don't forget — Write yourself a note ("Don't forget your lunch") or put reminders at the top of your to do list.
- Round to-its — The easiest way to get "a round to-it" is to schedule a task. If the lawn needs mowing, put it on your to do list.
- First things first – Prioritize your tasks and then schedule each one at the appropriate time. For instance, you may have to wait until after work to mow the lawn. Although it may be your "top priority" for the day, it needn't be at the top of your list!
- Learn to say no! — Frequently, we consider that saying "no" is discourteous, but you can be frank without being rude. "I can't now, but I could (insert when) "or "I'm sorry, but I just can't manage that today" is just good time management.
- The pause that refreshes – Do make breaks a scheduled part of your day. A small break at the end of a large task or series of small tasks refreshes you and helps you to wind down and focus on "what's next?"
- Be flexible — Effective time management will take some time to get used to. No matter what you did or didn't get done today, there is always tomorrow.

TIME MANAGEMENT SKILLS

Introductory Overview

Understanding Time Management

> "We all have time to either spend or waste and it is our decision what to do with it. But once passed, it is gone forever."
>
> —*Bruce Lee ("Zen in the Martial Arts" by Joe Hyams)*

Every individual on earth has the same amount of time - 60 seconds in a minute; 60 minutes in an hour; 1,440 minutes in a day; and 525,600 minutes in a year. While a vast majority of people confesses faltering to come to grips with it, extremely few can claim to have made the most of it. How is it that they have got it all done? It's because they have managed a way to figure out how to manage their time effectively. Time Management is more than just managing time. It is about controlling the use of the most valuable - and undervalued - resource. It is managing oneself in relation to time. It is setting priorities and taking charge of the situation and time utilization. It means changing those habits or activities that cause waste of time. It is being willing to adopt habits and methods to make maximum use of time. With good time management skills one is in control of one's time, stress and energy levels. One can maintain balance between one's work and personal life. One finds enough flexibility to respond to surprises or new opportunities. It is not how much time one has, but rather the way one uses it. The bottom line is how well one manages time. Internationally known authority on time management Dr. Alec Mackenzie in his book The Time Trap argues that the very idea of time management is a misnomer because one really cannot manage time in the way other resources can be managed: financial capital, physical capital, human capital, information and time. While each of the first four can be augmented, reduced, transferred or otherwise controlled, Time cannot be manipulated. Dr. Mackenzie contends that when it comes to time, one can only manage oneself in relation to it. One cannot control time as one can control other resources – one can only control how one uses it. In the world in which we live, time cannot be replaced or re-created. It is therefore not for us to choose whether we spend or save time but to choose only how we spend it.

Misconceptions about Time

There are several misconceptions which we all have about time. They affect everyone including those persons who may be considered quite successful and effective. Here are some of the misconceptions identified by Dr. Mackenzie:

- Time management is simple - all it requires is common sense. While it is true that the concept is simple, the self-discipline required to practice effective time management is not easy.
- Work is best performed under pressure. Psychological studies show this to be no more than an excuse for procrastination. One does not work well under pressure

  - only does the best one can under the circumstances. Pressure and challenge must not be confused. Lara's performance when the West Indies Team is in trouble has more to do with application and determination rather than pressure.
- I use a diary, a to-do list and have a secretary to keep me organized. One has to keep oneself organized - no one can do it

for others. The trouble with the disorganized person is that he hardly has time to listen to his secretary or look at his diary.

- I do not have the time. The effective worker or manager often gets more work done in the earlier hours of the morning than most laggards get done in the whole day. He then no longer has to work against tight deadlines and under stress which contributes to heart problems and not unusually the ultimate reduction of time on this earth.
- Time management might be good for some kinds of work but my job is creative. Time management is not about routine: it is about self-discipline. Lack of discipline prevents one from being great instead of simply good.
- Time management takes away the fun and freedom of spontaneity. Is working under stress, forgetting appointments, making constant excuses and apologies to be fun? Would it not be much more fun if by better organization one had one or two more hours every day to spend with the family, to play games, read a good book, plan for tomorrow and the day and week after or just relax?

Symptoms of Poor Time Management

Poor time management shows up by way of one or a combination of typical perceptible symptoms. Managers would do well to look for and reflect on whether they are subject to any of those symptoms with a view to take necessary corrective actions. The following are some of the indicators of poor time management:

- Constant rushing (e.g. between meetings or tasks)
- Frequent delays (e.g. in attending meetings, meeting deadlines)
- Low productivity, energy and motivation (e.g. 'I can't seem to get worked up about anything')
- Frustration (e.g. 'Oh, things just don't move ahead)
- Impatience (e.g. 'where the hell is that information I've asked him for?')
- Chronic vacillation between alternatives (e.g. 'whichever option I choose it is going to put me at a big disadvantage. I don't know which way to jump')
- Difficulty setting and achieving goals (e.g. 'I'm not sure what is expected of me')

Why do/will I have so little time ? Management by crisis

- Lack of Planning

- Incomplete information
- Personal disorganization
- Attempting too much
- Inability to Say No
- Responsibility unclear
- Ineffective delegation
- Inadequate staff & resources
- Paperwork
- Poor communication
- Poorly organized meetings
- Leaving tasks unfinished
- Inadequate controls
- Lack of self-discipline
- Socializing
- Drop-in visitors
- Telephone interruptions

The Eleven Time Thieves

Dr. Donald E. Wetmore ("Time Thieves: The 11 Biggest Time-wasters Revealed") lists out the eleven 'inconsiderate troupe' of eleven thieves that gang up to steal some of the precious time away from productive use of managers.

1. Poor Planning: Failure to see the value of planning and getting impatient to get something done are the causes of poor planning. Absence of a plan of action is likely to trigger off a false start, resulting in unproductive time utilization on the critical path of the task being undertaken. Consequently, the managers might not find enough time for completing the task.
2. Crisis Management: Most often, crisis management is an offspring of lack of prioritization of tasks. As a result of the inability to distinguish between the urgent, the important and the unnecessary tasks, unimportant tasks are likely to get done first at the cost of important tasks. Consequently, the managers are not likely to find enough time to get around to the important things.
3. Procrastination: It is easy to put off tasks if they are not due right away. The trouble is, tasks pile up and can force managers to run into a time crunch later. Procrastination is generally triggered off by the fear of failure / success, perfectionism,

wanting to do it all or incorrect priorities. It is a virtue to want to do a good job. But some people become so anxious about getting a job done perfectly that they never complete it. Managers should examine whether their efforts to get the job done perfectly are really improving things or preventing them from getting the job done.

4. Interruptions: Interruptions and distractions arise due to lack of planning, poor concentration and lack of control over environment. They are unnecessary thieves of a manager's time and come in many forms – drop-in visitors, telephones, e-mails unscheduled meetings, poor communications and confused chain of authority etc. Managers should be less willing to automatically give away their time just because they demand it. They should learn to avoid distractions if they are to get work done. They should work in areas where they are less likely to be disturbed and tell people when they are busy and cannot be disturbed.
5. Not Delegating: Wanting-to-do-all by oneself is yet another thief that could let the managers lose control. They feel that employees can never do anything as well as they can. They fear that something will go wrong if someone else takes over a job. They lack time for long-range planning because they are bogged down in day-to-day operations.
6. Unnecessary Meetings: If a meeting is held without a specific agenda and nothing productive comes out of it, clearly that meeting was unnecessary. Obviously, such meetings are thieves as the time is wasted and things just do not get started.
7. The "shuffling blues": Managers often waste much time because of disorganization. Keeping things that they need in a specific place, eliminating clutter, making sure that they have all the materials or information that they need before starting on the task and following a day-planner or schedule will help keep the 'shuffling blues' away at the work place.
8. Poor Physical Setup: Not having the things that the managers need frequently within easy reach and having a lot of the things that they seldom require close-by results in wastage of a lot of time, wearing out the carpet, retrieving what they frequently need. And of course, as they pass others they will often pull them aside to steal some of their time.
9. Poor Networking: Quality relationships with employees and others can be a substantial time-saver as they open doors for the managers with all kinds of opportunities. Failing to develop

a good network base will cause them to waste time creating what they might have had through their network.

10. Bad Attitude: Nothing sinks a day more effectively than having a poor attitude. It causes the managers to dwell on the problems and not the solutions and makes it possible to throw the day away. When they are burdening others with their problems and complaints they are forfeiting their valuable time.
11. Negative People: Being surrounded by negative people could mean the managers are spending a lot of their time listening to them but getting nothing much or purposeful from them. Obviously, avoiding such people will help the managers to minimize wasted hours and get some of their productive time back.

How much time do your spend each day on the following time stealers?

- Watching TV
- Reading Newspapers / Magazines excessively
- Idle chat, gossip and telephonic talk
- Opening and sorting mail
- Returning telephone calls
- Meetings
- Paying bills
- Day-dreaming
- Fretting over personal problems
- Caught in traffic snarls
- Planning how to change things
- Waiting for things to happen
- Taking naps
- Eating snacks between meals
- Drinking
- Smoking
- Shopping
- Wagering money

Saboteur Time Styles

The other aspect is self-inflicted thieves – 'saboteur time styles' that steal time. Based on the typical patterns of behaviour that tend to sabotage people's attempts at effective time management, Susan Ward ("Are You Sabotaging Your Time Management Efforts") classifies managers into different personality types and prescribes the following simple exercise, intended to help managers discover their standard behavioural responses to events and provide them with some clues for effective time management. The Firemen - For them, every event is a crisis. They are always seen busy dousing the fires. They find scarcely any time for anything else and do not spare a thought on time-management. Tasks keep piling up around them, while they are seen rushing from fire to fire all day. The Over-Committers – They just cannot say 'No' to anybody. They oblige and try to please everybody. All that anyone has to do is just ask, and they will chair another committee, take on another project, or organize yet another community event. Consequently, none of the tasks receives complete attention and remains half-done. The Aquarians - There is such a thing as being too "laid-back" - especially when it starts interfering with their ability to finish tasks or bother to return phone calls. Getting to things that is when they get to them is not time management; it is simple task avoidance. The Chatty Kathys - Born to socialize, they have astounding oral communication skills and cannot resist exercising them at every opportunity. Every interaction becomes a long drawn out conversation - especially if there is an unpleasant task dawning that they would like to put off. The Perfectionists – Exactitude is their watchword, and they feel that no rushed job can be a good job. Finishing tasks to satisfaction is such a problem; they need more time zones, not just more time.

Price of Time Inefficiency

What is the price of inefficient time management for an organization? That is a crucial question managers should ask and promptly address. Statistics show that a person - on the average - loses at least one hour of productivity each day due to disorganization and inefficiency. Accordingly calculated, the aggregate monetary value of loss caused by inefficient time management by all the employees in an organization amounts to:

- 1 hour X one person's hourly salary = Rs. ___________
- 6 days a week X ___________ Rs. lost today = Rs. lost this week.
- 48 weeks X Rs lost this week + ________ ____ Rs. lost this year.
- Number of persons X __ Rs. lost this year = Rs (total) _________

The Six D's

"When's the last day you didn't have a high-priority phone call, an urgent email or a stressed-out colleague begging for attention?" asks Tom Gegax, founder of Gegax Management Systems and author of the best –seller "By the Seat of Your Pants:

The No-Nonsense Business Management Guide

He says: "Getting pulled off-course is in every leader's job description. That's why enlightened managers must have a strategy for dealing with daily interruptions." Gegax bases his time-management principles on the "Six D's" - don't do it, delay it, deflect it, delegate it, do it imperfectly and do it. "When something pops up, rather than robotically just doing it, I start with the first option," Gegax says. "If that doesn't apply, I move on to the second. I keep cruising down the list until I reach the appropriate action." For instance, many seemingly urgent tasks disappear if you don't do them or delay them, he says, leaving you more time and energy to focus on the tasks that matter. And while some contingencies need immediate attention, your involvement isn't always required. Carefully consider whether to deflect the situation to another department or delegate it to a subordinate, Gegax advises. If you do opt to tackle the problem yourself, Gegax cautions against automatically shifting into "perfectionist mode." "A large number of my projects could hardly be described as perfect, yet were successful nevertheless," he says. Of course, reserve the final "D" — do it — for the tasks you've determined will keep you moving toward your goals.

Monochronic and Polychronic Views of Time

Just as a person's overall personality is made up of and represented by his or her traits, a person's time personality is made up of a series of time styles – monochronic or polychronic. It is expected that a person's awareness of the monochronic/polychronic side of personal time style affects his or her overall approach to time use, perceptions of time pressure and the amounts and order of time spent on tasks. This, in turn, affects his or her personal efficiency. Monochronic approach to time management is essentially objective and lays emphasis on promptness, speed, brevity and punctuality. It is a very efficient and focused way to manage work and life. Monochronic time managers are those who thrive on detailed planning and organization. They prefer to focus on one task at a time and they follow a schedule from which they don't like to deviate.

They tend to get upset by distractions or interruptions and are inclined to put new tasks off until a later date, when they can be worked into the schedule. Polychronic approach to time management is subjective and lays emphasis on inspiration, imagination, flexibility, intuition and dedication. Trust, bonding, pleasure and quality of life influence more strongly the decisions of a person who 'ticks' in polychronic time. Polychronic time managers prefer to have many projects under way simultaneously, enjoy changing from activity to activity and are unflustered by distractions and interruptions. Unlike their monochronic counterparts, polychronic managers believe they perform well under pressure.

Monochronic Managers	Polychronic Managers
do one thing at a time	do many things at once
concentrate well	are highly distractible and subject to interruptions
take time seriously	consider time commitments and objective to be achieved, if possible
low context, need information	high context, have information
are committed to the job	are committed to the people
adhere religiously to plans	change plans often and easily
are concerned with not disturbing	are more concerned with others closeness than privacy
seldom borrow or lend	borrow and lend easily
emphasize promptness	base promptness on the relationship
are accustomed to short-term relationships	strong tendency to build lifetime relationships

Clearly, monochronic approach is better suited for dealing with routine and predictable tasks, while polychronic approach is better suited in dealing with things such as creating a new concept or resolving an argument. Conflict arises when managers apply a monchronic style to a situation that demands polychronic time, or managers prefer polychronic style while the situation warrants the use of monchronic style. So how do the managers cope with a healthy need for subjective, polychronic, self-imposed time and at the same time fit in with the monochronic and objective time measures? The only way managers can figure out which method works best in a given situation is based on sound reasoning and acumen. How can you get an extra hour out of each day? Here are some tips to help you squeeze those extra minutes out of your day. Of course, you can adapt these so that they will fit in with your situation.

1. Get up earlier
2. Watch less TV (I mean how many Law & Order spinoffs does one need to watch?)
3. Avoid allowing others to waste your time
4. If you don't have to drive to work, use that time to study or plan. If you do drive to work listen to a motivational tape on the way to work instead of that mindless dj talk.
5. Organize your work; do it systematically.
6. Make creative use of lunchtime.
7. Delegate authority if, possible.
8. Spend less time on unimportant phone calls.
9. Think first, and then do the task.

10. Do what you dream about doing, instead of just dreaming about it.
11. Work hardest when you're the most mentally alert
12. Eliminate activities that make the smallest contributions to your life.
13. Always do the toughest jobs first.
14. Before each major act ask, "Is this really necessary?"
15. Choose interesting and constructive literature for spare time reading.
16. Learn how to sleep. Sleep soundly, then work refreshed.
17. Skip desserts.
18. Stop smoking.
19. Write notes or letters while waiting for others.
20. Always carry an envelope with paper in it and a few stamps.
21. Combine tasks that are done in the same area.
22. Be prompt for all appointments.
23. Lay out your clothes the night before.(I need to remember this myself)
24. Call on specialists to do work that you cannot do efficiently
25. Learn to read more rapidly.
26. Take a nap after dinner. Then take a shower. Begin the evening hours relaxed and refreshed.
27. Avoid interruptions.
28. Avoid making a big production out of tiny tasks.
29. Search out job shortcuts.
30. Know your limitations.
31. Work to your full capacity. I know it's tough to break bad habits. However, it is necessary to make sacrifices so that your business can be successful.

Don't try to implement all of these ideas at once. Implement them one at a time and repeat them until they become a part of your daily routine.

Source: http://EzineArticles.com/?expert=DeAnna_ Spencer

The 'Five Time Zone' Concept

To accelerate the ability to manage their time, managers need to strike a proper balance between monochronic and polychronic aspects of time management. The 'Five Time Zone Concept' advocated by Lewis,

Justus and Storz, Moni Laui (Switch on Your Mind: Accelerative Learning Strategies at Work.) enables managers to bring about that balance. The five links in the 'Five Time Zone' approach are - vision, plans, personal organization systems, commitment and energy.

- Developing Zone 1 - Vision and Goals: Managers must search for visions, not tasks. These visions are guided by their personal standards and values, and the direction they want to take. Once their visions are crystallized, they need to do some thinking to create goals from their visions and action steps from their goals.

My vision and goals . . .

- What is most important to me?
- What would I like to do if there were no limitations?
- What things in my life would I like to be different?
- My visions for myself are . . .

Developing Zone 2 - Plans: Having established goals, managers now can move into zone two - plans. A plan is needed to turn visions and goals into action. Writing things down and using some form of planning 'tool' are keys to successful planning. Once they have drawn up the plan, they need to review it. They should plan for highpayoff and low-payoff activities for high and low priorities.

- Developing Zone 3 – Personal Organization Systems (POS): Zone three encompasses a manager's personal organization system. Organizing the desk, follow-up, paperwork, physical environment are all part of personal organization system. The personal organization system should focus on –
- Creating an interesting and relaxing work-space
- Providing easy access to basic tools and materials
- Grouping similar tasks together to optimize time

Devising a good follow-up system that works well

- Enabling efficient handling of each piece of paper
- Ensuring a wider reach of people.

Developing Zone 4 – Commitment: The fourth time zone is the zone of commitment, in which managers correct any tendencies they might have towards procrastination. Procrastination can be overcome by identifying why one is procrastinating, breaking the mental blocks and visualizing the successful completion of a task while in a relaxed state. One way to do this it to identify the real reason for the procrastination - personal, logical, emotional or ethical barrier to action. Once this has surfaced from the subconscious to the conscious, strategies can be brought into play to deal with it. Developing Zone 5 – Energy: The final factor that keeps the chain together is zone five, the energy zone. Managers must check their office surroundings, as the environment they work in can sap or strengthen their energy levels. They must also identify the prime time - the time of day when they are most energetic and alert – they can schedule high-priority, high-payoff tasks or activities for these times.

- Find your prime time
- Internal and external prime time
- Cognitive tasks for the morning
- Complete high-energy tasks in high-energy periods
- Take energy breaks

Time Management Matrix

Time management experts like Stephen Covey S R (The Seven Habits of Highly Effective People; Simon & Schuster) have developed a model called a time management matrix. From a study of the Time Management Matrix, the following observations can be made:

1. Activities in Quadrant I and Quadrant II may be equally important. Some activities in Quadrant II may even be more important than activities in Quadrant I, but not necessarily more urgent.
2. Activities in Quadrant I assume critical importance and top priority.
3. Spending most of the time on Activities in Quadrant I results in stress and burnout.
4. Focusing on activities in Quadrant II can reduce the activities in Quadrant I, in the long run.
5. Focusing on activities in Quadrant II will mean avoiding all unimportant activities in Quadrant III and IV.

Elements of Effective Time Management

Time goes by at the same rate no matter what one does. One can not speed it up or slow it down. Unlike the other resources that one manages, there is no way to control time. The best one can do is take charge of oneself in the framework of time, investing oneself in those things that matter most in one's life. Effective time management requires reducing the impact of the time stealers and increasing the effectiveness of a manager in getting the things done that need to be done. The following are the important elements that combine to enable a manager eliminate distractions, interruptions and inefficiencies in the work process to make the most of time management.

A. Evaluating How Time is Used

The first step of effective time management is identifying how a manager is using his time.

This can be done by –

I. Activity Time Log: The first step to managing time better is to find out how managers are currently spending their time. Keeping a Time Log is a very effective way to do this. Through an Activity Time Log, managers can make a list of the activities or tasks that they spend time on. The very act of measuring is often enough to raise their unconscious habits into their consciousness, where they then have a chance to scrutinize and change them.

Pick activity categories that will encompass the entire day. Label those below and add up the total time spent on that particular activity category. Include a miscellaneous category for things that do not fit well into typical categories. Keeping the Activity Log for several days helps managers analyze their time and answer questions like:

- What is the most productive period of time?
- What is the least productive time?
- Did they achieve their goals?
- How could they have done what they were doing more effectively?

Activity logs are valuable tools for scrutinizing the way managers use their time. They can also help managers to track changes in their energy, alertness and effectiveness throughout the day. By examining their activity log, they will be able to discover and obviate timewasting or low-yield jobs. They will also know the times of day at which they are the most effective, so that they can carry out their most important tasks during those times. Studies reveal that managers do a miniscule of real work per day – 1.5 hours of actual work per day. The rest of the time is spent socializing, taking coffee breaks, eating, engaging in non-productive communication, shuffling papers and other preventable time-wasters.

Analyzing The Daily Time Log

After completing your Daily Time Log, take a few moments to analyze your results. This analysis will give you a clear picture on how you spend your time and how you can improve.

1. Did you have a plan for each day with clear priorities in writing?
2. Were you doing the right job at the right time?
   - What did you do that should not have been done at all?
   - Could it have been done more effectively at another time?
   - Could it have been delegated? If so, to whom can it be delegated?
3. What could be done in a better way?
   - Faster
   - More simply
   - In less detail
   - With better results
4. Concerning interruptions:
   - How are you interrupted (phone, visitors, meetings, crises, self, boss, clients)?
   - How often are you interrupted?
   - For how long have you been interrupted?
   - How important were the interruptions?
   - How long does it take to recover—to get back on track?
   - How many interrupted tasks were left unfinished at the end of the day?
5. Concerning contacts/ communications with others:
   - How important is time spent in accordance with your real priorities?
   - Who (with the right person) are they?
   - How often do you spend with them?
   - How long?

   Source: Mackenzie, R. Alec. The Time Trap, 2nd rev. ed., NY: ANACOM, American Management Association, 1990.
6. To what extent did you reach your goals?

Based on the analysis of Activity Time Log over some period, it is possible for managers to calculate their daily efficiency ratio. Daily efficiency ratio is the amount of time spent b managers on the work divided by the total amount of time they spent in the office. Efficiency Ratio = (Time Doing "Real Work") / (Time Spent "At Work") Assuming that managers have done only 15 hours of actual productive time in a week (60 hrs), the Daily Efficiency Ratio of a manager is only 25% of the time.

B. Goal-Setting

Why is goal-setting so important in time management? From the time management perspective, a person's life is a sequence of big and small choices and decisions. It is those choices that a person really manages, not the flow of time. A key difference between successful and unsuccessful managers is the quality and practicality of the goals they set for themselves. Goals state clearly the measurable and specific results to be accomplished by the managers and the timeframe to attain them. Goal-setting is the wisdom that comes from practical experience that helps managers direct their conscious and subconscious decisions towards success. The process of setting goals helps managers choose where they want to go in personal and professional life. By being aware of precisely what they want to achieve, they know the efforts required for it. Goals help in monitoring the day to day activities and ensure the activities are progressing in the right direction. There are two types of goals managers can set for themselves – rational goals and directional goals. Rational goals are specific, short-time goals focusing on the questions-

- What do I want to accomplish?
- Why am I doing this task?
- Who are all involved in the task?
- What are the expected outcomes of this task?
- When can this task be expected to be completed?

Directional goals (also known as domain planning) are long-term goals with no predictable outcomes, focusing on the question - What do I want to accomplish? To stay focused, managers should aim and visualize these goals. They should identify possible quarters from where they can pool up the support and required resources needed to put together and accomplish those goals. The above six top priority goals should occupy a manager's time for one month. Next month, they should make a new list. Some goals will remain top priority while others will drop off.

The goals will always be accompanied by a list of specific, easy to accomplish steps. They should set aside a certain time each day to work on top priority goals. Emphasis should be on results rather than activity. What makes a good goal? A good goal is one that when followed, offers a reasonably high probability of success in the defined time-frame. Gene Donohue ("Goal Setting Powerful Written Goals in 7 Easy Steps!") lays down the following 7 goal setting steps for the managers to follow that help in building the road map to good goals.

1. Make sure the goal you are working for is something you really want, not just something that sounds good: When setting goals

it is very important for the managers to remember that the goals are compatible with their personal interests and values. Any inherent conflict or incompatibility will cause unwarranted friction and adversely impact accomplishment of the goals.

2. A goal cannot contradict any of your other goals: Non-integrated thinking can also sabotage all the hard work managers put into their goals. Non-integrated thinking can also hamper their everyday thoughts. Managers should continually strive to eliminate contradictory ideas from their thinking.
3. Develop goals in the 6 areas of life: Setting goals in each area of life will ensure a more balanced life as managers begin to examine and change the fundamentals of everyday living. Setting goals in each area of life also helps in eliminating the non-integrated thinking. The six areas of life that need goal-setting include –
   - Family and Home
   - Physical and Health
   - Mental and Educational
   - Financial and Career
   - Spiritual and Ethical
   - Social and Cultural
4. Write down your goals: The difference between a goal and a dream is the written word. Writing down the goals creates the roadmap to success. Although the mere act of writing them down can set the process in motion, it is also extremely important to review the goals frequently. The more focused the managers are on their goals, the more likely they are to accomplish them.
5. Write your goal in the positive instead of the negative: The subconscious mind can not determine right from wrong and it does not judge. It's only function is to carry out its instructions. The more positive instructions one gives it, the more positive results one will get.
6. Write your goal out in complete detail. Writing down goals in details is once again giving the subconscious mind a detailed set of instructions to work on. The more information one gives it, the more clear the final outcome becomes. The more precise the outcome, the more efficient the subconscious mind can become.
7. By all means, make sure your goal is high enough: Keeping in view the time and resources at their disposal, managers should

set fairly high but practicable goals. Lower goals are indicators of lower motivational levels on the part of managers. Higher goals are pointers to the zest managers have toward their work.

Apart from the above, traditional goal-setting wisdom teaches that a good goal must be believable, specific and measurable, and have a deadline. Managers must believe that it is possible for them to achieve the goal or they will not be motivated to try. The goals should also be measurable and specific enough for them to know unambiguously whether they have been completed yet or not. For goals to be meaningful, managers must know the time-frame by when they are to be accomplished. Reviewing your goals daily is a crucial part of a manager's success and must become part of his/her routine. At the beginning of each day, they must take stock of the list of goals and identify the efforts required on their part, for the day, to accomplish each of the goals by the set deadline. Each night, they should review the goals to ascertain whether the required work has been done or not. This process will set their subconscious and conscious minds working towards the goal. This will also begin to replace any of the negative self-talk they may indulge in and replace it with positive self-talk. A manager's time can best be directed by using goals. Without goals, they become easily side-tracked and waste time.

C. Defining Priorities

Prioritizing means "taking conscious control of one's choices and deciding to spend more time on the activities and tasks that are important and valuable, and less time on the ones that are not...." The importance of prioritizing tasks or activities is best driven home by the popular 'pebbles and jar' parable. One day, an expert in time management was speaking to a group of managers. As he stood in front of the group of high-powered over-achievers he said, "Okay, time for a quiz" and he pulled out a one-gallon, wide-mouth mason jar and set it on the table in front of him. He also produced about a dozen fist-sized rocks and carefully placed them, one at a time, into the jar. When the jar was filled to the top and no more rocks would fit inside, he asked,

"Is this jar full?" Everyone yelled, "Yes."

The time management expert replied, "Really?" He reached under the table and pulled out a bucket of gravel. He dumped some gravel in and shook the jar causing pieces of gravel to work themselves down into the spaces between the big rocks. He then asked the group once more, "Is the jar full?"

"Probably not," one of them answered.

"Good!" he replied. He reached under the table and brought out a bucket of sand. He started dumping the sand in the jar and it went into all of the spaces left between the rocks and the gravel. Once more he asked the question, "Is this jar full?"

"No!" the audience shouted.

Once again he said, "Good." Then he grabbed a pitcher of water and began to pour it in until the jar was filled to the brim. Then he looked at the spectators and asked, "What is the point of this illustration?" One eager beaver raised his hand and said, "The point is, no matter how full your schedule is, if you try really hard you can always fit some more things in it!"

"No," the speaker replied, "that's not the point. The truth this illustration teaches us is, "If you don't put the big rocks in first, you'll never get them in at all.

What are the 'big rocks' in your life, time with loved ones, your faith, your education, your dreams, a worthy cause, teaching or mentoring others?

Remember to put these BIG ROCKS in first or you'll never get them in at all. So, tonight, or in the morning, when you are reflecting on this short story, ask yourself this question, "What are the 'big rocks' in my life?" Then, put those in your jar first. Time management expert Alec Mackenzie in The Time Trap narrates an anecdote that underscores the importance of prioritizing activities. As the story goes, an efficiency consultant by the name of Ivy Lee was meeting with the president of a large steel mill. The president, one Charles Schwab, was interested to find out how he could increase performance. Lee was telling Schwab how he could provide him with advice to better manage the company. Schwab, however, was not interested because he did not want more knowledge. Instead, he wanted to find out how to get more done within available time, and he was willing to pay anything within reason for such advice. Lee said that he could help him increase his efficiency by at least 50% provided he could have about 20 minutes of his time. After Schwab consented, Lee gave him a blank piece of paper and told him to write down the six most important things he wanted to accomplish tomorrow. Schwab thought about it and completed the task in about three minutes. Then Lee instructed him to order these things from most important to least important. That, too, took very little time. Now the executive was instructed to keep the list until the following morning, at which time he was asked to look at the first item and to start working on it until it was completed. After that he was told to work on task number two and so on until the end of the day. Lee further advised Schwab not to worry about those tasks that he could not get done, since it didn't matter because they would not have gotten done anyway. Then Schwab was asked to repeat this process every working day. Lee then told him to try this system as long as he likes. Lee also asked Schwab to have his employees try this system and, if it worked, to send him a check for whatever the idea was worth to him and the company. After several months, Lee received a check for $25,000 and a letter in which Schwab said that this was one of the most profitable ideas that he had ever been taught. It is further reputed that the consistent application of this strategy helped to turn this small steel mill into Bethlehem Steel. Managers must realize that they cannot simply do task or activity they take up. Given the constraints of time and resources, they have to be selective and consciously choose to spend time on what is most important to them. They have to keep in mind is that whenever they start an activity or task, they are inevitably ruling out everything else they could have done with that time. When managers have to choose among several tasks, they can use several prioritization tools. The key ones are summarized below. It can be very helpful at times to break out of their routine way of looking at things and to use a tool that they do not use all of the time.

Covey's Quadrants

Discussed earlier under Time Matrix, Steven Covey describes a high-level prioritization Time Management Grid in his book The Seven Habits of Highly Effective People. In this grid, tasks are categorized by four quadrants:

- Quadrant 1 represents things which are both urgent and important - labelled "firefighting". The activities need to be dealt with immediately, and they are important.
- Quadrant 2 represents things which are important, but not urgent - labelled "Quality Time". Although the activities here are important, and contribute to achieving the goals and priorities - they do not have to be done right now. As a result, they can be scheduled when they can be given quality thought to them. A good example would be the preparation of an important talk, or mentoring a key individual. Prayer time, family time and personal relaxation/recreation are also part of Quadrant 2.
- Quadrant 3 represents distractions. They must be dealt with right now, but frankly, are not important. For example, when a person answers an unwanted phone call, - he/she has had to interrupt whatever he/she is doing to answer it.
- The final quadrant, Quadrant 4, represents things which are neither urgent nor important. Some meetings could fall into

this category – they have been scheduled in advance, but if they achieve nothing, then they have simply wasted time. Other examples could include driving time and low quality relaxation or family time.

Using the Tool

Managers must strive to maximize Quadrant 2 time. They should allocate time in the diary to carry out these tasks when they are at their best. Doing so can reduce the amount of time taken up by firefighting quadrant 1 activities, since many quadrant 1 activities could have been quadrant 2 if they had been done earlier. Managers can also seek to reduce time spent in Quadrant 3 by improving the systems and processes for dealing with distractions, and they can eliminate as much as possible of quadrant 4 activities, by either not spending time on these things, or changing the nature of them to make them more productive. For example, driving can be quadrant 4 if the time is unproductive, but there are a number of ways of making this time more productive by learning new skills, planning and so on.

Ken Blanchard's Quadrants

Ken Blanchard - the author of the popular book "The One Minute Manager" and "The On- Time, On-Target Manager" – sets out his quadrants a little differently:

- Have to Do, Want to Do
- Have to Do, Don't Want to Do
- Don't Have to Do, Want to Do
- Don't Have to Do, Don't Want to Do

Most of the managers do not have a problem with Quadrants 1 and 4. If It is Quadrant 1, they will willingly do it. If it is Quadrant 4, they never do it. It is Quadrants 2 and 3 where the conflict is likely to arise and most of the managers are likely to be attracted to Quadrant 3, meaning things that do not have to be done get done. The Blanchard advice for the managers is to take up tasks in the order of Quadrant 2 and Quadrant 1, and spend little or no time on Quadrant 3 items. To use this model, managers have to chart out to-do list and plan accordingly.

Paired Comparison

The Simple Paired Comparison method uses a simple scoring system for comparing activities. The following example illustrates how this method can be applied: Here is the list of example tasks or activities to be performed:

1. Call home about dinner plans
2. Fire Venkat
3. Draft budget report
4. Respond to e-mails

Compare the following and put a check mark against the relatively important task of each comparison:

- 1 to 2, 1 to 3, 1 to 4
- 2 to 3, 2 to 4
- 3 to 4

Let's say the result is as follows:

1. Call home about dinner plans XX
2. Fire Venkat XXX
3. Draft budget report X
4. Respond to e-mails

So, the order you would do the tasks in would be 2, 1, 3, 4.

The ABC Method

The ABC method ranks tasks into the following categories:

- 'A' are activities which Absolutely must get done now
- 'B' are those that Better get done soon
- 'C' are those that could wait for now
- 'D' are those that can be Delegated but require follow up

Then it subdivides tasks in these categories into A1, A2, A3, ..., B1, B2, ... and so forth. A lot of people find this prioritization method helpful.

The Payoff Versus Time Method

With this method, the managers have to weigh each task by the payoff they expect from it versus the time it takes to do it. Tasks that have high payoff and that take little time are the ones they would take up first. Correspondingly, tasks that have low payoff and that take a lot of time are ones they would do last or not do them at all. Whichever method one uses - whether a particular method listed above, a combination of methods, or one of one's own design – a manager should use it not only to rank the order in which they will do things, but also to defer or eliminate items that are not important or of least priority.

Scheduling Activities

After identifying the activities and prioritizing them, it is time to create a schedule. When scheduling, it is important to plan a weekly schedule as well as a daily schedule. The weekly schedule is important for the overall success of the activities and tasks, but it is the daily planning that will help one to track one's progress and determine whether or not one is on schedule. Managers should try using significant project milestones in their weekly planning but for daily planning break each milestone down into the necessary components and plan the completion of those components on a daily basis. It is helpful to keep one's schedule in an appointment book or electronic organizer, but for purposes of planning one can use a scheduling grid as follows.

Time Management Tools

- Master List
- Calendar
- Prioritized Task List
- Paper
- Directory

The following points demonstrate why scheduling is so critical to success.

- Scheduling can greatly reduce your stress quotient. Proper scheduling gives one the peace of mind of knowing that one has formulated a feasible plan of action and that one's goals are attainable.
- Scheduling also helps one to be prepared for obstacles because part of the scheduling process is creating a contingency plan for unexpected problems.
- Scheduling serves as a way to evaluate your progress as you work. Planning your daily and weekly activities will clearly illustrate whether or not you are staying on schedule.

Tool 1: Master List

- Begin with items from your desktop
- Quick reference of ongoing activities
- Include due dates
- Include personal and professional goals

Tool 1: Master List

- Keep track of delegated work
- Establish and set goals
- Orgnize larger projects
  - Break down into smaller task
  - Daily task lists
  - Expect the unexpected

When scheduling the activities, ideally managers should follow the below procedure:

- Block out times on the schedule for each of the major activities.
- Start with recurring activities that occur at a fixed time
- Then block out time for activities that they want to do on a regular basis
- Allot ample time for each activity, especially high priority activities.
- Take into account when they are most effective. Morning people might schedule more activities early in the day. Night owls might schedule things later.

Essential Steps in Using a Planner

Outlined below is a step-by-step approach for using a day planner to manage time effectively.

1. Select a Compatible Time Planner: A day planner is a device that includes a calendar, space to write "to-do" lists, and space to write telephone numbers, addresses, and other/ reference information. It can be a Franklin Planner (simple paper-and-pencil type), Day Timer, a fancy electronic organizer or time management software on a computer. If techno-savvy, a manager can pick an electronic organizer. If not, a manager can choose the paper-and-pencil method.

2. Find a Single, Accessible Place to Keep the Planner: Having selected a planner, managers should cultivate the habit of keeping it in an exclusively designated and easily accessible place at home and workplace. An ideal place to keep the planner could be near the telephone or on the office desk.

3. Enter the Basic in the Day Planner: Managers should consider what vital information might be useful to enter in the Planner – such as insurance policy numbers, computer passwords, telephone numbers, equipment numbers - and arrange the information in alphabetical order.

Tool 1: Your Calender

- Maintain your own calendar
- Keep one calendar for everything
- Take calendar wherever you go
- Know your energy cycle
- Plan every day

4. Carry the Planner at All Times: Carrying the planner at all times means that the managers have all the vital information they need with them all the time. Ideally, the Day Planner should be their integral part and constant companion of managers.

5. Refer to the Day Planner Regularly: Managers should make it a habit to refer to the Day Planner thrice a day – at the start of the day to be sure of the things to be done, afternoon to monitor the progress of their activities, and night to take stock of the status of the activities for the day.

6. Use the Day Planner as a Calendar for Everything: Appointments, and activities for the day on personal, family and professional fronts should be listed in the planner. It is advisable that activities relating to family and professions are highlighted using different colours. It is also essential that crucial activities or tasks that need personal attention and close scrutiny are highlighted using different colours to review their progress from time to time.

7. Use Day Planner as a 'Brain Dump' to Capture Ideas: Day Planner also doubles up as a Brain-Dump for managers as they can put down the ideas as they surface in the planner. That way it helps to refer to them and weigh their value and feasibility at the appropriate time.

Tool 2: Your Calender

- Don't plan every minute
- Prioritize
- Save peak energy periods for yurself
- Schedule time for routine taks
- Schedule your rewards

8. Conduct a Daily Planning Session: The goal of this session is to plan the upcoming day's activities and develop a plan of attack and to carry out the same. In addition to listing priorities and reviewing schedules, the planning session is the time to consider exactly how each task will be accomplished. What materials will be needed? What obstacles are likely to be encountered? How can these obstacles be overcome? The planning session will thus provide a mental map that guides them in carrying out the tasks on the list

9. Prioritize 'To-Do' List and Action in Accordance with Priorities: There are many ways to prioritize a "to do" list. One way is to number all of the items on the list in order of decreasing priority. Another way is to classify items into one of three categories: "Essential," "Important," and "Do only if I have extra time." The managers should pick the method that best fits their style, and begin prioritizing their daily "to do" list.

Tool 3: Daily Task List

- List everything you'd like to accomplish
- Assign value using "ABC" system
- Assign numerical value to each item

Tool 4: Notes

- Carry paper at all times
- Make notes
- Use full-sized paper
- Date notes
- File in action file folders

10. Generate a List of Long-Term Goals and Break the Long-Term Goals into Small, Manageable Chunks: First, generate a list of all long-term goals. These are broad goals to be accomplished over many months and years. Then, take one goal at a time and break it down into small chunks or sub-goals that might be accomplished on a monthly basis. Assign one sub-goal to each month of the year. At the beginning of the month, conduct a monthly planning session to decide how to accomplish the sub-goal over the course of the month. Assign various tasks to each week of the month. At the beginning of each week, conduct a weekly planning session to decide how to assign aspects of that week's sub-goal to the daily task lists for the entire week. During each daily planning session, plan the details of the assigned task that will be performed that day.

Tool 4: Telephone/ Address Directory

- Carry It
- Maintain one directory
- Transfer business card infomration
- Include e-mail, fax, home address/phone

E. Personal Action Plan with a Follow-Up

In order to eliminate the time wasters in the work-process, managers need to act to change them. For them to act and take corrective measures, they need to draw up an action plan.

Getting Oriented to Manage Time

To get ready to manage their time better, managers should answer the following questions:

- What is my time worth? How much do I get paid per hour? If I could save one hour a day, what would this amount to, in the course of one year?
- What is my job? What results are expected of me? Am I meeting a predetermined, definable purpose, or am I just drifting?
- What have I been doing? At the end of a day, am I able to account for my time, or do I say to myself, "Where did the day go? I don't feel I have accomplished anything."
- Have I been doing the right things? Am I involved in work activities that rightfully fall under the responsibility of my subordinates? What are the five most important tasks I have to do?
- How am I spending/ investing my time? What results do I see for the time I spend on each activity? What would happen if some of these things were not done?
- Am I goal-oriented? Am I working toward quantified objectives? Have I established performance standards for myself? For my people?
- Have I done any planning? When I arrive on the job in the morning, do I know what it is I want to accomplish during that particular day? Have I established priorities? Have I determined a hierarchy of importance?
- Have I tried to manage, schedule, control my work and time? Is the job running me or am I running the job? Am I suffering from "brief caseitis," i.e., bringing home more and more of my work?
- Do I delegate all possible tasks? Am I able to hand over more tasks to my coworkers or staff at work and to my spouse or children at home?
- Does the time I spend on the job affect my lifestyle? Am I enjoying life and having fun, or am I so stressed from the pressures of poor time management on the job that the tension carries over into my everyday life?

b. Drop-in Visitors: Taking time-log of visits and implementing a plan to arrange and screen appointments is an effective way of dealing with drop-in visitors. Managers can also have 'Open Door' and 'Quiet Hour" timings fixed so that they are not distracted when certain of their tasks demand undivided personal attention.

c. Meetings: Setting a clear agenda before will provide the right direction to the meetings and elicit positive outcomes from them. Selecting an appropriate location and assessing the needs of participation, information and coordination are also important prerequisites in conducting meetings. Concise minutes summarizing decisions, assignments and deadlines followed by effective follow-up on decisions make meetings purposeful.

Time - Saving Tips: Interruptions

- Close your door
- Distinguish between necessary visits and interruptions
- Use different techniques
  - Visit others
  - Arrange appointment
  - Leave your office
  - Establish regular meeting time

Overcoming Barriers to Effective Time Management

a. Telephone Interruptions: Delegation of authority and responsibility is an ideal way of controlling telephone interruptions. Also fixing specific time slots for socializing and business will help the managers effectively reduce the telephone interruptions. Implementation of the screening procedures also lessen the burden of unwanted telephone intrusions.

Time - Saving Tips: Interruptions

- Close your door
- Distinguish between necessary visits and interruptions
- Use different techniques
  - Visit others
  - Arrange appointment
  - Leave your office
  - Establish regular meeting time

b. Drop-in Visitors: Taking time-log of visits and implementing a plan to arrange and screen appointments is an effective way of dealing with drop-in visitors. Managers can also have 'Open Door' and 'Quiet Hour" timings fixed so that they are not distracted when certain of their tasks demand undivided personal attention.

c. Meetings: Setting a clear agenda before will provide the right direction to the meetings and elicit positive outcomes from them. Selecting an appropriate location and assessing the needs of participation, information and coordination are also important prerequisites in conducting meetings. Concise minutes summarizing decisions, assignments and deadlines followed by effective follow-up on decisions make meetings purposeful.

Time - Saving Tips: Meetings

- Request agenda
- Arrive early
- Notify chair if your will be late
- Avoid routine, emergency, impromptu meetings
- Avoid Monday mornings, Friday afternoons

d. Lack of Priorities: Putting first things first helps managers spend relatively more time on activities that are important. Managers must realize that most of the problems arise due to action without thought. Defining clearly the objectives and priorities and deadlines in the form of a Daily Planner will help managers effectively use their time.

e. Personal Disorganization: Managers must recognize that personal disorganization, indecision, procrastination, insecurity, confusion of priority, and inability to meet deadlines are mostly due to lost documents. Uncluttered desk, orderly filing system and simplified procedures will help the managers make the most of time management. Through a system in place for screening junk mails, minimizing paperwork and emphasis on brevity, managers can overcome their personal disorganization.

Time - Saving Tips: Managing E-mails

- Know your system's special features
- List serves
- Same time every day
- Use Web services - (examples)
  - IFAP.ed.gov
  - NASFAA Today New

f. Ineffective Delegation: Managers must ensure that clear, unambiguous instructions are given to the subordinates. They should establish plans, schedules with details, progress reports, monitoring of deadlines, and emphasize goalaccomplishment methods and procedures. They should measure results rather than activity and track progress of an activity to take timely corrective actions.

g. Attempting too much: Managers must set their objectives, priorities, and deadlines daily so that they must plan, start early and always remember Murphy's 2nd Law: "Recognize that everything takes longer than you think". They must limit their response to the urgent and important demands. They should learn to say "No" when necessary.

h. Unclear Communication: Managers must assess the legitimate needs for information and check for interference, noise or activity in the flow of information. They should also assess potential impact of unclear communication, take preventive steps and minimize organizational levels. If it is difficult to minimize organizational levels, they should facilitate easy flow of information across the organization.

i. Inadequate, Inaccurate or Delayed Information: Managers must determine what information is needed for planning, decisions and feedback on results. Then they should ensure its availability, reliability and timeliness.

j. Indecision/ Procrastination: Managers must set deadlines on all objectives and priorities, use reminders, have the secretary check on the progress, reward themselves (no coffee until they finish). They should avoid fixing blame; ask what's been learned and how repetition can be avoided.

k. Confused Authority / Responsibility: Managers must lay emphasis on accountability for results; through recognition and reward for exercise of initiative; through citation, consideration in performance and salary review, promotion, etc.

l. Inability to say 'No': Managers must recognize that inability to say 'No' is a major cause of time wastage. They should understand that saying "Yes" may betray feelings of insecurity and low self-worth and should resist this urge. They should take time log recording all "Yes" responses that could have been "No" and assess the time wasted. They should learn to say "No", especially to inappropriate or thoughtless requests.

Summary

Now that we have come towards the end of the book we have realized that how our time gets wasted because we never thought of managing time in an effective manner. It is said that time and tide waits for none so our attempts would be to make the best use of time and prevent others from wasting our time too. This chapter winds up all our observations on time management in this book. It summarizes as to what causes us to waste our time and suggests solutions to save time as much as possible. It also offers tips to make the best use of time. As with all the precious resources, time is a scarce resource. The wisdom lies in making the most of it. Horace Mann says:

> "Lost, yesterday,
> Somewhere between sunrise and sunset,
> Two golden hours,
> Each set with sixty diamond minutes.
> No reward is offered,
> For they are gone forever"

Which of the following Time Enhancers have you tried lately?

- Listen to radio and TV news shows to keep up on the latest news; this should enable you to skim through newspapers and magazines.
- Limit recreational TV watching to one hour a day.
- Limit all casual, idle, or gossip chatter to five minutes.
- Open and sort through mail as soon as it arrives at your desk or home; handle each piece only once.
- Using the "automatic dialing and redial" telephone to speed up making and returning phone recalls.
- Use a timer to help you limit phone calls to less than five minutes.
- Hold as few meetings as possible; use an agenda and stick to it; limit the time to no more than one hour for each meeting.
- Pay each bill on the day it arrives in the mail, keeping the entries in your checkbook accurate and up to date.
- Use daydreaming as a form of stress release or relaxation, and limit it to a total of fifteen minutes per day.
- Get professional help for personal problems if you find thinking about them occupies a lot of your free time.
- Use a tape recorder with ear phones to listen to motivational tapes, relaxation tapes, or soft relaxing music when in traffic or on a commuter bus, train, plane, etc.
- Use a daily schedule book or "date minder" to create a log of scheduled activities to help you review your success at managing your time.
- Bring books and mail to read or a tape recorder to listen to when you have appointments where you know you will be waiting for a length of time.

- Eliminate naps and extend your nightly sleep time or increase your daily exercise schedule to increase your energy level.

Eliminate snacking between meals; eat three balanced meals a day

- Give up smoking (cigarettes, cigars or pipes).
- Give up the need for a "quick one" at your local bar, tavern, or lounge.
- Exchange alcoholic consumption time for exercise or some other time enhancer.
- Go shopping with a list, stick to the list, and leave when you have completed your list.
- Avoid browsing shopping unless it is a planned social, couple, or family shopping activity.
- Find alternative leisure activities that require no betting of legal tender.

Study your answer and take steps necessary to eliminate your time wasters.

Time Tips

1. Count all your time as time to be used and make every attempt to get satisfaction out of every moment.
2. Find something to enjoy in whatever you do.
3. Try to be an optimist and seek out the good in your life.
4. Find ways to build on your successes.
5. Stop regretting your failures and start learning from your mistakes.
6. Remind yourself, "There is always enough time for the important things." If it is important, you should be able to make time to do it.
7. Continually look at ways of freeing up your time.
8. Examine your old habits and search for ways to change or eliminate them.
9. Try to use waiting time-review notes or do practice problems.
10. Keep paper or a calendar with you to jot down the things you have to do or notes to yourself.
11. Examine and revise your lifetime goals on a monthly basis and be sure to include progress towards those goals on a daily basis.
12. Put up reminders in your home or office about your goals.

13. Always keep those long term goals in mind.
14. Plan your day each morning or the night before and set priorities for yourself.
15. Maintain and develop a list of specific things to be done each day, set your priorities and then get the most important ones done as soon in the early part of the day as you can. Evaluate your progress at the end of the day briefly.
16. Look ahead in your month and try and anticipate what is going to happen so you can better schedule your time.
17. Try rewarding yourself when you get things done as you had planned, especially the important ones.
18. Do first things first.
19. Have confidence in yourself and in your judgement of priorities and stick to them no matter what.
20. When you catch yourself procrastinating-ask yourself, "What am I avoiding?"
21. Start with the most difficult parts of projects, then either the worst is done or you may find you don't have to do all the other small tasks.
22. Catch yourself when you are involved in unproductive projects and stop as soon as you can.
23. Find time to concentrate on high priority items or activities.
24. Concentrate on one thing at a time.
25. Put your efforts in areas that provide long term benefits.
26. Push yourself and be persistent, especially when you know you are doing well.
27. Think on paper when possible-it makes it easier to review and revise.
28. Be sure and set deadlines for yourself whenever possible.
29. Delegate responsibilities whenever possible.
30. Ask for advice when needed.

SOURCE OF TIME MANAGEMENT SKILLS

Work Smarter and Improve Time Utilization

This section discusses personal time management skills. These are essential skills for effective people. People who use these techniques routinely are the highest achievers in all walks of life, from business to sport to public service. If you use these skills well, then you will be able to function effectively, even under intense pressure. At the heart of time management is an important shift in focus:

Concentrate on results, not on being busy

Many people spend their days in a frenzy of activity, but achieve very little because they are not concentrating on the right things.

The 80:20 Rule

This is neatly summed up in the Pareto Principle, or the '80:20 Rule'. This argues that typically 80% of unfocussed effort generates only 20% of results. *The remaining 80% of results are achieved with only 20% of the effort.* While the ratio is not always 80:20, this broad pattern of a small proportion of activity generating non-scalar returns recurs so frequently as to be the norm in many areas. By applying the time management tips and skills in this section you can optimize your effort to ensure that you concentrate as much of your time and energy as possible on the high payoff tasks. This ensures that you achieve the greatest benefit possible with the limited amount of time available to you.

Time Management Tools

By the end of this section, you should have a much clearer understanding of how to use time to its greatest effect. These tools and many, many more are explained in Mind Tools' Make Time For Success! This contains more than 100 pages of time tested tips, techniques and secrets to improve your time management skills and get the most that life has to offer. You will learn how to set realistic goals, generate a life plan and leverage all of the opportunities that life has to offer. Many of the lessons include workbook exercises so that you really understand how to put these invaluable skills to work in your life.

GOOD TIME MANAGEMENT

How often do you find yourself running out of time? Weekly, daily, hourly? For many, it seems that there's just never enough time in the day to get everything done. When you know how to manage your time you gain control. Rather than busily working here, there, and everywhere (and not getting much done anywhere), effective time management helps you to choose what to work on and when. This is essential if you're to achieve anything of any real worth. We've put together an interactive Time Management Quiz to help you identify the aspects of time management that you need most help with. The results will point you to the specific tools you need to use to gain control of your time, and start working efficiently.

Extent of Goodness of Ones Time Management

Instructions:

For each statement, click the button in the column that best describes you. Please answer questions as you actually are (rather than how you think you should be), and don't worry if some questions seem to score in the 'wrong direction'. When you are finished, please click the 'Calculate My Total' button at the bottom of the test.

Top of Form

	Question	*Not at all*	*Rarely*	*Some times*	*Often*	*Very Often*
1	Are the tasks you work on during the day the ones with the highest priority?	0	0	0	0	0
2	Do you find yourself completing tasks at the last minute, or asking for extensions?	0	0	0	0	0
3	Do you set aside time for planning and scheduling?	0	0	0	0	0
4	Do you know how much time you are spending on the various jobs you do?	0	0	0	0	0
5	How often do you find yourself dealing with interruptions?	0	0	0	0	0
6	Do you use goal setting to decide what tasks and activities you should work on?	0	0	0	0	0
7	Do you leave contingency time in your schedule to deal with "the unexpected"?	0	0	0	0	0
8	Do you know whether the tasks you are working on are high, medium, or low value?					
9	When you are given a new assignment, do you analyze it for importance and prioritize it accordingly?	0	0	0	0	0

10	Are you stressed about deadlines and commitments?	0	0	0	0	0
11	Do distractions often keep you from working on critical tasks?	0	0	0	0	0
12	Do you find you have to take work home, in order to get it done?	0	0	0	0	0
13	Do you prioritize your "To Do" list or Action Program?	0	0	0	0	0
14	Do you regularly confirm your priorities with your boss?	0	0	0	0	0
15	Before you take on a task, do you check that the results will be worth the time put in?	0	0	0	0	0
				Total	**= 0**	

Score Interpretation

Score	*Comment*
46-75	You're managing your time very effectively! Still, check the sections below to see if there's anything you can tweak to make this even better.
31-45	You're good at some things, but there's room for improvement elsewhere. Focus on the serious issues below, and you'll most likely find that work becomes much less stressful.
15-30	Ouch. The good news is that you've got a great opportunity to improve your effectiveness at work, and your long term success! However, to realize this, you've got to fundamentally improve your time management skills. Start below!

As you answered the questions, you probably had some insight into areas where your time management could use a pick-me-up. The following is a quick summary of the main areas of time management that were explored in the quiz, and a guide to the specific tools you can use for each.

Note: There are a lot of links to follow here! To save relevant links for reading later, hover over the green "+" button – like this – to the right of each link and click the "Add to Favourites" button that appears.

Goal Setting

(Questions 6, 10, 14, 15)

To start managing time effectively, you need to set goals. When you know where you're going, you can then figure out what exactly needs to be done, in what order. Without proper goal setting, you'll fritter your time away on a confusion of conflicting priorities. People tend to neglect goal setting because it requires time and effort. What they fail to consider is that a little time and effort put in now saves an enormous amount of time, effort and frustration in the future. Mind Tools has two great articles on goal setting that are must-reads for everyone. If you are serious about time management, we suggest you start with Personal Goal Setting and The Golden Rules of Goal Setting. We also recommend Treasure Mapping.

Prioritization

(Questions 1, 4, 8, 9, 13, 14, 15)

Prioritizing what needs to be done is especially important. Without it, you may work very hard, but you won't be achieving the results you desire because what you are working on is not of strategic importance. Most people have a "to-do" list of some sort. The problem with many of these lists is they are just a collection of things that need to get done. There is no rhyme or reason to the list and, because of this, the work they do is just as unstructured. So how do you work on To Do List tasks – top down, bottom up, easiest to hardest? To work efficiently you need to work on the most important, highest value tasks. This way you won't get caught scrambling to get something critical done as the deadline approaches. For information on how to start prioritizing your tasks, see our articles on Activity Logs, Prioritized To Do Lists, Prioritization, The Action Priority Matrix, and The Urgent/Important Matrix.

Managing Interruptions

(Questions 5, 9, 11, 12)

Having a plan and knowing how to prioritize it is one thing. The next issue is knowing what to do to minimize the interruptions you face during your day. It is widely recognized that managers get very little uninterrupted time to work on their priority tasks. There are phone calls, information requests, questions from employees, and a whole host of events that crop up unexpectedly.

Some do need to be dealt with immediately, but others need to be managed. Two excellent tools that discuss how to minimize your interrupted time are The Urgent/Important Matrix and Managing Interruptions. However, some jobs need you to be available for people when they need help – interruption is a natural and necessary part of life. Here, do what you sensibly can to minimize it, but make sure you don't scare people away from interrupting you when they should.

Procrastination

(Questions 2, 10, 12)

"I'll get to it later" has led to the downfall of many a good employee. After too many "laters" the work piles up so high that any task seems insurmountable. Procrastination is as tempting as it is deadly. The best way to beat it is to recognize that you do indeed procrastinate. Then you need to figure out why. Perhaps you are afraid of failing? (And some people are actually afraid of success!) Once you know why you procrastinate then you can plan to get out of the habit. Reward yourself for getting jobs done, and remind yourself regularly of the horrible consequences of not doing those boring tasks! For more help on recognizing and overcoming procrastination see our guide to Beating Procrastination.

Scheduling

(Questions 3, 7, 12)

Much of time management comes down to effective scheduling of your time. When you know what your goals and priorities are, you then need to know how to go about creating a schedule that keeps you on track, and protects you from stress. This means understanding the factors that affect the time you have available for work. You not only have to schedule priority tasks, you have to leave room for interruptions, and contingency time for those unexpected events that otherwise wreak chaos with your schedule. By creating a robust schedule that reflects your priorities and well as supports your personal goals, you have a winning combination: One that will allow you to control your time and keep your life in balance. To learn specific scheduling skills, see Pickle Jar Theory and Scheduling Skills.

Key Points

Time management is an essential skill that helps you keep your work under control, at the same time that it helps you keep stress to a minimum. We would all love to have an extra couple of hours in every day. Seeing as that is impossible, we need to work smarter on things that have the highest priority, and then creating a schedule that reflects our work and personal priorities. With this in place, we can work in a focused and effective way, and really start achieving those goals, dreams and ambitions we care so much about.

COMMON TIME MANAGEMENT MISTAKES

How well do you manage your time? If you're like many people, your answer may not be completely positive! Perhaps you feel overloaded, and you often have to work late to hit your deadlines. Or maybe your days seem to go from one crisis to another, and this is stressful and demoralizing. Many of us know that we could be managing our time more effectively; but it can be difficult to identify the mistakes that we're making, and to know how we could improve. When we do manage our time well, however, we're exceptionally productive at work, and our stress levels drop. We can devote time to the interesting, high-reward projects that can make a real difference to a career. In short, we're happier! In this article, we're looking at ten of the most common time management mistakes, as well as identifying strategies and tips that you can use to overcome them. These ten mistakes are:

Failing to Keep a To-Do List

Do you ever have that nagging feeling that you've forgotten to do an important piece of work? If so, you probably don't use a To-Do List to keep on top of things. (Or, if you do, you might not be using it effectively!) The trick with using To-Do Lists effectively lies in prioritizing the tasks on your list. Many people use an A - F coding system (A for high priority items, F for very low priorities). Alternatively, you can simplify this by using A through D, or by using numbers. If you have large projects on your list, then, unless you're careful, the entries for these can be vague and ineffective. For instance, you may have written down "Start on budget proposal." But what does this entail? The lack of specifics here might cause you to procrastinate, or miss key steps. So make sure that you break large tasks or projects down into specific, actionable steps - then you won't overlook something important. You can also use Action Programs to manage your work when you have many large projects happening at once. (Action Programs are "industrial strength" versions of To-Do Lists.)

Not Setting Personal Goals

Do you know where you'd like to be in six months? What about this time next year, or even 10 years from now? If not, it's time to set some personal goals! Personal goal setting is essential to managing your time well, because goals give you a destination and vision to work toward. When you know where you want to go, you can manage your priorities, time, and resources to get there. Goals also help you decide what's worth spending your time on, and what's just a distraction. To learn how to set SMART, effective goals, read up on Locke's Goal Setting Theory. Here, you'll learn how to set clearly defined goals that will keep you motivated. You might also enjoy our Book Insight into "Long Fuse, Big Bang" by Eric Haseltine. This book teaches you how to focus on your long-term goals without overlooking your short term priorities.

Not Prioritizing

Your assistant has just walked in with a crisis that she needs you to deal with right now, but you're in the middle of brainstorming ideas for a new client. You're sure that you've *almost* come up with a brilliant idea for their marketing campaign, but now you risk losing the thread of your thinking because of this "emergency." Sometimes, it's hard to know how to prioritize, especially when you're facing a flood of seemingly-urgent tasks. However, it's essential to learn how to prioritize tasks effectively if you want to manage your time better. One tool that will help you prioritize effectively is the Urgent/Important Matrix. This helps you understand the difference between urgent activities, and important activities. You'll also learn how to overcome the tendency to focus on the urgent. The Action Priority Matrix is another useful tool, which will help you determine if a task is high-yield and high-priority, or low-value, "fill in" work. You'll manage your time much better during the day if you know the difference. You might also want to go through our Bite-Sized Training Class, How to Prioritize, to further enhance your skills.

Failing to Manage Distractions

Do you know that some of us can lose as much as two hours a day to distractions? Think how much you could get done if you had that time back! Whether they come from emails, IM chats, colleagues in a crisis, or phone calls from clients, distractions prevent us from achieving flow, which is the satisfying and seemingly effortless work that we do when we're 100 percent engaged in a task. If you want to gain control of your day and do your best work, it's vital to know how to minimize distractions and manage interruptions effectively. For instance, turn off your IM chat when you need to focus, and let people know if they're distracting you too often. You should also learn how to improve your concentration, even when you're faced with distractions. Additionally, our article on managing email effectively teaches you how to gain control of your email, so that it doesn't eat up your entire day.

Procrastination

Procrastination occurs when you put off tasks that you should be focusing on right now. When you procrastinate, you feel guilty that you haven't started; you come to dread doing the task; and, eventually, everything catches up with you when you fail to complete the work on time. Start by taking our Procrastination Quiz to find out if procrastination is a problem in your life. If it is, then learn the strategies you need to beat procrastination. For instance, one useful strategy is to tell yourself that you're only going to start on a project for ten minutes. Often, procrastinators feel that they have to complete a task from start to finish, and this high expectation makes them feel overwhelmed and anxious. Instead, focus on devoting a small amount of time to starting. That's all! You might also find it helpful to use Action Plans. These help you break large projects down into manageable steps, so that it's easy to see everything that you need to get done, and so that you can complete small chunks at a time. Doing this can stop you from feeling overwhelmed at the start of a new project.

Tip:

Our Bite-Sized Training session, Overcoming Procrastination, gives you more in-depth strategies and tips for dealing with procrastination.

Taking on too Much

Are you a person who has a hard time saying "no" to people? If so, you probably have far too many projects and commitments on your plate. This can lead to poor performance, stress, and low morale. Or, you might be a micromanager: someone who insists on controlling or doing all of the work themselves, because they can't trust anyone else to do it correctly. (This can be a problem for everyone - not just managers!) Either way, taking on too much is a poor use of your time, and it can get you a reputation for producing rushed, sloppy work. To stop this, learn the subtle art of saying "yes" to the person, but "no" to the task. This skill helps you assert yourself, while still maintaining good feelings within the group. If the other person starts leaning on you to say "yes" to their request, learn how to think on your feet, and stay cool under pressure.

Thriving on "Busy"

Some people get a rush from being busy. The narrowly-met deadlines, the endless emails, the piles of files needing attention on the desk, the frantic race to the meeting... What an adrenaline buzz! The problem is that an "addiction to busyness" rarely means that you're effective, and it can lead to stress. Instead, try to slow down, and learn to manage your time better.

Tip:

"Do More Great Work", by Michael Bungay Stanier, is full of ideas and tips to reduce the "busywork" that you're doing, so that you're more excited and engaged in the work that matters. Click here for our Book Insight on it.

Multitasking

To get on top of her workload, Linda regularly writes emails while she chats on the phone to her clients. However, while Linda thinks that this is a good use of her time, the truth is that it can take 20-40 percent more time to finish a list of jobs when you multitask, compared with completing the same list of tasks in sequence. The result is also that she does both tasks poorly - her emails are full of errors, and her clients are frustrated by her lack of concentration. So, the best thing is to forget about multitasking, and, instead, focus on one task at a time. That way, you'll produce higher quality work. Our Expert Interview with Dave Crenshaw, looking at The Myth of Multitasking, will give you an enlightening look at multitasking, and will help you explore how you can manage simultaneous projects more effectively.

Not Taking Breaks

It's nice to think that you can work for 8-10 hours straight, especially when you're working to a deadline. But it's impossible for anyone to focus and produce really high-quality work without giving their brains some time to rest and recharge. So, don't dismiss breaks as "wasting time." They provide valuable down-time, which will enable you to think creatively and work effectively. If it's hard for you to stop working, then schedule breaks for yourself, or set an alarm as a reminder. Go for a quick walk, grab a cup of coffee, or just sit and meditate at your desk. Try to take a five minute break every hour or two. And make sure that you give yourself ample time for lunch - you won't produce top quality work if you're hungry!

Ineffectively Scheduling Tasks

Are you a morning person? Or do you find your energy picking up once the sun begins to set in the evening? All of us have different rhythms, that is, different times of day when we feel most productive and energetic. You can make best use of your time by scheduling high-value work during your peak time, and low-energy work (like returning phone calls and checking email), during your "down" time. Our article, Is This a Morning Task? will teach you how to do this.

Key Points

One of the most effective ways of improving your productivity is to recognize and rectify time management mistakes. When you take the time to overcome these mistakes, it will make a huge difference in your productivity - and you'll also be happier, and experience less stress!

Tip:

To continue improving your time management skills, take our Time Management Quiz, which will help you identify where your strengths and weaknesses lie. You can also take our Bite-Sized Training class, the Time Management Audit, to hone your skills to the next level.

WAYS TO MAKE ONESELF PRODUCTIVE

When we want to get more done, many of us simply work longer hours, move deadlines around, and multi-task. Although these strategies can provide some short-term relief, they aren't sustainable in the long term. Pretty soon, this approach becomes a way of life, leading to high levels of stress and eventually, poor productivity. Productivity is a measure of how much you accomplish – not how busy you are. So it's far better to learn how to work intelligently, and to use leverage to achieve more with your time and resources. This will increase your productivity – and help you find extra time to do other things.

The quiz below will help you to understand how productive you are. Then, the discussion and resources that follow will help you identify strategies that you can use to increase your productivity, so that you can do more, with less stress.

Instructions

For each statement, click the button in the column that best describes you. Please answer questions as you actually are (rather than how you think you should be), and don't worry if some questions seem to score in the 'wrong direction'. When you are finished, please click the 'Calculate My Total' button at the bottom of the test.

	Question	*Not at all*	*Rarely*	*Some times*	*Often*	*Very Often*
1	I use the leverage of other people's time to work efficiently.	0	0	0	0	0
2	I organize my day to take advantage of natural highs and lows in my energy and motivation.	0	0	0	0	0
3	I actively look for ways to improve the flow of my work, and the way that I approach tasks.	0	0	0	0	0
4	I can maintain focus on one task for a significant period of time.	0	0	0	0	0
5	I spend lots of time looking for information or documents, or locating missing items.	0	0	0	0	0
6	I actively look for ways to avoid wasting time and effort – both for myself and for my team.	0	0	0	0	0
7	I multitask regularly.	0	0	0	0	0
8	I use the talents, time, and expertise of other people on my team to help get the work done.	0	0	0	0	0
9	I use techniques like skimming and note taking to identify the key points from the documents that I receive.	0	0	0	0	0
10	I use a formal tracking system to understand how I spend my time.	0	0	0	0	0
11	I have a clear plan for dealing with disruptions and interruptions.	0	0	0	0	0
12	The volume of correspondence and documentation that I receive on a daily basis overwhelms me.	0	0	0	0	0

13	I delay difficult or unpleasant tasks until the last minute – or until the issue disappears on its own.	0	0	0	0	0
14	To ensure that things are done right, I keep close track of the activities and decisions of others on my team.	0	0	0	0	0
15	I find that my mind wanders, and it's hard to concentrate for long.	0	0	0	0	0
16	I do all of the tasks that are assigned to me, and hope that I can keep up with the volume of work.	0	0	0	0	0
				Total	**=**	**0**

Extent of Ones' Productiveness Bottom of Form: Score Interpretation

Score	*Comment*
16-36	You have some work to do to become more productive. It's inefficient simply to fill your day with tasks or to try to do too much without considering your limits and priorities. Use the information and resources below as your motivation to work smarter, not harder. The good news: you'll soon be accomplishing very much more, in less time.
37-58	You're on the right track with your productivity efforts, and you probably get your most important work done. However, you could be more productive. Use the productivity techniques and resources outlined below to become more productive and efficient in your daily life.
59-80	Fantastic! You have a clear understanding of your priorities, and you use your time to maximize your output. You also think about how to use leverage to get the most from your time, and to use it to the organization's advantage. This makes you a real asset. Where appropriate, use the resources below to continue to build on and improve your productivity skills.

This quiz highlights five key elements of working productively – organization, attitude, delegation, information integration, and effective use of systems. We'll look at these key areas below. By increasing your performance and effectiveness in these areas, you'll accomplish more in your day. You'll also begin to understand where to focus your time and energy to improve your productivity, and get better results.

Organization

(Questions 2, 5, 7, 10)

The first step in any productivity improvement plan is to get organized. Think about how to arrange your physical space so that it helps, rather than hurts, your performance. Messy desks and drawers affect your productivity because you spend valuable time searching through piles of documents, instead of doing high-value activities. Learning how to be organized is an art, and you need to work on it every day. From organizing email to organizing your files, there are many great systems that can help you order your working environment. Organization also involves self-awareness, and becoming aware of how you spend your time is essential for improving productivity.

An Activity Log shows you exactly where you use your time well and where you waste time handling low-priority work, interruptions and distractions. Activity logs also uncover whether you rely on multitasking: doing more than one thing at a time actually decreases productivity. Self-awareness also helps you to understand when you do your best work. Some people do their best work early in the morning, and others aren't fully productive until the afternoon or evening. Understanding your work pattern preferences will help you schedule important priority tasks for the times of day when you perform the best. Our article Is This a "Morning Task"? explores this in more detail.

Attitude

(Questions 4, 11, 13, 15)

The next part of improving productivity is related to your attitude and approach to your work. Self-motivation is very important if you want to maximize your productivity. Learn what motivates you to do your best work – and then create the best environment possible so that you to do so. Also, when you create an environment that supports productivity, you can get "in flow." This is a state that allows you to focus intensely on your work to achieve incredible results. To get into this high-productivity zone, you must also minimize or eliminate disruptions. Have a plan for managing interruptions, managing your stress, and improving your concentration. As you take positive steps to control your time and schedule, you'll likely reduce your stress, which will allow you to experience more positive energy.

This is essential for getting "in flow", so that your whole productivity plan supports and improves itself once you get started. Your mindset is fundamentally important for increasing productivity and improving overall time management. Think positively, and take small actions to improve your performance. This will give you the motivation and inspiration that you need to continue moving forward with your plan. Start now by adopting a positive perspective, and by believing that you can, indeed, be productive and accomplish your goals.

Delegation

(Questions 1, 8, 14)

Being productive is not a lone sport. To be truly productive in a work setting, you must rely on your team to help you. That's why work teams are the preferred way to reach goals – together, you can achieve much more than with the single efforts of individuals. To use the power of teamwork, you must know how to delegate effectively. Delegating isn't simply having others do your work – successful delegation ensures that the right person performs the task, regardless of who is ultimately responsible for getting it done. When people are able to work on their high-priority tasks, then everybody – and your organization – wins. If you spend too much time doing work that other people could do, and you have no time to make progress on your own key objectives, then you need to reevaluate who should be doing what on a regular basis.

Delegating effectively means providing sufficient support and resources so that another person can complete the job well. It doesn't mean micromanaging the process and checking every 10 minutes that things are being done right (in other words, "your way"). To delegate successfully, learn how to let go and trust people to do what must be done. When you do this on a regular basis and build a team of people who all help one another as needed, your productivity levels will increase radically.

Information Integration

(Questions 9, 12)

Your productivity will also increase when you master how to identify and use information quickly. Emails, memos, trade magazines, published studies, status reports, operating statistics, financial results – these are just some of the information categories that you may receive on a regular basis. If you try to read each of these in detail, it might take a day or more each week! So, look at strategies for overcoming information overload. You must approach information with a critical mind. What do you need to know? What type of information will a particular document provide? How will you use this information to improve the way that you work? Your answers to questions like these will help you determine the level of detail you need from each document. You may simply be able to ignore some items, or quickly skim topics and headings of others. Use these and other active reading strategies to help you reduce the time that you spend dealing with information and documentation. If you must read a lot of information in detail, learn how to speed read. Our article on the subject reviews several ways to read material quickly, and you can practice speed reading on your own. If you process and integrate information quickly and effectively, it will help you work more productively.

Productive Systems

(Questions 1, 3, 6, 16)

Finally, to increase your productivity, improve the way that you and your team work. Improving organizational systems not only helps you accomplish more – it can also help your organization leverage its assets effectively, to achieve its objectives and be more successful. Consider continuous improvement through practices like Kaizen and other techniques like Kanban and Job Analysis. These will encourage you to look at everyday tasks, processes and practices, and review how you can do things better. Also, learn from lean manufacturing approaches, and ask "How can we do what we do with less waste?" Whether it's reducing bottlenecks in a process or running meetings more effectively, anything that contributes to a more efficient work environment will ultimately make you more productive.

Key Points

No matter how well you're performing right now, you can almost always improve productivity. When you're more productive, you contribute strongly to the overall success and profitability of your organization. And it feels good to be in control of your time, and know that you can produce the results that are expected of you. To be more productive, get organized, have the right attitude, manage information you receive effectively, and actively seek ways to improve your working systems. Taking this approach will help you to increase your personal productivity and effectiveness.

ROLE OF PRIORITIZATION

Prioritization is the essential skill you need to make the very best use of your own efforts and those of your team. It's also a skill that you need to create calmness and space in your life so that you can focus your energy and attention on the things that really matter. It is particularly important when time is limited and demands are seemingly unlimited. It helps you to allocate your time where it is most-needed and most wisely spent, freeing you and your team up from less important tasks that can be attended to later. or quietly dropped. With good prioritization (and careful management of deprioritized tasks) you can bring order to chaos, massively reduce stress, and move towards a successful conclusion. Without it, you'll flounder around, drowning in competing demands.

Simple Prioritization

At a simple level, you can prioritize based on time constraints, on the potential profitability or benefit of the task you're facing, or on the pressure you're under to complete a job:

- Prioritization based on project value or profitability is probably the most commonly-used and rational basis for prioritization. Whether this is based on a subjective guess at value or a sophisticated financial evaluation, it often gives the most efficient results.

- Time constraints are important where other people are depending on you to complete a task, and particularly where this task is on the critical path of an important project. Here, a small amount of your own effort can go a very long way.
- And it's a brave (and maybe foolish) person who resists his or her boss's pressure to complete a task, when that pressure is reasonable and legitimate.

Prioritization Tools

While these simple approaches to prioritization suit many situations, there are plenty of special cases where you'll need other tools if you're going to be truly effective. We look at some of these below:

Paired Comparison Analysis

Paired Comparison Analysis is most useful where decision criteria are vague, subjective or inconsistent. It helps you prioritize options by asking you to compare each item on a list with all other items on the list individually. By deciding in each case which of the two is most important, you can consolidate results to get a prioritized list. Click here to find out more about Paired Comparison Analysis.

Grid Analysis

Grid Analysis helps you prioritize a list of tasks where you need to take many different factors into consideration. Click here to learn how to use it.

The Action Priority Matrix

This quick and simple diagramming technique asks you to plot the value of the task against the effort it will consume. By doing this you can quickly spot the "quick wins" which will give you the greatest rewards in the shortest possible time, and avoid the "hard slogs" which soak up time for little eventual reward. This is an ingenious approach for making highly efficient prioritization decisions. Click here to find out more.

The Urgent/Important Matrix

Similar to the Action Priority Matrix, this technique asks you to think about whether tasks are urgent or important. Frequently, seemingly urgent tasks actually aren't that important. And often, really important activities (like working towards your life goals) just aren't that urgent. This approach helps you cut through this. Click here to find out more.

The Ansoff Matrix and the Boston Matrices

These give you quick "rules of thumb" for prioritizing the opportunities open to you. The Ansoff Matrix helps you evaluate and prioritize opportunities by risk. The Boston Matrix does a similar job, helping you prioritize opportunities based on the attractiveness of a market and your ability to take advantage of it.

Pareto Analysis

Where you're facing a flurry of problems needing to be solved, Pareto Analysis helps you identify the most important changes to make. It firstly asks you to group together the different types of problem you face, and then asks you to count the number of cases of each type of problem. By prioritizing the most common type of problem, you can focus your efforts on resolving it. This clears time to focus on the next set of problems, and so on.

Nominal Group Technique

Nominal Group Technique is a useful technique for prioritizing issues and projects within a group, giving everyone fair input into the prioritization process. This is particularly useful where consensus is important, and where a robust group decision needs to be made. Using this tool, each group participant "nominates" his or her priority issues, and then ranks them on a scale, of say 1 to 10. The score for each issue is then added up, with issues then prioritized based on scores. The obvious fairness of this approach makes it particularly useful where prioritization is based on subjective criteria, and where people's "buy in" to the prioritization decision is needed. To learn more about the Nominal Group Technique and how you and your team can use it to prioritize issues and projects, click here. *To understand how prioritization fits into a comprehensive and effective time management system, click here see our Make Time for Success time management and personal effectiveness self-study course.*

UNDERSTANDING URGENT/IMPORTANT MATRIX

Using Time Effectively, Not just Efficiently

We've all been there: The project is due for today's meeting and we are only three quarters done. We're anxious, we can't concentrate, everything is a distraction, and then, finally, we blow. Time stressors are the most pervasive source of pressure and stress in the workplace and they happen as a result of having too much to do in too little time. With this kind of pressure all too common, effective time management is an absolute necessity. You probably use a day-planner and to-do list to manage your time.

These tools are certainly helpful, but they don't allow you to drill down to one of the most essential elements of good time management: distinguishing between what is important and what is urgent. Great time management means being effective as well as efficient. Managing time effectively, and achieving the things that you want to achieve, means spending your time on things that are important and not just urgent. To do this, and to minimize the stress of having too many tight deadlines, you need to understand this distinction:

- Important activities have an outcome that leads to the achievement of your goals.
- Urgent activities demand immediate attention, and are often associated with the achievement of someone else's goals.

Urgent activities are often the ones we concentrate on. These are the "squeaky wheels that get the grease." They demand attention because the consequences of not dealing with them are immediate. The Urgent/Important Matrix is a useful tool for thinking about this. The idea of measuring and combining these two competing elements in a matrix has been attributed to both former US President Eisenhower and Dr Stephen Covey. Eisenhower's quote, "What is important is seldom urgent and what is urgent is seldom important," sums up the concept of the matrix perfectly. This so-called "Eisenhower Principle" is said to be how Eisenhower organized his tasks. As a result, the matrix is sometimes called the Eisenhower Matrix. Covey brought the idea into the mainstream and gave it the name "The Urgent/Important Matrix" in his 1994 business classic, "The 7 Habits of Highly Effective People".

Ways to Use the Tool

The Urgent/Important Matrix is a powerful way of thinking about priorities. Using it helps you overcome the natural tendency to focus on urgent activities, so that you can keep clear enough time to focus on what's really important. This is the way you move from "firefighting", into a position where you can grow your business and your career. The steps below help you use the matrix to prioritize your activities:

1. The first step is to list all the activities and projects you feel you have to do. Try to include everything that takes up your time at work, however unimportant. (If you manage your time using an Action Program, you'll have done this already.)
2. Next, assign importance to each of the activities – you can do this on, say, a scale of 1 to 5: remember, this is a measure of how important the activity is in helping you meet your goals.

and objectives. Try not to worry about urgency at this stage, as this helps get to the true importance.

3. Once you have assigned importance to each activity, evaluate the urgency of each activity. As you do this, you can plot the listed items on the matrix according to the assigned importance and urgency.
4. Now study the matrix using the strategies described below to schedule your priorities.

Strategies for Different Quadrants of the Matrix

Urgent and Important

There are two distinct types of urgent and important activities: Ones that you could not foresee, and others that you have left to the last minute. You can avoid the latter by planning ahead and avoiding procrastination. Issues and crises, on the other hand, cannot always be foreseen or avoided. Here, the best approach is to leave some time in your schedule to handle unexpected issues and unplanned important activities. And if a major crisis arises, some other activity may have to be rescheduled. If this happens, identify which of you urgent-important activities could have been foreseen and think about how you could schedule similar activities ahead of time, so they do not become urgent.

Urgent and Not Important

Urgent but not important activities are things that stop you achieving your goals, and prevent you from completing your work. Ask yourself whether these tasks can be rescheduled, or whether someone else could do them. A common source of such interruptions is from other people in your office. Sometimes it's appropriate to say "No" to people, or encourage them to solve the problem themselves. Alternatively, try allocating time when you are available so that people only interrupt you at certain times (a good way of doing this is to schedule a regular meeting so that all issues can be dealt with at the same time.) By doing this, you'll be able to concentrate on your important activities for longer periods of time.

Not Urgent, but Important

These are the activities that help you achieve your personal and professional goals, and complete important work. Make sure that you have plenty of time to do these things properly, so that they do not become urgent. And remember to leave enough time in your schedule to deal with unforeseen problems. This will maximize your chances of keeping on schedule, and help you avoid the stress of work becoming more urgent that necessary.

Not Urgent and Not Important

These activities are just a distraction, and should be avoided if possible. Some can simply be ignored. Others are activities that other people may want you to do, but they do not contribute to your own desired outcomes. Again, say "No" politely and firmly if you can. If people see you are clear about your objectives and boundaries, they will often not ask you to do "not important" activities in the future.

Key Points

The Urgent/Important Matrix helps you look at your task list, and quickly identify the activities you should focus on. By prioritizing using the Matrix, you can deal with truly urgent issues, at the same time that you keep on working towards your goals.

UNDERSTANDING ACTION PRIORITY MATRIX

The Action Priority Matrix is a simple diagramming technique that helps you choose which activities to prioritize and which ones you should drop if you want to make the most of your time and opportunities. It's useful because most of us have many more activities on our "wish lists" – whether these are bright ideas to pursue, exciting opportunities or interesting possibilities – than we have time available. By choosing activities intelligently, you can make the very most of your time and opportunities. However by choosing badly, you can quickly bog yourself down in time-consuming, low-yield projects that close down opportunities and stop you moving forwards.

ROLE OF EFFECTIVE SCHEDULING

So far in this section of Mind Tools, we have looked at your priorities and your goals – these define what you aspire to do with your time. Scheduling is where these aspirations meet the reality of the time you have available. Scheduling is the process by which you look at the time available to you, and plan how you will use it to achieve the goals you have identified. By using a schedule properly, you can:

- Understand what you can realisticaly achieve with your time.
- Plan to make the best use of the time available.
- Leave enough time for things you absolutely must do.
- Preserve contingency time to handle 'the unexpected'.
- Minimize stress by avoiding over-commitment to yourself and others.

Ways to Use the Tool

There are many good scheduling tools available, including diaries, calendars, paper-based organizers, PDAs and integrated software suites like MS Outlook or GoalPro 6. The scheduling tool that is best for you depends on your situation, the current structure of your job, your taste and your budget: The key things are to be able to enter data easily, and to be able to view an appropriate span of time in the correct level of detail. Scheduling is best done on a regular basis, for example at the start of every week or month. Go through the following steps in preparing your schedule:

1. Start by identifying the time you want to make available for your work. This will depend on the design of your job and on your personal goals in life.
2. Next, block in the actions you absolutely must take to do a good job. These will often be the things you are assessed against.
3. For example, if you manage people, then you must make time available for dealing with issues that arise, coaching, and supervision. Similarly, you must allow time to communicate with your boss and key people around you. While people may let you get away with 'neglecting them' in the short-term, your best time management efforts will surely be derailed if you do not set aside time for those who are important in your life.
4. Review your To Do List, and schedule in the high-priority urgent activities, as well as the essential maintenance tasks that cannot be delegated and cannot be avoided.
5. Next, block in appropriate contingency time. You will learn how much of this you need by experience. Normally, the more unpredictable your job, the more contingency time you need. The reality of many people's work is of constant interruption: Studies show some managers getting an average of as little as six minutes uninterrupted work done at a time.
6. Obviously, you cannot tell when interruptions will occur. However, by leaving space in your schedule, you give yourself the flexibility to rearrange your schedule to react effectively to issues as they arise.
7. What you now have left is your "discretionary time": the time available to deliver your priorities and achieve your goals. Review your Prioritized To Do List and personal goals, evaluate the time needed to achieve these actions, and schedule these in.

By the time you reach step 5, you may find that you have little or no discretionary time available. If this is the case, then revisit the assumptions you used in the first four steps. Question whether things are absolutely necessary, whether they can be delegated, or whether they can be done in an abbreviated way. Remember that one of the most important ways people learn to achieve success is by maximizing the 'leverage' they can achieve with their time.

They increase the amount of work they can manage by delegating work to other people, spend money outsourcing key tasks, or use technology to automate as much of their work as possible. This frees them up to achieve their goals. Also, use this as an opportunity to review your To Do List and Personal Goals. Have you set goals that just aren't achievable with the time you have available? Are you taking on too many additional duties? Or are you treating things as being more important than they really are? If your discretionary time is still limited, then you may need to renegotiate your workload. With a well-thought through schedule as evidence, you may find this surprisingly easy.

Key Points

Scheduling is the process by which you plan your use of time. By scheduling effectively, you can both reduce stress and maximize your effectiveness. Before you can schedule efficiently, you need an effective scheduling system. This can be a diary, calendar, paper-based organizer, PDA or a software package like MS Outlook or GoalPro 6. The best solution depends entirely on your circumstances. Scheduling is then a five-step process:

1. Identify the time you have available.
2. Block in the essential tasks you must carry out to succeed in your job.
3. Schedule in high priority urgent tasks and vital "house-keeping" activities.
4. Block in appropriate contingency time to handle unpredictable interruptions.
5. In the time that remains, schedule the activities that address your priorities and personal goals.

If you have little or no discretionary time left by the time you reach step five, then revisit the assumptions you have made in steps one to four.

UNDERSTANDING PICKLE JAR THEORY

Pickle Jar Theory" uses the analogy of an empty pickle jar to think about how we use the fixed amount of time available to us each day. If we think of it as we plan our schedule, we can get important work done while still leaving time for the small things that make life fun.

Imagine a Huge Empty Pickle Jar...

Firstly, forget about time management altogether, and just imagine that you have a huge empty pickle jar (think of the largest pickles you have ever seen). Now, imagine filling the jar with golf balls. And, when you get it to the point you think it can hold no more, try adding another golf ball or two. Even though it seems full, you're not done yet. You're going to now squeeze in a handful of marbles. Give your pickle jar a shake and as the golf balls and marbles start to settle and create more room, add in a bit of sand. Now, fill your pickle jar to the tip-top by adding back in some of the pickle juice.

UNDERSTANDING "MORNING" TASK

Like many of us, Alys's job has a mix of regular, routine duties that are usually urgent – as well as longer-term, more important tasks that are usually less urgent. She spends her mornings on the urgent tasks that she must get done. These routine tasks are a bit boring, so her motivation is to get them finished and off of her To Do List as soon as possible. This leaves her afternoons free from these details, so that she can work on longer-term, more creative tasks – like researching, planning, and writing presentations. The problem is that she's a morning person. By the time she finishes her routine tasks, she's at her low point of energy in the afternoon. And, to make matters worse, she works in the UK – so in the afternoon, she gets tons of distracting emails and phone calls from her colleagues in the U.S. As a result, her creative tasks are often pushed to the side, and she's forced to work on them at the very end of the day, when she's feeling at her worst. Alys clearly needs to change the way she organizes her day! In this article, we'll examine how to find your best time of day (or week), and how to schedule tasks around that.

TOWARDS MANAGING INTERRUPTIONS

Everyday interruptions at work can be a key barrier to managing your time effectively and, ultimately, can be a barrier to your success. Think back to your last workday, and consider for a minute the many interruptions that occurred. They may have been phone calls, emails, hallway conversations, colleagues stopping by your office, or anything else that unexpectedly demanded your attention and, in doing so, distracted you from the task at-hand. Because your day only has so many hours in it, a handful of small interruptions can rob you of the time you need to achieve your goals and be successful in your work and life. More than this, they can break your focus, meaning that you have to spend time re-engaging with the thought processes needed to successfully complete complex work. The key to controlling interruptions is to know what they are and whether they are necessary, and to plan for them in your daily schedule. The tips that follow will help you do that, and so prevent interruptions from frustrating you and jeopardizing your success.

Using the Tool

Use the following tips to understand and manage interruptions:

1. Keep an Interrupters Log

If interruptions consistently rob you of time and energy, or if they frequently push you off schedule and cause delays, it's time to keep an Interrupters Log. This is a simple record of the interruptions you experience in the course of a day. Keep your Interrupters Log with you every day for at least a week, recording every interruption you experience, and marking down the person interrupting you; the date and time it occurs; what the interruption is; whether it was valid; and whether it was urgent (or whether someone could have waited until a better time.) Once you have recorded the interruptions for a week, sit down with your log and analyze the information.

Which interruptions are valid and which are not?

You need to deal with the valid interruptions. We'll show you below how you can schedule them into your day so that they get the attention they need, while you still have the time you need to adequately address your daily work. As for the interruptions that are not valid, you must find a way to block these out in the future.

2. Analyze and Conquer Interruptions

To analyze and conquer the interruptions you find in your Interrupters Log, firstly look at whether the interruption is valid or not. Could someone have avoided interrupting you by waiting for a routine meeting? Or was it something they should have asked you about at all? If not, deal with this politely but assertively. Next, look at how urgent the interruptions were, and whether they could have been pre-empted. You can pre-empt many interruptions by holding routine meetings with people: If they're confident that they'll have access to you at a defined point in the near future, they'll learn to save up non-urgent issues until this meeting.

However, some interruptions are both urgent and valid. You need to be interrupted, and you need to deal with the situation. From your

Interrupters Log, you'll see how much time is taken up by these urgent, valid interruptions. Block this time into your schedule as "contingency time", and only take on as much other work as you can fit into the remaining time. You'll have to juggle this other work around the interruptions, but at least you won't be overloaded and stressed by the things that you haven't done because they've been displaced by emergencies.

3. Put Your Phone to Work for You (Not Against You)

A little bit of planning can go a long way in working to control telephone interruptions, which many people experience all day long. If you are on a deadline or your focus needs to be intense (and not interrupted), use your voice mail to screen calls, or have an assistant deal with messages for you. This way, you can deal with calls by priority, and at times that suit you. In fact, this telephone time can be planned into your schedule, and so become a normal part of your working day.

4. Catch Your Breath

When interrupted, it's easy to get caught up in the "rush" of the person who is interrupting, for they undoubtedly feel their request is urgent. In reality, however, most interruptions are not genuinely crisis-driven, and it can serve everyone best to take a little time before taking action.

Take a few minutes to consider the situation. Catch your breath and clear your head. A small delay, even one of just a few minutes, goes a long way in assessing the situation accurately and reacting appropriately.

5. Learn to Say "No"

It's often acceptable to say "no" to requests or tasks if you are busy when someone else can handle it, if it is not an important task, or if it can be done later. When this is the case, saying "no" in a courteous and sincere way, followed by a short explanation is the best course of action to take: "I am working against a very tight deadline on an important project right now so, I am sorry, but I can not jump in and help".

6. "Available" and "Unavailable" Time

Simple yet effective: Let people know when you are available. and when you are not. Make sure that people know that during your "unavailable time", they should only interrupt you if they have to. You and your co-workers can also agree on a signal that everyone in the office can use when unavailable, like turning the nameplate on the door around, or simply closing the door. This alleviates interruptions and can avoid hurt feelings.

Tip:

Be careful here. If you're a manager, an important part of your job is to be available to people, to handle urgent issues which arise, and to coach your team so that people are as effective as possible. If you put up barriers that are too high, you won't be able to do these jobs. By all means, use "unavailable time", but don't over use it, and make sure people know they can interrupt you if there is a genuine crisis.

7. "Invitation Only" Time

Schedule regular check-in times for the individuals you talk to most often. Ask these people to keep a running list of things that they need to discuss, so you can cover all the points at one time. And, force yourself to do the same. An open-door policy is good, but you should limit the number of people you invite to your work area. For instance, if you're scheduling a meeting, offer to meet your co-worker in his or her office or a conference room. This way, you can excuse yourself after you accomplish your purpose. Additionally, it's much easier to get up and leave than it is to get people to leave your office once they're seated and comfortable.

8. Uncontrollable Interruptions

There are interruptions that, no matter how hard you try, you simply cannot control. Most people are happy to schedule a more convenient time, but when this does not work, quickly set the parameters by saying something like, "I only have five minutes to talk about this right now," and stick to it. Do not ask the interrupter to sit down and do not engage in small talk. Encourage the interrupter to get right to the point and if a solution cannot be reached before the allotted time runs out, set a time for getting back to them and, again, stick to it.

TOWARDS DEALING WITH LATENESS

Do you have a colleague who regularly arrives late for meetings? It's an annoying habit, and it's even worse if everyone else must wait for him because he's a key person in the decision-making process. Or perhaps you have a colleague who frequently turns up late at the office, complaining about "nightmare traffic" on her drive to work. Worse still, are you the person who is always late? Lateness is bad for team productivity or team morale, and it may point to a wider lack of responsibility. So, what can you do to stop it?

TOWARDS ORGANIZING DISORGANIZED PEOPLE

Imagine this scenario: After a week of hard work, you send an important report to your colleague. His task is to edit the wording and make a few key decisions to finalize some of the content. The deadline is still three weeks away, but you hope he'll finish it early because you'll have more work to do once he gives you his input. Your colleague, however, delays making the changes. After numerous reminders from you, he sends it back the day before your deadline.

This means that you have to rush to complete your final changes in time. His delay has caused you some serious stress, and it's not the first time that this has happened. Working with disorganized people can be a stressful experience, especially when it starts impacting your own productivity. But what can you do about it? Is it your responsibility to help them get organized? If yes, how do you do it tactfully? In this article, we'll look at how to help other people get organized. Whether they're colleagues, team members, or even your manager, we'll explore strategies to help you to help them.

TOWARDS MINIMIZING DISTRACTIONS

How often are you distracted at work?

It's a question that's almost laughable, right? Most of us are distracted several times, if not dozens of times, every day. We get emergency emails and phone calls. We take breaks to browse the Internet. Co-workers walk into our office for a quick chat, or send us amusing instant messages. It doesn't matter where you work or what you do, you probably deal with distractions on a daily basis. And these distractions are costly:

A 2007 study by Basex estimated that distractions cost U.S. businesses $588 billion per year, and this high cost is likely repeated in organizations around the world. What's more (and depending on the complexity of our work), regaining concentration after a distraction can take quite a few minutes. If we're distracted 10 times a day, multiply the time lost by 10, and it's easy to see why we sometimes don't get much quality work done. Learning how to minimize distractions can dramatically increase your productivity and effectiveness, as well as reduce your stress.

Without distractions, you can get into flow, produce high-quality work, and achieve much more during the day. In this article, we'll discuss the most common distractions we face at work, and we'll look at strategies for minimizing or eliminating them.

Email

While email is incredibly useful, it's also one of the biggest work distractions we face. Many of us could spend entire days simply reading and responding to emails.

- Schedule "email" times – Minimize this distraction by scheduling specific times to check and respond to emails. For instance, you could check email when you first arrive at work, at lunch, and right before you leave, and specify a half-hour slot every day to respond to your emails. (If you do this, it may be useful to let co-workers and customers know that they will need to contact you another way if they need you urgently.)
- Check and respond to email at "low productivity" times – Remember that there are certain times of day when you probably do your best work. Some people work best in the morning, and others late at night. Schedule your email check-in during your less-productive times – and save your peak hours for doing creative, high-value work.
- Turn emails into actions – If an email will take more than a few minutes to action or respond to, add it as a new action on your To-Do List or Action Program.
- Keep your email program closed – When you're not using your email program, close it entirely – or at least turn off the visual or audible alerts that distract you. This eliminates the temptation to check it constantly.
- Most email programs will also allow you to fetch new email manually with a "send/receive" button, or will allow you to set it to get new email automatically at certain times of the day (every three hours, for example).

Disorganization

A disorganized desk or office can be very distracting. When your work space or work life is disorganized, it can be difficult to think and plan clearly. Getting organized is a topic that could easily fill books, and it does! We have several good resources here at Mind Tools. Our articles How to Be Organized, Actions Programs, The Art of Filing, and The 5S System will help you to organize your office and work life, so you can be more productive – and less distracted – during the day.

Instant Messaging

Instant messaging can be useful, but many times it's also a way for co-workers to interrupt you without having to get up and walk into your office. If you use instant messaging (it's very powerful if used in a disciplined way), get into the habit of using it for small, quick queries. It's often better to use email or the phone for more complex ones. Also, if you find yourself distracted by IM, consider setting specific times during the day for being "online." Then, when you don't want to be contacted, leave it off or set your status to "busy." If people need to contact you, make sure they know your "hours" for IM.

Phone Calls

The ring of the phone has become almost like Pavlov's bell for some people - we think we must answer it, even if we're concentrating on something important. Minimize phone call distractions by turning off your phone during your peak work hours. Or, let your team know that you won't take non-essential calls between specific times, such as from noon to 2 pm. Alternatively, get people into the habit of using IM to check with co-workers that they are OK to take a call. If co-workers are deep in concentration, they can ask to "talk in 10 minutes" without losing the thread of their work.

The Internet

Browsing the web can take up enormous amounts of time from our day, and when we start looking on the Internet for one thing, it's easy to get lost for 20 minutes or more.

- Read the news before the start of the day – Visit news sites or read newspapers before work, so that you know the news. That way, you won't be distracted as much during the day.
- Close your Internet browser – Eliminate Internet distractions by keeping your browser closed when you're not using it. If you repeatedly check personal email, or go on social networking sites like Facebook or Twitter, then log out of your account. If you're forced to take those few extra seconds to log in each time, it may remind you that you're not focusing on work.
- (However, bear in mind that tools like Twitter are increasingly useful for staying in touch with events in your industry. Just make sure that you only check it at set times of the day - for instance, before lunch and at the end of the day.)
- Use special software – There are some useful software applications such as Freedom and Anti-Social that help eliminate online distractions. You can specify which websites you want to block, and set a timer for how long you want the block to remain active. Using technology like this to block access for yourself can be a big help.
- Take short Internet breaks – Remember that taking little breaks, especially after working for an hour or more in deep concentration, can be quite useful for resting your mind. These tiny breaks allow you to return to focus with renewed energy. Use casual Internet browsing as a reward for every hour you

devote to high-quality, focused work – and you'll feel as if you've earned the time.

Other People

Co-workers often create the greatest distractions.

- Close your door – Close your office door to keep people from casually stopping by. If they knock or come in anyway, explain that when your door is closed, you shouldn't be disturbed unless there's an emergency. A sign on your office door may also help. (If you're a manager, there's clearly a tension between this and – very importantly – making sure that your "door is always open" to members of your team. Consider working from home or in a conference room when you don't want to be disturbed.)
- Use headphones – If you're in a cubicle or open office environment, people are less likely to interrupt you if you're wearing headphones. (You don't even have to be listening to music!)
- Talk to the disrupter – If you share an office with someone who often disrupts your day, talk to the person about the problem: he may not realize he's distracting you. Or, if a co-worker often comes in, sits down, and chats for a while, don't allow her to do it - place a pile of papers on the chair she'd use, or stand up immediately when she comes into your office or cubicle.

Work Environment

Windows, a busy highway, or loud co-workers may all contribute to a distracting work environment.

- Work in another location – If possible, work in a conference room or empty office to regain your concentration. If your job allows it, working in a different setting, such as at home, at a library, or in a coffee shop, may also help you to focus more.
- Use "white noise" – If noise is a problem, install padded partitions, or consider buying a sound machine that produces white noise to cover annoying sounds. Noise-canceling headphones with soft music can also improve your focus. You can also download white noise files from the Internet and set them on "repeat." Having white noise play constantly helps block unwanted sounds.

Other Projects and Tasks

An overwhelming To-Do List may be a major distraction during the day. You may then procrastinate on those tasks, simply because you have so much to do, which further lowers your productivity.

- Prioritize your To-Do List – Commit to accomplishing the two most important tasks on your list every day.
- Track your day – Pick one day to keep track of everything you spend your time doing. You might discover that you spend five hours managing interruptions and dealing with emergencies, and four hours doing actual work. This assessment would then show you that you have only four productive hours each day to achieve your most important tasks.
- Delegate – Learn how to delegate effectively. This is important for managing an overwhelming list of tasks and projects.

Tiredness

Coming to work well rested is vital to having a productive day.

- Get enough sleep – Many people don't get enough sleep at night. When you're tired, it's very easy to become distracted.
- Stay hydrated – When you don't drink enough water and you become dehydrated, you may not think clearly. Dehydration can also make you feel tired and less alert. Keep a water bottle on your desk, and drink regularly during the day.
- Go for a walk – If you're tired at work, go outside for a walk. Getting some fresh air and moving your body can give you more energy, and can make you feel more alert.
- Watch your diet – Your diet may also influence how tired you feel. For example, avoid heavy lunches – and instead eat smaller, healthy snacks throughout the day.

Key Points

We all face distractions on a daily basis. Distractions not only lower our productivity, they also increase our stress. You probably already know what distracts you the most – phone calls, emails, instant messages, Internet browsing, interrupting co-workers, and so on. Strategies like scheduling email checks, turning off your phone, and leaving the office for a quieter environment may eliminate distractions so that you get more done.

ART OF CONCISE CONVERSATIONS

Does this sound familiar? One of your colleagues phones you for advice about her project. However, instead of getting right to the point, she spends 20 minutes telling you about her son's latest baseball game, your boss's recent promotion, and the office manager's new shoes. Or even worse, there's your co-worker who makes a point, and then spends the next half hour saying it over and over in several different ways – or he keeps going over the same conclusions you've both already agreed on. It seems like your clothes will go out of style before the conversation ends. Have you been in situations like these? The business world (and the world in general) is filled with people who don't seem to know how to stick to the subject.

This not only affects your working relationships, it can also waste a lot of your time. However, it's important to build relationships with your colleagues. A lot of this happens in unstructured conversations – the same conversations that may be considered "time wasters." So how do you find the right balance? How can you have productive conversations, and still leave room to have a little fun and establish relationships with your co-workers and clients? We'll give you some practical approaches to different types of conversational "time wasters".

CREATING TIME IN ONES' DAY

Time - it's something that money can't really buy, and something that many of us would like more of! And, with the breakneck pace of work today far outweighing what we had to contend with even a few decades ago, many of us could achieve so much more with a little more time on our hands. In this article, we're looking at strategies that you can use to create more time for yourself. With these, you can get more done at work, or spend time doing more of things that you enjoy. It's unlikely that every one of these strategies will fit your own circumstances. However, some of these strategies are sure to help!

TOWARDS IMPROVING ONES' CONCENTRATION

How many times have you sat at your desk and tried to focus on a task, only to find that your mind is wandering? Despite your best intentions, you just can't concentrate. We've all been in this familiar, frustrating situation, and it's something that can really undermine your performance. In this article, we'll review strategies to improve your concentration and reduce your daily distractions.

Environment

Your personal work environment plays a large role in your ability to concentrate. The more comfortable and welcoming your environment is, the easier it will likely be for you to stay there and focus. Here are some ideas for improving your physical environment:

- Make sure you're comfortable – Start by ensuring that your chair and desk are at the right height for you to work comfortably.

If your chair is too high or your desk is too low, you'll be uncomfortable, and you'll be tempted to use this as an excuse to get up and walk away.

- Put up pictures – Viewing a natural scene or watching wildlife can help improve concentration. If you're able to put up pictures in your office or work area, then choose landscapes or natural images that you enjoy. This can help your focus, especially if you can see the pictures from your desk.
- Shut out distractions as much as possible – Listening to music can help, especially if it's instrumental music. Some people even use noise machines in their offices – these produce a steady "white noise," like ocean waves or falling rain. This steady background noise can drown out other noise, helping you focus better and ignore distractions.

Nutrition

Follow some simple nutritional tips:

- Drink water – Many of us don't think about drinking water while we're at work, yet dehydration can make us feel tired, irritable, slow, or even sick. When our brains don't have enough fluid, they can't operate at peak performance. Staying hydrated is an easy way to help improve your concentration during the day.
- Eat breakfast – Start your day with a healthy breakfast. It's much harder to concentrate when you're hungry, so eat a well-rounded meal before you go to work. You can also help your concentration throughout the day by keeping healthy snacks at your desk. Almonds, whole-grain crackers, fresh fruit, and vegetables are good choices.
- Get up and move around – Do you walk around during the day? If you're like many people, you probably don't move around enough. Research has shown that regular walking can help increase your focus during the day.

Mindset

Constant distractions, and the low productivity that's associated with these distractions, have become so commonplace in today's offices that doctors have even given it a name: Attention Deficit Trait, or ADT. And, they say that entire organizations can suffer from it. Follow some of these guidelines to help focus your mind:

- Set aside time to deal with worries – Many of us have trouble concentrating during the day because we're constantly worrying about other things. It could be an approaching deadline for a project you haven't started, a new colleague who's causing problems, or just the amount of work on your desk. If you find yourself distracted by worries, then note these down so that you don't need to hold them in your mind. Then schedule time to deal with these issues.

- Focus on one task at a time – It can be much harder to focus if you take minibreaks (15–30 seconds) to answer emails, send text messages, or take quick phone calls. Some researchers believe that it can take up to 15 minutes for us to regain complete focus after a distraction.
- Close your email box and chat program – Let your voice mail do its job. If your office allows it, close your office door or put up a "Do Not Disturb" sign to let colleagues know you need to focus. (If you're a manager and you want to operate an open door policy, then consider working from home or from elsewhere.)
- Switch between high- and low-attention tasks – This can give your brain a rest after heavy concentration. For instance, if you spend two hours working on your department's budget, you'll probably feel tired afterward. You can recharge your energy by working on a low-attention task, like filing, for 15 minutes before going back to your budget.
- Prioritize – Having too much to do can be distracting, and this sometime causes procrastination. Or, you may quickly jump from task to task, creating the illusion of work – but in reality, you're not accomplishing very much. If you're not sure which tasks to start or which are most important, take 10 or 15 minutes to prioritize your to-do list. Our article Overcoming Procrastination can also help.

Limiting distractions allows you to get into the flow of your work – so you get more done. If you'd like to learn about improving your focus, read the Mind Tools articles In Flow and Managing Interruptions.

More Tips for Improving Your Concentration

- Take short breaks – We can be masters at focusing, but eventually we're going to need a break. Our minds can struggle to focus intensely on tasks for eight hours a day. This is where it can be better to divide your work into one-hour segments, with a 5–10 minute break between tasks. This short break will allow your mind to rest before focusing again.

- Do your hardest tasks when you're most alert – This will help you maximize your concentration. Do you want to learn how to schedule your tasks around your energy levels? Read our article "Is This a Morning Task?"
- Use a phone headset – If you have a headset for your phone, consider using it for a few hours each day. If your colleagues think you're on the phone, they're less likely to interrupt you.
- Promise yourself a reward – For instance, make a rule that if you focus intensively for 45 minutes on one task, you can take a break to get a cup of coffee when you're done. Little "self-rewards" can often be great motivators.
- Schedule email downloads – It can be tremendously distracting to have emails pinging into your inbox every few minutes – you're tempted to stop what you're doing, and answer them right away. If you can, schedule your email to download only a few times each day, and deal with all of your emails in one go.

Key Points

Sitting down to focus on one task can be difficult, especially when you're constantly interrupted. To help increase your focus, start with a good breakfast, and drink plenty of water throughout the day. Don't multitask, close your door, and listen to music if it helps you concentrate. Although it may sound somewhat counter-intuitive, taking short, regular breaks throughout the day can also help you focus.

TOWARDS MAXIMIZING PRODUCTIVITY THROUGH IMPROVED FOCUS

Focus

Let's take an example. Have you ever seen a hassled mom trying to get her young daughter to leave whatever she is doing and do something else? It's a common enough sight: Young children can get so wrapped up in whatever they're doing that it takes a lot of persuasion to get them to switch their attention. This ability to focus totally on one thing comes naturally to young children, but it's one of the biggest challenges that most of the rest of us face. We struggle to concentrate and, because of this, fail to get on with the work we're doing. Some people, though, seem able to focus intensely on what they're doing, and perform exceptionally well as a result.

Modern psychologists refer to this state of absolute absorption or concentration in what we are doing, as being "in flow." Mihaly Csikszentmihalyi, who first described the concept, suggests that this state of being able to achieve total focus applies to almost every field of activity. According to Csikszentmihalyi, flow involves *"being completely involved in an activity for its own sake. The ego falls away. Time flies. Every action, movement, and thought follows inevitably from the previous one, like playing jazz. Your whole being is involved, and you're using your skills to the utmost"*. So how do we enter this "ecstatic" state?

REFERENCES

Allen, David: Ready For Anything: 52 Productivity Principles for Work and Life. London: Viking Penguin, 2003.

Amos, Julie-Ann: Making the Most of Your Time. Oxford: How to Books, Ltd., 1999.

Amos, Julie-Ann: Managing Your Time: What To Do And How To Do It In Order To Do More. Oxford: How To Books, Ltd., 1998.

Bly, Robert W: 101 Ways To Make Every Second Count: Time Management Tips And Techniques For More Success With Less Stress. Franklin Lakes: The Career Press, 1999.

Boehme, Ann J: Planning Successful Meetings and Events: A Take-Charge Assistant Book. New York: AMACOM Books, 1999.

Covey, Stephen R., Roger A. Merrill & Rebecca A. Merrill: First Things First, New York: Simon & Schuster, 1994.

Dobson, Ann: Managing Meetings: How to Prepare For Them, How to Run Them, and How to Follow Up the Results. Oxford: How to Books, Ltd., 1999.

Gryna, Frank M: Work Overload: Redesigning Jobs to Minimize Stress and Burnout. Milwaukee: Quality Press, 2004.

Mackenzie, R. Alec: The Time Trap, New York: AMACOM, 1997. Marley, Patty & Jan Bailey: Time Management Made Easy. Lincolnwood: NTC Contemporary, 1998.

Mayer, Jeffrey J: Time Management For Dummies. 2nd Ed. Foster City: IDG Books Worldwide, 1999.

Mina, Eli: The Business Meetings Sourcebook: A Practical Guide To Better Meetings and Shared Decision Making. New York: AMACOM Books, 2002.

Olson, Jeff: The Agile Manager's Guide To Getting Organized. Bristol: Velocity Business Publishing, 1997.

Rogak, Lisa: Smart Guide to Managing Your Time. New York: John Wiley & Sons, Inc., 1999.

Rogers, Tim & Fiona Graham: Responding To Stress. Oxford: How to Books, Ltd., 1999.

Taking Control Of Your Time, Boston: Harvard Business School Press, 2005.

Time Management: Increase Your Personal Productivity and Effectiveness. Boston: Harvard Business School Press, 2005.

Williams, Paul B: Getting A Project Done On Time: Managing People, Time, And Results. New York: AMACOM Books, 1996.

6

Major Time Management Models, Theories and Methods

> "Those who make the worst of their time most complain about its shortness."
>
> —*La Bruyere*

OVERVIEW OF FLOW MODEL ANALYZING THE FLOW MODEL

Have you ever been so involved in doing something that you lost track of time? Everything around you – from the ringing of phones to the people passing in the hallways – seemed to fade away. Your attention was focused entirely on what you were doing, and you were so engaged that you might even have missed lunch. You felt energized, even joyful, about what you were doing. Most of us have had this experience at one time or another. Psychologists call this "flow." When it happens, we lose our sense of self, and move forward on instinct, completely devoted to the task before us. In this article, we'll examine flow in detail by looking into the Flow Model. We'll review how the model can help us understand why we find some tasks much easier than others. We'll also look at how you can use the ideas behind the Flow Model to experience flow more often, so that you can be more productive.

The Flow Model was first introduced by positive psychologist Mihaly Csíkszentmihályi. He wrote about the process of flow in his book "Flow: The Psychology of Optimal Experience." The model shows the emotional states that we're likely to experience when trying to complete a task, depending on the perceived difficulty of the challenge, and our perceptions of our skill levels. For example, if the task isn't challenging and doesn't require a lot of skill, we're likely to feel apathy towards it. But facing a challenging task without the required skills could easily result in worry and anxiety. To find a balance, and to perform at our best, we need a challenge that is significant and interesting, and we need well-developed skills, so that we're confident that we can meet the challenge. This moves us to a position where we can experience "flow" (being totally involved and engaged in the activity). This state of flow is often observed in people who have mastered their business, art, sport, or hobby. They make whatever they're doing look easy, and they're totally engaged with it.

Main Components of Flow

How do you know when you're experiencing flow? Csíkszentmihályi identified 10 experiences that go with the state of being in flow:

1. Having a clear understanding of what you want to achieve.
2. Being able to concentrate for a sustained period of time.
3. Losing the feeling of consciousness of one's self.
4. Finding that time passes quickly.
5. Getting direct and immediate feedback.
6. Experiencing a balance between your ability levels, and the challenge.
7. Having a sense of personal control over the situation.
8. Feeling that the activity is intrinsically rewarding.
9. Lacking awareness of bodily needs.
10. Being completely absorbed in the activity itself.

Remember that all of these factors and experiences don't necessarily have to be in place for flow to happen. But you're likely to experience many of them when flow occurs.

Three Conditions

Csíkszentmihályi also identified three things that must be present if you want to enter a state of flow:

1. Goals – Goals add motivation and structure to what you're doing. Whether you're learning a new piece of music or creating a presentation, you must be working towards a goal to experience flow.
2. Balance – There must be a good balance between your perceived skill and the perceived challenge of the task. If one of these weighs more heavily than the other, flow probably won't occur.
3. Feedback – You must have clear, immediate feedback, so that

you can make changes and improve your performance. This can be feedback from other people, or the awareness that you're making progress with the task.

Using the Flow Model

To improve your chances of experiencing flow, try the following:

- Set goals – Goal setting is important in experiencing flow. Learning to set effective goals can help you achieve the focus you need.
- Improve your concentration – Many things may distract you from your work, and achieving flow is more difficult when your focus is interrupted. Use strategies to improve your concentration so that you're more productive and focused during the day.
- Build self-confidence – If you don't have confidence in your skills, tasks may seem much harder than they actually are. Our article Building Self-Confidence will show you how to develop yourself for success.
- Get feedback – Remember, feedback is an important requirement for flow. Make sure that appropriate technical feedback systems are in place, and learn how to give and receive feedback so that you can help yourself – and others – to improve.
- Make your work more challenging – Consider strategies such as job crafting, and explore ways of creating more job satisfaction.

Tip:

Remember that simply increasing the amount of challenge doesn't guarantee flow. Csíkszentmihályi stressed that you experience flow only when you perceive the right opportunities. It happens because you're in the right mindset, not because you have "perfect conditions."

- Improve Your Skills – Doing a personal SWOT Analysis, can help you identify the skills that you need to work on to be successful. You can then develop a plan for improving your skills to help you complete more challenging tasks. Our Personal Development Plan Workbook guides you through this process in more detail.
- Coach yourself – If you don't have a mentor or coach to help you through challenging tasks, learn how to coach yourself.

The Inverted-U Model

There's a potential conflict of ideas between the Flow Model and the Inverted-U Model – a popular and widely respected model that helps explain the relationship between performance and pressure. In the inverted-U graph, the vertical axis represents someone's level of performance, while the horizontal axis represents the pressure that he or she is under. According to the model, there's a "perfect medium" of pressure where people perform at their best. The Flow Model doesn't explain the loss of performance that occurs when pressure is too high – for example, when we're scared, or when we're overwhelmed by work. At these times, your productivity can drop and negative emotions like anxiety will increase dramatically. By using both of these models together, you're most likely to be able to enter and enjoy the state of flow.

Key Points

Flow is a state we reach when our perceived skills match the perceived challenge of the task that we're doing. When we're in a state of flow, we seem to forget time. The work we do may fill us with joy, and we lose our sense of self as we concentrate fully on the task. This is the state that we're in when we're doing our best work, and when we're at our most productive. The Flow Model shows the relationship between task complexity and your perceived skill level. You can use the model to discover why you're not achieving flow. It can also help you discover whether you need to improve your skills, or increase the challenge or certain tasks, to help achieve flow.

FOCUS ON WORKING HOME

Staying Focused Amid Distractions

Mark's organization has allowed him to work at home three days a week, and it's his first full day of "telecommuting." He sets his computer up on his dining room table, and is ready to get to work. Three hours later, however, he's shocked to realize that he's completed very little. What's he been doing? Well, he had to make coffee. Then he did a load of laundry, took a phone call from a friend, and sorted through the mail when it arrived. One thing led to another, and now he's really behind! Working from home can be incredibly productive. But it's also full of distractions. If you work from home, it's up to you to make sure you're doing a full day of focused, productive work. In this article, we'll discuss the benefits and challenges of working from home, and we'll provide some tips to help you be at your most productive during the day.

IMPORTANCE OF PERSONAL GOAL SETTING

Planning to Live Your Life Your Way Setting Goals Starting to Set Personal Goals

Many people feel as if they're adrift in the world. They work hard, but they don't seem to get anywhere worthwhile. A key reason that they feel this way is that they haven't spent enough time thinking about what they want from life, and haven't set themselves formal goals. After all, would you set out on a major journey with no real idea of your destination? Probably not! Goal setting is a powerful process for thinking about your ideal future, and for motivating yourself to turn your vision of this future into reality. The process of setting goals helps you choose where you want to go in life. By knowing precisely what you want to achieve, you know where you have to concentrate your efforts. You'll also quickly spot the distractions that can, so easily, lead you astray.

Goal setting is used by top-level athletes, successful business-people and achievers in all fields. Setting goals gives you long-term vision and short-term motivation. It focuses your acquisition of knowledge, and helps you to organize your time and your resources so that you can make the very most of your life. By setting sharp, clearly defined goals, you can measure and take pride in the achievement of those goals, and you'll see forward progress in what might previously have seemed a long pointless grind. You will also raise your self-confidence, as you recognize your own ability and competence in achieving the goals that you've set.

You set your goals on a number of levels:

- First you create your "big picture" of what you want to do with your life (or over, say, the next 10 years), and identify the large-scale goals that you want to achieve.
- Then, you break these down into the smaller and smaller targets that you must hit to reach your lifetime goals.
- Finally, once you have your plan, you start working on it to achieve these goals.

This is why we start the process of goal setting by looking at your lifetime goals. Then, we work down to the things that you can do in, say, the next five years, then next year, next month, next week, and today, to start moving towards them.

Step 1: Setting Lifetime Goals

The first step in setting personal goals is to consider what you want to achieve in your lifetime (or at least, by a significant and distant age in the future). Setting lifetime goals gives you the overall perspective that shapes all other aspects of your decision making. To give a broad, balanced coverage of all important areas in your life, try to set goals in some of the following categories (or in other categories of your own, where these are important to you):

- Career - What level do you want to reach in your career, or what do you want to achieve?
- Financial - How much do you want to earn, by what stage? How is this related to your career goals?
- Education - Is there any knowledge you want to acquire in particular? What information and skills will you need to have in order to achieve other goals?
- Family - Do you want to be a parent? If so, how are you going to be a good parent? How do you want to be seen by a partner or by members of your extended family?
- Artistic - Do you want to achieve any artistic goals?
- Attitude - Is any part of your mindset holding you back? Is there any part of the way that you behave that upsets you? (If so, set a goal to improve your behaviour or find a solution to the problem.)
- Physical - Are there any athletic goals that you want to achieve, or do you want good health deep into old age? What steps are you going to take to achieve this?
- Pleasure - How do you want to enjoy yourself? (You should ensure that some of your life is for you!)
- Public Service - Do you want to make the world a better place? If so, how?

Spend some time brainstorming these things, and then select one or more goals in each category that best reflect what you want to do. Then consider trimming again so that you have a small number of really significant goals that you can focus on. As you do this, make sure that the goals that you have set are ones that you genuinely want to achieve, not ones that your parents, family, or employers might want. (If you have a partner, you probably want to consider what he or she wants - however, make sure that you also remain true to yourself!)

Step 2: Setting Smaller Goals

Once you have set your lifetime goals, set a five-year plan of smaller goals that you need to complete if you are to reach your lifetime plan. Then create a one-year plan, six-month plan, and a one-month plan of progressively smaller goals that you should reach to achieve your lifetime goals. Each of these should be based on the previous plan. Then create a daily To-Do List of things that you should do today to work towards your lifetime goals. At an early stage, your smaller goals might be to read books and gather information on the achievement of your higher level goals. This will help you to improve the quality and realism of your goal setting. Finally review your plans, and make sure that they fit the way in which you want to live your life.

Staying on Course

Once you've decided on your first set of goals, keep the process going by reviewing and updating your To-Do List on a daily basis. Periodically review the longer term plans, and modify them to reflect your changing priorities and experience. (A good way of doing this is to schedule regular, repeating reviews using a computer-based diary.)

Smart Goals

A useful way of making goals more powerful is to use the SMART mnemonic. While there are plenty of variants (some of which we've included in parenthesis), SMART usually stands for:

- S - Specific (or Significant).
- M - Measurable (or Meaningful).
- A - Attainable (or Action-Oriented).
- R - Relevant (or Rewarding).
- T - Time-bound (or Trackable).

For example, instead of having "To sail around the world" as a goal, it's more powerful to say "To have completed my trip around the world by December 31, 2015." Obviously, this will only be attainable if a lot of preparation has been completed beforehand!

Further Goal Setting Tips

The following broad guidelines will help you to set effective, achievable goals:

- State each goal as a positive statement - Express your goals positively – "Execute this technique well" is a much better goal than "Don't make this stupid mistake."
- Be precise: Set precise goals, putting in dates, times and amounts so that you can measure achievement. If you do this, you'll know exactly when you have achieved the goal, and can take complete satisfaction from having achieved it.
- Set priorities - When you have several goals, give each a priority. This helps you to avoid feeling overwhelmed by having too many goals, and helps to direct your attention to the most important ones.
- Write goals down - This crystallizes them and gives them more force.

- Keep operational goals small - Keep the low-level goals that you're working towards small and achievable. If a goal is too large, then it can seem that you are not making progress towards it. Keeping goals small and incremental gives more opportunities for reward.
- Set performance goals, not outcome goals - You should take care to set goals over which you have as much control as possible. It can be quite dispiriting to fail to achieve a personal goal for reasons beyond your control!
- In business, these reasons could be bad business environments or unexpected effects of government policy. In sport, they could include poor judging, bad weather, injury, or just plain bad luck.
- If you base your goals on personal performance, then you can keep control over the achievement of your goals, and draw satisfaction from them.
- Set realistic goals - It's important to set goals that you can achieve. All sorts of people (for example, employers, parents, media, or society) can set unrealistic goals for you. They will often do this in ignorance of your own desires and ambitions.
- It's also possible to set goals that are too difficult because you might not appreciate either the obstacles in the way, or understand quite how much skill you need to develop to achieve a particular level of performance.

Goals Achieving

When you've achieved a goal, take the time to enjoy the satisfaction of having done so. Absorb the implications of the goal achievement, and observe the progress that you've made towards other goals. If the goal was a significant one, reward yourself appropriately. All of this helps you build the self-confidence you deserve. With the experience of having achieved this goal, review the rest of your goal plans:

- If you achieved the goal too easily, make your next goal harder.
- If the goal took a dispiriting length of time to achieve, make the next goal a little easier.
- If you learned something that would lead you to change other goals, do so.
- If you noticed a deficit in your skills despite achieving the goal, decide whether to set goals to fix this.

Tip:

Our article, Golden Rules of Goal Setting, will show you how to set yourself up for success when it comes to your goals. If you're still having trouble, you might also want to try Backward Goal Setting. Failing to meet goals does not matter much, just as long as you learn from the experience. Feed lessons learned back into your goal setting. Remember too that your goals will change as time goes on. Adjust them regularly to reflect growth in your knowledge and experience, and if goals do not hold any attraction any longer, consider letting them go.

Goal Setting Example

For her New Year's Resolution, Susan has decided to think about what she really wants to do with her life. Her lifetime goals are as follows:

- Career - "To be managing editor of the magazine that I work for."
- Artistic - "To keep working on my illustration skills. Ultimately I want to have my own show in our downtown gallery."
- Physical - "To run a marathon."

Now that Susan has listed her lifetime goals, she then breaks down each one into smaller, more manageable goals. Let's take a closer look at how she might break down her lifetime career goal - becoming managing editor of her magazine:

- Five-year goal: "Become deputy editor."
- One-year goal: "Volunteer for projects that the current Managing Editor is heading up."
- Six-month goal: "Go back to school and finish my journalism degree."
- One-month goal: "Talk to the current managing editor to determine what skills are needed to do the job."
- One-week goal: "Book the meeting with the Managing Editor."

As you can see from this example, breaking big goals down into smaller, more manageable goals makes it far easier to see how the goal will get accomplished.

Tip:

A good way of getting going with this is to use the Mind Tools Life Plan Workbook. Supported by worksheets and advice, this guides you through a simple 5-step process for setting your life goals, and for organizing yourself for success.

Key Points

Goal setting is an important method of:

- Deciding what you want to achieve in your life.
- Separating what's important from what's irrelevant, or a distraction.
- Motivating yourself.
- Building your self-confidence, based on successful achievement of goals.

Set your lifetime goals first. Then, set a five-year plan of smaller goals that you need to complete if you are to reach your lifetime plan. Keep the process going by regularly reviewing and updating your goals. And remember to take time to enjoy the satisfaction of achieving your goals when you do so. If you don't already set goals, do so, starting now. As you make this technique part of your life, you'll find your career accelerating, and you'll wonder how you did without it!

FOCUS ON LOCKE'S GOAL SETTING THEORY

Understanding SMART Goal Setting

Goal setting is a powerful way of motivating people, and of motivating yourself. The value of goal setting is so well recognized that entire management systems, like Management by Objectives, have goal setting basics incorporated within them. In fact, goal setting theory is generally accepted as among the most valid and useful motivation theories in industrial and organizational psychology, human resource management, and organizational behaviour. Many of us have learned – from bosses, seminars, and business articles – to set SMART goals. It seems natural to assume that by setting a goal that's Specific, Measurable, Attainable, Relevant, and Time-bound, we will be well on our way to accomplishing it.

But is this really the best way of setting goals?

To answer this, we look to Dr Edwin Locke's pioneering research on goal setting and motivation in the late 1960s. In his 1968 article "Toward a Theory of Task Motivation and Incentives," he stated that employees were motivated by clear goals and appropriate feedback. Locke went on to say that working toward a goal provided a major source of motivation to actually reach the goal – which, in turn, improved performance. This information does not seem revolutionary to us some 40 years later. This shows the impact his theory has had on professional and personal performance. In this article, we look at what Locke had to say about goal setting, and how we can apply his theory to our own performance goals.

Goal Setting Theory

Locke's research showed that there was a relationship between how difficult and specific a goal was and people's performance of a task. He found that specific and difficult goals led to better task performance than vague or easy goals. Telling someone to "Try hard" or "Do your best" is less effective than "Try to get more than 80% correct" or "Concentrate on beating your best time." Likewise, having a goal that's too easy is not a motivating force. Hard goals are more motivating than easy goals, because it's much more of an accomplishment to achieve something that you have to work for. A few years after Locke published his article, another researcher, Dr Gary Latham, studied the effect of goal setting in the workplace.

His results supported exactly what Locke had found, and the inseparable link between goal setting and workplace performance was formed. In 1990, Locke and Latham published their seminal work, "A Theory of Goal Setting and Task Performance." In this book, they reinforced the need to set specific and difficult goals, and they outlined three other characteristics of successful goal setting.

Five Principles of Goal Setting

To motivate, goals must have:

1. Clarity.
2. Challenge.
3. Commitment.
4. Feedback.
5. Task complexity.

Let's look at each of these in detail.

1. Clarity

Clear goals are measurable and unambiguous. When a goal is clear and specific, with a definite time set for completion, there is less misunderstanding about what behaviours will be rewarded. You know what's expected, and you can use the specific result as a source of motivation. When a goal is vague – or when it's expressed as a general instruction, like "Take initiative" – it has limited motivational value. To improve your or your team's performance, set clear goals that use specific and measurable standards. "Reduce job turnover by 15%" or "Respond to employee suggestions within 48 hours" are examples of clear goals. When you use the SMART acronym to help you set goals, you ensure the clarity of the goal by making it Specific, Measurable and Time-bound.

2. Challenge

One of the most important characteristics of goals is the level of challenge. People are often motivated by achievement, and they'll judge a goal based on the significance of the anticipated accomplishment. When you know that what you do will be well received, there's a natural motivation to do a good job. Rewards typically increase for more difficult goals. If you believe you'll be well compensated or otherwise rewarded for achieving a challenging goal, that will boost your enthusiasm and your drive to get it done. Setting SMART goals that are Relevant links them closely to the rewards given for achieving challenging goals. Relevant goals will further the aims of your organization, and these are the kinds of goals that most employers will be happy to reward. When setting goals, make each goal a challenge. If an assignment is easy and not viewed as very important – and if you or your employee doesn't expect the accomplishment to be significant – then the effort may not be impressive.

Note:

It's important to strike an appropriate balance between a challenging goal and a realistic goal. Setting a goal that you'll fail to achieve is possibly more de-motivating than setting a goal that's too easy. The need for success and achievement is strong, therefore people are best motivated by challenging, but realistic, goals. Ensuring that goals are Achievable or Attainable is one of the elements of SMART.

3. Commitment

Goals must be understood and agreed upon if they are to be effective. Employees are more likely to "buy into" a goal if they feel they were part of creating that goal. The notion of participative management rests on this idea of involving employees in setting goals and making decisions. One version of SMART – for use when you are working with someone else to set their goals – has A and R stand for Agreed and Realistic instead of Attainable and Relevant. Agreed goals lead to commitment. This doesn't mean that every goal has to be negotiated with and approved by employees.

It does mean that goals should be consistent and in line with previous expectations and organizational concerns. As long as the employee believes that the goal is consistent with the goals of the company, and believes the person assigning the goal is credible, then the commitment should be there. I nterestingly, goal commitment and difficulty often work together. The harder the goal, the more commitment is required. If you have an easy goal, you don't need a lot of motivation to get it done. When you're working on a difficult assignment, you will likely encounter challenges that require a deeper source of inspiration and incentive.

As you use goal setting in your workplace, make an appropriate effort to include people in their own goal setting. Encourage employees to develop their own goals, and keep them informed about what's happening elsewhere in the organization. This way, they can be sure that their goals are consistent with the overall vision and purpose that the company seeks.

4. Feedback

In addition to selecting the right type of goal, an effective goal program must also include feedback. Feedback provides opportunities to clarify expectations, adjust goal difficulty, and gain recognition. It's important to provide benchmark opportunities or targets, so individuals can determine for themselves how they're doing. These regular progress reports, which measure specific success along the way, are particularly important where it's going to take a long time to reach a goal. In these cases, break down the goals into smaller chunks, and link feedback to these intermediate milestones. SMART goals are Measurable, and this ensures that clear feedback can be provided. With all your goal setting efforts, make sure that you build in time for providing formal feedback. Certainly, informal check-ins are important, and they provide a means of giving regular encouragement and recognition. However, taking the time to sit down and discuss goal performance is a necessary factor in long-term performance improvement. See our article on Delegation for more on this.

5. Task Complexity

The last factor in goal setting theory introduces two more requirements for success. For goals or assignments that are highly complex, take special care to ensure that the work doesn't become too overwhelming. People who work in complicated and demanding roles probably have a high level of motivation already. However, they can often push themselves too hard if measures aren't built into the goal expectations to account for the complexity of the task. It's therefore important to do the following:

- Give the person sufficient time to meet the goal or improve performance.
- Provide enough time for the person to practice or learn what is expected and required for success.

The whole point of goal setting is to facilitate success. Therefore, you want to make sure that the conditions surrounding the goals don't frustrate or inhibit people from accomplishing their objectives. This reinforces the "Attainable" part of SMART.

Key Points

Goal setting is something most of us recognize as necessary for our success. By understanding goal setting theory, you can effectively apply the principles to goals that you or your team members set. Locke and Latham's research confirms the usefulness of SMART goal setting, and their theory continues to influence the way we measure performance today. Use clear, challenging goals, and commit yourself to achieving them. Provide feedback on goal performance. Take into consideration the complexity of the task. If you follow these simple rules, your goal setting process will be much more successful, and your overall performance will improve.

FOCUS ON BACKWARD GOAL-SETTING

Using Backward Planning to Set Goals

If your goal is to become an account director within the next five years, where do you start your planning process? Or if your team needs to redesign the company's organizational structure, where do you begin? In planning, most of us would usually start building our plan from start to finish. What do you have to do first, second, third, and so on? And by what date does each step need to be completed? This is a solid form of Personal Goal Setting that works very well. When combined with the Golden Rules of Goal Setting, you have a motivating formula that can help you actively move yourself forward.

A New Approach

However, there's another simple but lesser-used method of goal setting that can be equally as powerful. It's called backward planning, backward goal-setting, or backward design, and it's used quite often in education and training.

UNDERSTANDING GOLDEN RULES OF GOAL SETTING

Five Rules to Set Yourself Up for Success

Have you thought about what you want to be doing in five years' time?... Are you clear about what your main objective at work is at the moment?... Do you know what you want to have achieved by the end of today? If you want to succeed, you need to set goals. Without goals you lack focus and direction. Goal setting not only allows you to take control of your life's direction; it also provides you a benchmark for determining whether you are actually succeeding. Think about it: Having a million dollars in the bank is only proof of success if one of your goals is to amass riches.

If your goal is to practice acts of charity, then keeping the money for yourself is suddenly contrary to how you would define success. To accomplish your goals, however, you need to know how to set them. You can't simply say, "I want" and expect it to happen. Goal setting is a process that starts with careful consideration of what you want to achieve, and ends with a lot of hard work to actually do it. In between there are some very well defined steps that transcend the specifics of each goal. Knowing these steps will allow you to formulate goals that you can accomplish. Here are our Five Golden Rules of Goal Setting:

The Five Golden Rules

Rule #1: Set Goals that Motivate You

When you set goals for yourself, it is important that they motivate you: this means making sure that they are important to you, and that there is value in achieving them. If you have little interest in the outcome, or they are irrelevant given the larger picture, then the chances of you putting in the work to make them happen are slim. Motivation is key to achieving goals. Set goals that relate to the high priorities in your life. Without this type of focus, you can end up with far too many goals, leaving you too little time to devote to each one.

Goal achievement requires commitment, so to maximize the likelihood of success, you need to feel a sense of urgency and have an "I must do this" attitude. When you don't have this, you risk putting off what you need to do to make the goal a reality. This in turn leaves you feeling disappointed and frustrated with yourself, both of which are de-motivating. And you can end up in a very destructive "I can't do anything or be successful at anything" frame of mind.

Tip:

To make sure your goal is motivating, write down *why* it's valuable and important to you. Ask yourself, "If I were to share my goal with others, what would I tell them to convince them it was a worthwhile goal?" You can use this motivating value statement to help you if you start to doubt yourself or lose confidence in your ability to actually make the goal happen.

Rule #2: Set SMART Goals

You have probably heard of "SMART goals" already. But do you always apply the rule? The simple fact is that for goals to be powerful, they should be designed to be SMART. There are many variations of what SMART stands for, but the essence is this – goals should be:

Specific
Measurable
Attainable

Relevant

Time Bound

Set Specific Goals

You goal must be clear and well defined. Vague or generalized goals are unhelpful because they don't provide sufficient direction. Remember, you need goals to show you the way. Make it as easy as you can to get where you want to go by defining precisely where you want to end up.

Set Measurable Goals

Include precise amounts, dates, etc in your goals so you can measure your degree of success. If your goal is simply defined as "To reduce expenses" how will you know when you have been successful? In one month's time if you have a 1% reduction or in two years' time when you have a 10% reduction? Without a way to measure your success you miss out on the celebration that comes with knowing you have actually achieved something.

Set Attainable Goals

Make sure that it's possible to achieve the goals you set. If you set a goal that you have no hope of achieving, you will only demoralize yourself and erode your confidence. However, resist the urge to set goals that are too easy. Accomplishing a goal that you didn't have to work hard for can be anticlimactic at best, and can also make you fear setting future goals that carry a risk of non-achievement. By setting realistic yet challenging goals, you hit the balance you need. These are the types of goals that require you to "raise the bar" and they bring the greatest personal satisfaction.

Set Relevant Goals

Goals should be relevant to the direction you want your life and career to take. By keeping goals aligned with this, you'll develop the focus you need to get ahead and do what you want. Set widely scattered and inconsistent goals, and you'll fritter your time – and your life – away.

Set Time-Bound Goals

You goals must have a deadline. Again, this means that you know when you can celebrate success. When you are working on a deadline, your sense of urgency increases and achievement will come that much quicker.

Rule #3: Set Goals in Writing

The physical act of writing down a goal makes it real and tangible. You have no excuse for forgetting about it. As you write, use the word "will" instead of "would like to" or "might". For example, "I will reduce my operating expenses by 10% this year", not "I would like to reduce my operating expenses by 10% this year." The first goal statement has power and you can "see" yourself reducing expenses, the second lacks passion and gives you an excuse if you get sidetracked.

Tip 1:

Frame your goal statement positively. If you want to improve your retention rates say, "I will hold on to all existing employees for the next quarter" rather than "I will reduce employee turnover." The first one is motivating; the second one still has a get-out clause "allowing" you to succeed even if some employees leave.

Tip 2:

If you use a To Do List, make yourself a To Do List template that has your goals at the top of it. If you use an Action Program, then your goals should be at the top of your Project Catalog.)

Post your goals in visible places to remind yourself every day of what it is you intend to do. Put them on your walls, desk, computer monitor, bathroom mirror or refrigerator as a constant reminder. You can even post them in the Mind Tools Career Excellence Club forum, and share them with other members for added motivation.

Rule #4: Make an Action Plan

This step is often missed in the process of goal setting. You get so focused on the outcome that you forget to plan all of the steps that are needed along the way. By writing out the individual steps, and then crossing each one off as you complete it, you'll realize that you are making progress towards your ultimate goal. This is especially important if your goal is big and demanding, or long-term. Read our article on Action Plans for more on how to do this.

Rule #5: Stick With It!

Remember, goal setting is an ongoing activity not just a means to an end. Build in reminders to keep yourself on track, and make regular time-slots available to review your goals. Your end destination may remain quite similar over the long term, but the action plan you set for yourself along the way can change significantly. Make sure the relevance, value, and necessity remain high.

Key Points

Goal setting is much more than simply saying you want something to happen. Unless you clearly define exactly what you want and understand why you want it the first place, your odds of success are considerably reduced. By following the Five Golden Rules of Goal Setting you can set goals with confidence and enjoy the satisfaction that comes along with knowing you achieved what you set out to do.

FOCUS ON WELL-FORMED OUTCOMES

Many of us set goals at the beginning of a new year, at our annual performance reviews, or when something major happens, and we want to assess where we are and where we want to go. Yet sometimes, even with the best of intentions, we grind to a halt with these goals. Before we realize it, weeks and months have gone by – and we still haven't achieved the results we wanted. So how can you give yourself the best chance of successfully achieving your goals and your dreams? One way to do this is to create a "Well-Formed Outcome" that motivates you to move forward. By building a complete picture of that goal, and creating a strong internal representation of it, you can make the difference that speeds you to success. The Well-Formed Outcomes structure is based on NeuroLinguistic Programming (NLP) principles, and it was modeled from studies of successful people. It involves asking a set of questions that identify and clarify your intentions, actions, and thoughts, so that you can define your goal in a "well-formed" way.

UNDERSTANDING PERSONAL MISSION STATEMENTS

Defining Your Goals

One of the most important things that corporate leaders do is define their organization's purpose, and identify what they ultimately want it to accomplish. They communicate this information in corporate mission and vision statements. These set a clear course for the organization, tell employees how they should focus their efforts, and prevent people going "off mission". If mission and vision statements are so important to organizations, why don't we spend any time creating them for ourselves? In this article, we'll look the benefits of creating personal mission and vision statements. We'll show you how to create them, and highlight how you can use them to bring clarity to your own objectives and goals.

Reasons for Creating Mission and Vision Statements

All of us have very different ideas about success. What's important, however, is that you spend time defining your version of success. Otherwise, how will you understand what you should be working toward, and how will you know if your decisions are helping you move toward your goals? Used as part of your personal approach to goal setting, mission and vision statements are useful for bringing sharp focus to your most important goal, and for helping you to quickly identify which opportunities you should pursue. Shaping this goal into a mission statement helps you keep it at the front of your mind, and helps you focus your energy and resources upon it.

Without this focus, you can be distracted, or you can spread your effort too thinly across multiple competing goals. By creating a personal mission statement, you make one of your personal goals supremely important. This gives you the best possible chance of achieving it, which is essential for some types of goal. However, if you focus exclusively on one goal, you'll inevitably have to de-emphasize others. Make sure that you're happy to do this, and make sure that people who are important to you don't suffer as a consequence.

Mission Versus Vision

So, what's the difference between a mission statement and a vision statement?

- Mission statement – This defines your purpose. It's what you ultimately want to achieve in your life or career, expressed in a specific, measurable way.
- Vision statement – This is a bit more emotional. Here, you define your core values, and how you'll apply those values to your mission.

As your career develops, your goals and objectives are likely to change too. So make sure you revisit your mission and vision statements regularly, and update them as required.

VISUALIZATION

Imagining and Achieving Goals

Have you ever wondered what Olympic athletes think about right before they compete? Imagine this for a moment: They're in front of thousands, or even millions, of people. They're feeling nervous, watching their competition, and considering all the things that might go wrong and how to avoid them. Sounds reasonable, right? After all, that's probably what we would do in their position. However, if they did that, their odds of losing the competition would probably be quite high. Well-trained athletes know they should never visualize mistakes, especially right before a competition. Why? Because picturing, or visualizing, mistakes - imagining poor performance - increases the likelihood that the athletes will actually do those things during the event, even when they don't mean to.

Instead, most top athletes are trained to visualize their goals right before a competition. They see themselves winning the game, running the fastest race, or scoring the winning point. They're trained to 'picture' what they WANT to happen, instead of what they DON'T want to happen. When they do this, their chances for success increase dramatically. This is the power of visualization - and you, too, can use this technique every day to help you achieve your goals and dreams. In this article, we outline what visualization is, and how you can start using it in your life.

Visualization

Visualization is simply a technique that you can use to create a strong mental image of a future event. With good use of visualization, you can practice in advance for the event, so that you can prepare properly for it. And by visualizing success, you can build the self-confidence you need to perform well. For instance, imagine you have a major job interview next week. You're nervous already, and it's easy to worry about giving poor answers to the interviewer's questions, speaking awkwardly about your past accomplishments, and forgetting your letters of recommendation. Does this sound familiar? We've all probably experienced negative thinking like this.

However, instead of thinking negatively, you could use visualization to imagine that the interview goes well. You could picture yourself talking confidently, easily describing all of your past achievements, and providing letters of recommendation to the interviewer. That vision feels a lot better, doesn't it? Visualization offers several benefits:

- Visualizing outcomes that you want can increase your confidence. 'Seeing' yourself succeed helps you believe that it can - and will - happen.
- Visualization helps you 'practice' success. When you imagine every step of an event or activity going well, you get your mind and body ready to take those steps in real life.
- Anyone can benefit from visualization. You don't have to be a life coach or personal development expert to use visualization to achieve your goals.

Using Visualization to Achieve Goals

The great thing about visualization is that you can use it in so many areas of your life. Do you want a promotion? Do you want to make more friends at the office? Do you want to start your own business? Visualization can help you in all of these areas. This is why so many highly effective people use the technique to help them achieve their goals and dreams.

UNDERSTANDING TREASURE MAPPING

Visualizing Your Goal for Greater Achievement

When you want to achieve something really badly, have you ever tried closing your eyes and imagining yourself "there"? You touch it, feel it and see it clearly. You scan every detail in your mind's eye. This is a powerful and important technique for motivating yourself and building the self-confidence needed to achieve your goals. Yet when you open your eyes, the vivid image start fades, and it can take real concentration to recreate your visualization each time you want some inspiration. What if you could keep hold of that vivid image and refer to it when ever you need a little motivation, or a reminder of what you are working towards? Treasure mapping is a simple tool to help you do just that. Visualization itself is a very powerful technique.

And Treasure Mapping can be the icing on the visualization cake! It's a very simple but effective idea: Treasure Mapping involves creating a physical representation or collage of what you want to achieve. It acts as a constant reminder and representation of your goals. And so it intensifies the effects of visualization, which acts on your subconscious mind to motivate and encourage you towards achieving those goals. Let's say you have the ambition to get fitter and run a marathon: Your "treasure map" could include pictures of runners, people crossing the marathon finishing line, and athletes training hard; perhaps it could also include pictures of the foods that you need to eat (and those you need to avoid). If you are a salesperson with the ambition to beat sales records in your company, your treasure map could include a representation of the sales chart you hope to achieve, pictures of people signing deals with customers, pictures of your product standing proud; and perhaps a picture of someone receiving a prize.

Using the Tool

Your treasure map will represent how you visualize the achievement of your goals and your journey toward that achievement. The first step towards creating your treasure map is to clarify your goals and then visualize what will happen, or what you will have, once you have achieved the goal. (For further help on clarifying your goals, please refer to Mind Tools article on goal setting. Once you have are clear about what you want to achieve, write it down in detail and start to visualize your achievement: Ask yourself questions such as:

- What will I see when I have achieved my goal?
- What will I have? What will I be?

- How will I celebrate the achievement?
- How will other people see me and what I have achieved?

Now enjoy collecting images that represent this visualization and arrange these images on paper as a collage. These image of the ultimate achievement go in the most prominent position of you treasure map – at the top or in the middle. The next step is to visualize the journey towards achieving the goals. What will you have to do? What will you have to stop doing to achieve your goals? There may be important milestones or necessary sacrifices to achieving your goals. Visualize these too, and find images that represent them. Now arrange these on the collage too. Finally, paste the pictures of your goals, your journey towards them, and sacrifices on your collage. Make sure you arrange them in a way that helps imprint upon you the desire to achieve your goals. Hang your chart in a prominent place so that you see it daily: There it will help motivate and inspire you towards achieving your goals.

Key Points

Treasure mapping helps bring you goals to life and gives you a clear image of what you want to achieve and how you will achieve it. First clarify you goals and what you need to do to achieve them. Then visualize these. Choose images to represent how you see your achievement and make a collage; and use this as a constant reminder of what you want to achieve.

ROLE OF NEW YEAR'S RESOLUTIONS

Planning for a Year of Achievement

Are you busy making your New Year resolutions, or have you resolved never to make a New Year's resolution ever again? If the latter, you're not alone. Many people get demoralized when, year after year, they make resolutions that they keep for only a few weeks or maybe even just a few days. Why is this? After all, we all have the best intentions and the timing (new year, new start) couldn't be better. The problem may lie in the fact that we place a huge amount of pressure on ourselves. During the last week of December and the first week of January, all you hear is, "What're your New Year's resolutions?" "What are you going to work on this year?"

And the focus is on the "what" not the "how." When you are more concerned with the goal you set than on the specifics of how you are going to accomplish it, or even whether it is realistic and achievable, you can set yourself up for failure. So if you resolve to set successful New Year resolutions, read on. Let's focus on how, this year, you can set yourself up for a year of achievement!

IMPORTANCE OF MOTIVATING ONESELF

Practical Tools and Strategies Motivation Basics

Maybe you're continuing to ignore those overflowing filing cabinets, instead of taking some time out to reorganize them. Or, you're avoiding that difficult conversation with a person who is always late, choosing instead to tolerate the tardiness. Perhaps you keep rearranging your priorities, so that the tasks you hate always end up at the bottom of the list. The longer you delay doing something, the more stress and pressure you're likely to feel. After a while, you may even start to lose confidence in your ability to complete the task at all. Many of us sometimes need help getting motivated. And it can be very frustrating when we know we have to do something, but we just can't get around to making a start.

There are essentially two types of motivation:

- Intrinsic motivation – This is when you are motivated by "internal" factors to meet your own personal needs. Most hobbies and leisure activities are based on intrinsic motivation. We do them because we enjoy them, not because we have to.
- Extrinsic motivation – This is when you are motivated by "external" factors that are given or controlled by others, for example, by salary or by praise. Our jobs are usually based on extrinsic motivation, although there will be some intrinsic motivation involved if you enjoy aspects of what you do.

Most situations at work involve both types of motivation. If we do a job we enjoy, some of the work we do will be intrinsically motivating. Realistically though, we probably wouldn't go to work if we weren't being paid! Enjoying your job is intrinsically motivating, while being paid a salary to do it is extrinsically motivating. Even if we do a job we enjoy, problems can crop up when we need to do something that we don't inherently like – such as filing, speaking with staff about performance issues, completing reports, and so on. We have to do undesirable tasks as part of our job, so we have to find a way to motivate ourselves to complete them. That's where self-motivation is necessary.

ROLE OF PROCRASTINATION

In psychology, procrastination refers to the act of replacing high-priority actions with tasks of low-priority, and thus putting off important tasks to a later time. Some Psychologists cite such behaviour as a mechanism for coping with the anxiety associated with starting or completing any task or decision.

Other psychologists indicate that anxiety is just as likely to get people to start working early as late and the focus should be impulsiveness. That is, anxiety will cause people to delay only if they are impulsive. Schraw, Wadkins, and Olafson have proposed three criteria for a behaviour to be classified as procrastination: it must be counterproductive, needless, and delaying. Similarly, Steel (2007) reviews all previous attempts to define procrastination, indicating it is "to voluntarily delay an intended course of action despite expecting to be worse off for the delay." Procrastination may result in stress, a sense of guilt and crisis, severe loss of personal productivity, as well as social disapproval for not meeting responsibilities or commitments. These feelings combined may promote further procrastination. While it is regarded as normal for people to procrastinate to some degree, it becomes a problem when it impedes normal functioning. Chronic procrastination may be a sign of an underlying psychological disorder.

Etymology

The modern term comes from the Latin word *procrastinatus*, which is the past participle of *procrastinare* derived from *pro-* (forward) and *crastinus* (of tomorrow). Though descriptions of procrastination appear in ancient Egyptian, Greek and Roman texts, it first appears by name in the English language in 1548 Oxford English Dictionary.

Causes

Psychological

The psychological causes of procrastination are in debate. Drawing on clinical work, there appears to be a connection with issues of anxiety, low sense of self-worth, and a self-defeating mentality. On the other hand, drawing on meta-analytical correlational work, anxiety and perfectionism have no connection or at best an extremely weak connection with procrastination. Instead, procrastination is strongly connected with lack of self-confidence (e.g., low self-efficacy), disliking the task (e.g., boredom proneness), but especially impulsiveness. These characteristics are often facets of the personality trait conscientiousness while anxiety and irrational beliefs (such as perfectionism) are aspects of the personality trait neuroticism. Accordingly, Lee, Kelly and Edwards (2006) indicated that neuroticism has no direct links to procrastination and that any relationship is fully mediated by conscientiousness.

Physiological

Research on the physiological roots of procrastination mostly surrounds the role of the prefrontal cortex. Consistent with notion that procrastination is strongly related to impulsiveness, this area of the brain is responsible for executive brain functions such as planning, impulse control, attention, and acts as a filter by decreasing distracting stimuli from other brain regions. Damage or low activation in this area can reduce an individual's ability to filter out distracting stimuli, ultimately resulting in poorer organization, a loss of attention and increased procrastination. This is similar to the prefrontal lobe's role in attention-deficit hyperactivity disorder, where underactivation is common.

Mental Health

For some people, procrastination can be persistent and tremendously disruptive to everyday life. For these individuals, procrastination may be symptomatic of a psychological disorder such as depression or ADHD. Therefore, it is important for people whose procrastination has become chronic and is perceived to be debilitating, to seek out a trained therapist or psychiatrist to see if an underlying mental health issue may be present.

Perfectionism

Traditionally, procrastination has been associated with perfectionism, a tendency to negatively evaluate outcomes and one's own performance, intense fear and avoidance of evaluation of one's abilities by others, heightened social self-consciousness and anxiety, recurrent low mood, and "workaholism". According to Robert B. Slaney adaptive perfectionists (when perfectionism is egosyntonic) were *less* likely to procrastinate than non-perfectionists, while maladaptive perfectionists (people who saw their perfectionism as a problem; i.e., when perfectionism is egodystonic) had high levels of procrastination (and also of anxiety). Accordingly, meta-analytic review of 71 studies by Steel (2007) indicate that typically perfectionists actually procrastinate slightly less than others, with "the exception being perfectionists who were also seeking clinical counseling."

Academic Procrastination

More specifically, a 1992 study showed that "52% of surveyed students indicated having a moderate to high need for help concerning procrastination". It is estimated that 80%–95% of college students engage in procrastination, approximately 75% considering themselves procrastinators. One source of procrastination is underestimating the time required to analyze research. Many students devote weeks to gathering research for a term paper, but are unable to finish writing it because they have to review many contradictory opinions before they can offer their own perspective on the subject. Despite knowing how to consult resources, they struggle to perform their own analysis. "Student syndrome" refers to the phenomenon where a student will only begin to fully apply themselves to a task immediately before a deadline. This negates the usefulness of any buffers built into individual task duration estimates. Students also have difficulties when self-imposing deadlines.

Types

The Relaxed Type

The relaxed type of procrastinators view their responsibilities negatively and avoid them by directing energy into other tasks. It is common, for example, for relaxed type procrastinating children to abandon schoolwork but not their social lives. Students often see projects as a whole rather than breaking them into smaller parts. This type of procrastination is a form of denial or cover-up; therefore, typically no help is being sought. Furthermore, they are also unable to defer gratification. The procrastinator avoids situations that would cause displeasure, indulging instead in more enjoyable activities. They may not appear to be worried about work and deadlines, but this is simply an evasion of the work that needs to be completed.

The Tense-Afraid Type

The tense-afraid type of procrastinators usually feel overwhelmed with pressure, unrealistic about time, uncertain about goals, and many other negative feelings. They may feel a sense of malaise. Feeling that they lack the ability or focus to successfully complete their work, they tell themselves that they need to unwind and relax, that it's better to take it easy for the afternoon, for example, and start afresh in the morning. They usually have grandiose plans that aren't realistic. Their 'relaxing' is often temporary and ineffective, and leads to even more stress as time runs out, deadlines approach and the person feels increasingly guilty and apprehensive.

This behaviour becomes a cycle of failure and delay, as plans and goals are put off, pencilled into the following day or week in the diary again and again. It can also have a debilitating effect on their personal lives and relationships. Since they are uncertain about their goals, they often feel awkward with people who appear confident and goal-oriented, which can lead to depression. Tense-afraid procrastinators often withdraw from social life, avoiding contact even with close friends.

Stigma and Misunderstanding

Procrastinators often have great difficulty in seeking help, or finding an understanding source of support, due to the stigma and profound misunderstanding surrounding extreme forms of procrastination. One of the symptoms, known to psychologists as task-aversion, is often mischaracterised as laziness, a lack of willpower or loss of ambition.

WAYS OF OVERCOMING PROCRASTINATION

Manage Your Time - Get it All Done

If you've found yourself putting off important tasks over and over again, you're not alone. In fact, many people procrastinate to some degree – but some are so chronically affected by procrastination that it stops them fulfilling their potential and disrupts their careers. The key to controlling this destructive habit is to recognize when you start procrastinating, understand why it happens (even to the best of us), and take active steps to manage your time and outcomes better.

Understanding Procrastination

In a nutshell, you procrastinate when you put off things that you should be focusing on right now, usually in favour of doing something that is more enjoyable or that you're more comfortable doing. According to psychologist Professor Clarry Lay, a prominent writer on procrastination, procrastination occurs when there's "a temporal gap between intended behaviour and enacted behaviour." That is, procrastination is occurring when there's a significant time period between when people intend to do a job, and when they actually do it.

Ways to Overcome Procrastination

Follow these steps to deal with and control procrastination:

Step 1: Recognize That You're Procrastinating

If you're honest with yourself, you probably know when you're procrastinating. But to be sure, take our Are You a Procrastinator? self test. Here are some useful indicators that will help you know when you're procrastinating:

- Filling your day with low priority tasks from your To Do List.
- Reading e-mails several times without starting work on them or deciding what you're going to do with them.
- Sitting down to start a high-priority task, and almost immediately going off to make a cup of coffee.
- Leaving an item on your To Do list for a long time, even though you know it's important.
- Regularly saying "Yes" to unimportant tasks that others ask you to do, and filling your time with these instead of getting on with the important tasks already on your list.

- Waiting for the "right mood" or the "right time" to tackle the important task at hand.

Notes:

Putting off an unimportant task isn't necessarily procrastination: it may just be good prioritization! Putting off an important task for a short period because you're feeling particularly tired isn't necessarily procrastination either, so long as you don't delay starting the task for more than a day or so, and this is only an occasional event. If you have a genuine good reason for rescheduling something important, then you're not necessarily procrastinating. But if you're simply "making an excuse" because you really just don't want to do it, then you are. In his 1986 article "At Last, My Research Article on Procrastination", published in the *Journal of Research on Personality,* Lay noted that procrastinatory behaviour is independent of need for achievement, energy, or self-esteem. In other words, you may be a procrastinator even if you're confident in your own abilities, energetic, and enjoy achieving things.

Step 2: Work Out Why You're Procrastinating

Why you procrastinate can depend on both you and the task. But it's important to understand which of the two is relevant in a given situation, so that you can select the best approach for overcoming your reluctance to get going. One reason for procrastination is that people find a particular job unpleasant, and try to avoid it because of that. Most jobs have unpleasant or boring aspects to them, and often the best way of dealing with these is to get them over and done with quickly, so that you can focus on the more enjoyable aspects of the job. Another cause is that people are disorganized. Organized people manage to fend of the temptation to procrastinate, because they will have things like prioritized to-do lists and schedules which emphasize how important the piece work is, and identify precisely when it's due.

Step 3: Adopt Anti-Procrastination Strategies

Procrastination is a habit – a deeply ingrained pattern of behaviour. That means that you won't just break it overnight. Habits only stop being habits when you have persistently stopped practising them, so use as many approaches as possible to maximize your chances of beating procrastination. Some tips will work better for some people than for others, and for some tasks than others. And, sometimes, you may simply need to try a fresh approach to beat the "procrastination peril"! These general tips will help motivate you to get moving:

- Make up your own rewards. For example, promise yourself a piece of tasty flapjack at lunchtime if you've completed a certain task. And make sure you notice how good it feels to finish things!

- Ask someone else to check up on you. Peer pressure works! This is the principle behind slimming and other self-help groups, and it is widely recognized as a highly effective approach.
- Identify the unpleasant consequences of NOT doing the task.
- Work out the cost of your time to your employer. As your employers are paying you to do the things that they think are important, you're not delivering value for money if you're not doing those things. Shame yourself into getting going!
- Aim to "eat an elephant beetle" first thing, every day!

If you're pocrastinating because you're disorganized, here's how to get organized!

- Keep a To-Do list so that you can't "conveniently" forget about unpleasant or overwhelming tasks.
- Use an Urgent/Important Matrix to help prioritize your to-do list so that you can't try to kid yourself that it would be acceptable to put off doing something on the grounds that it's unimportant, or that you have many urgent things which ought to be done first when, in reality, you're procrastinating.
- Become a master of scheduling and project planning, so that you know when to start those all-important projects.
- Set yourself time-bound goals: that way, you'll have no time for procrastination!
- Focus on one task at a time.

If you're putting off starting a project because you find it overwhelming, you need to take a different approach. Here are some tips:

- Break the project into a set of smaller, more manageable tasks. You may find it helpful to create an action plan.
- Start with some quick, small tasks if you can, even if these aren't the logical first actions. You'll feel that you're achieving things, and so perhaps the whole project won't be so overwhelming after all.

If you're procrastinating because you find the task unpleasant:

- Many procrastinators overestimate the unpleasantness of a task. So give it a try! You may find that it's not as bad as you thought!

- Hold the unpleasant consequences of not doing the work at the front of your mind.
- Reward yourself for doing the task.

Finally, if you're procrastinating because you can't decide what action to take, and are putting off making a decision because you're nervous about making the wrong choice, see our decision-making section. This teaches a range of powerful and effective decision-making techniques. Remember: the longer you can spend without procrastinating, the greater your chances of breaking this destructive habit for good!

Key Points

To have a good chance of conquering procrastination, you need to spot straight away that you're doing it. Then, you need to identify why you're procrastinating and taken appropriate steps to overcome the block. *Part of the solution is to develop good time management, organizational and personal effectiveness habits, such as those described in Make Time for Success!This helps you establish the right priorities, and manage your time in such a way that you make the most of the opportunities open to you.*

REFERENCES

Ariely, Dan; Wertenbroch, Klaus (2002). "Procrastination, Deadlines, and Performance: Self-Control by Precommitment". *Psychological Science* 13 (3): 219–224.

Robert B. Slaney is a professor of counseling psychology in Penn State's College of Education

Schraw, G., Wadkins, T., Olafson, L. (2007). "Doing the things we do: A grounded theory of academic procrastination". *Journal of Educational Psychology* 99 (1): 12–25.

Steel, Piers (2007). "The nature of procrastination: a meta-analytic and theoretical review of quintessential self-regulatory failure". *Psycholgoical Bulletin* 131 (1): 65-94.

Steel, Piers (2007). "The Nature of Procrastination: A Meta-Analytic and Theoretical Review of". *Psychological Bulletin* 133 (1): 65–94.

Steel, Piers (2010). *The Procrastination Equation: How to Stop Putting Things Off and Start Getting Stuff Done.* New York: HarperCollins.

Strub, Richard L. (September 1989). "Frontal lobe syndrome in a patient with bilateral globus pallidus lesions". *Archives of Neurology* 46 (9): 1024–7.

7

Time Management Tools, Strategies and Help

"Time is the substance from which I am made. Time is a river which carries me along, but I am the river; it is a tiger that devours me, but I am the tiger; it is a fire that consumes me, but I am the fire"

—*Jorge Luis Borges*

UNDERSTANDING ESSENTIAL TIME MANAGEMENT TOOLS

In recent years time management tools have become big business. Whether the latest technological wizardry or a scrap of paper kept in a pocket, whatever helps people improve their time and task management will be popular. The trouble is, some of them do more harm than good, often costing a good deal more time and money than they claim to save. It's so easy to pay good money for something, only for it to sit in a desk drawer gathering dust.

So what time management tools can you depend on to genuinely help you to live well and work better? Here's how to choose and what to use...

Your time management tools can be as simple or as multi functional as you like, but they should all allow you to capture, store, organize and access information, quickly and easily. Whichever you use, they need to help you to manage the following:

1. Appointments. Your repeat and one off appointments need to be scheduled so you know where you're meant to be and what you're meant to be doing.
2. Deadlines. You need to know who wants what by when, to allow yourself time to plan, prepare and complete the project.

3. Dates. Personal or social dates that you want to remember need to be recorded. Some you may forget and get away with. Others you'd better remember!
4. Reminders. Built in to give you time to take action before an important date or deadline.
5. Thoughts and ideas. Do you ever have a fabulous idea and then lose it? Lock these down before they fly away.
6. Goals, projects and actions. Whatever you're working on or towards becomes less abstract and more concrete if it's out of your head, as well as being in it.
7. Reference. All the information you want to be access, as and when necessary.

Whatever you use to help you manage your time, ask yourself which of the following criteria they meet. The more they do, the better they will serve you:

- Simple. Technology is great when it saves you more time than you invest in it. But how much wasted technology do you own, or see at work? Learning how to operate a system has to justify itself. If it doesn't, ditch it for something simpler.
- Accessible. Can you get to it quickly and easily?You could own the most sophisticated gadget in the world, but if you can't keep it with you, you won't use it.
- Reliable. You need to be able to trust it to work, regardless of where you are or what you're doing.

A good way to quantify these is to rate whatever you use on a scale of 1 to 10 for each of the three criteria to give you a score up to 30. There are countless free time management tools available, online and off.

But which ones do you need?

'Must have' time management tools

1. Planners. Whether they're electronic or paper based, daily planners should form the backbone of personal organizational skills. Bear in mind that you'll only ever be as effective as the quality, planning and execution of the contents in yours.
2. Pen and paper. Small enough to keep with you — you never know when a thought or idea will strike, so make it a habit to keep them with you. This is particularly true if you're committed to keeping a time management log. A pocket notepad and pen mean you can jot down pretty much anything you want to act on, or commit to, later.

3. Computer. A double edged sword, this one. Your PC or notebook can do many things, online and off. How many save you time? As many as you want. Time spent improving your data storage and access by organizing computer files is time well spent. Manage you computer well and it will serve you. Don't, and it will start to own you.
4. Timer. Use a timer to establish limits on whatever you want to do more or less of (visual timers are particularly useful). For example, if you're habitually wasting time online, use a timer to help you put limits on the amount you do it. On the other hand, when you're having difficulty overcoming procrastination set it for a short time to get you going.
5. Digital voice recorder. When you're travelling, taking notes isn't always possible. Using a voice recorder allows you to capture thoughts and ideas when you're on the go. These really are portable, whether you're waiting, walking, driving, or even running (well you may be able to; you may end up sounding like a crank caller when you play it back later).
6. PDA (Personal Digital Assistant). More a luxury than a necessity? Some say they are. Do they justify the costs? Many people say they do. Discover the advantages of PDA tools for time management to decide for yourself.

Finally, there's one more tool you can use when you want to remember something but you find yourself without any of the capture tools mentioned above — what you're wearing. Change the way you wear something — turn your watch round, undo a button or untie a shoelace (be careful with that one!) Get creative so that later you ask yourself why you did it when you have the means to capture the thought on paper. You'll find it comes back to you. Bottom line? Choose what you'll use. A tool will only serve you if you apply it. The time management tools you choose are exactly the same. Make sure yours earn their keep.

ROLE OF TIME MANAGEMENT STRATEGIES

Building time management strategies is similar to planning a budget. Just as the goal of a budget is to put you in control of your money, your goal in time management is to regain control of your time. The first step in forming time management strategies is to analyze how you spend your time. For one week, list everything you do and the approximate time it takes. At the end of the week, you'll see how you "spent" your time. Now you're ready to begin planning. Humans are creatures of habit and chances are you'll find you adhere to some sort of daily routine.

Examine your routine and determine where you can make changes. Include all of your daily tasks, scheduling them at their usual times and allowing ample time to complete them. If you're normally five minutes late, schedule your time so that you are able to leave ten minutes earlier. At first, this may mean starting your day 15 minutes earlier, but effective time management strategies soon put you back in control of time that used to fall through the cracks. Frequently time management brings a picture to mind of a daily planner with every minute plotted from the time your alarm clock sounds until the time you crawl into bed. However, time management experts suggest that you planning only 50% of your time leaves you time to relax as well as time to cope with the unexpected.

Create a To Do List

After you've analyzed your time, begin planning by creating a To Do List for tomorrow. Divide the list into classes.

1. Today's schedule or high priority activities that you must complete today. Be sure to include personal appointments and social obligations like doctor's appointments. Just as important are activities like promised family outings or playtimes with children.
2. Projects with a deadline beyond today (tomorrow, this week, this month, etc.)
3. When I get around to it. (i.e. clean out the garage, the closets)

Your first inclination may be to put all small projects in the first category, but remember the first part of your list is for things you need to accomplish. You'll also optimize your time by including some small projects in number two or number three. Secondly, prioritize each of the three sections of your To Do List, listing items first by deadline (e.g. needs to be done in the a.m, p.m. or exact time or date). List Class 3 projects by their order of importance.

Class 1: Today's Schedule

Start planning your day using your routine as a guide. Pencil in times for Class 1 projects, making sure you give each one a generous block of time. If you estimate a job will take 15 minutes, give yourself half an hour to complete it. If you estimate it will take an hour, give yourself an hour and a half. If "today's projects" are few, fill in the rest of your day with Class 2 projects. Be flexible. As you work through your daily plan, if you finish a task ahead of schedule, either move on to your next scheduled task or work on part of an unscheduled Class 2 project. If a routine break is the next thing on your schedule, reward yourself with an early break, still allowing only the normal amount of time to give yourself an early start on your next task. Also, take advantage of multi-task opportunities. Work on a page of Friday's report while today's report is printing.

Refill your coffee cup when you pick up the fax from the office fax machine. Fold a load of laundry while the potatoes are boiling. When new things "crop up", either put them in a free block of time or add them to part two or part three of your list. Also, remember to leave 10 or 15 minutes at the end of your schedule to make your To Do List for tomorrow.

Class 2: Projects With a Deadline

Whenever possible, split up projects with a deadline. For instance, laundry needs to be done this week, but you can divide it into loads and finish it over several days. At work, long reports can be broken into pages. If you finish a task from today's schedule with time to spare, use the "extra time" to complete part of a Class 2 project. Throw tonight's load of laundry into the washer or work on a page of the report that's due on Friday. Cross off any parts of finished projects to avoid repetition and to help you see what you have accomplished as well as to stay focused on what you have left to do.

Class 3: When I Get A Round To-It

As you did with Projects With a Deadline, divide larger projects into smaller tasks whenever you can. For instance, you might want to detail the inside of your vehicle. Washing windows, cleaning the steering wheel, console, dash, upholstery and carpets can all be done separately. At first you may find "round to-its" are a rare breed. In that case, you may want to schedule a Class 3 project or part of one into your day. However, as you become more organized, you'll be hanging "round to-its" on the wall like trophies, especially if you take advantage or our Time Management Tips.

IMPORTANCE OF TIME MANAGEMENT HELP

There's no time like the present to pick up some time management tips! Learning how to manage your time won't buy you more time, but it will ultimately give you more time to spend on what you want to do vs. what you need to get done! In 1968, singer Judi Collins recorded the Sandy Denny song, *"Who Knows Where the Time Goes"*. During the pixilated Flower Power era time management was of little importance, but in today's fast-paced society time is an important commodity in the workplace and for students in school or college as well as at home. Although each day still begins with 24 hours, frequently it seems that forces out of our control erode our minutes.

- Work time, with short deadlines and large production quotas, is literally golden. Time mis-management can bleed away employers' profits and ultimately cost you your job.

- Drive time to and from work is bloated with gridlock.
- Extra curricular activities and heavy homework assignments leave kids with little free time.
- Frequently, household chores clean us out of personal time.

Time Management Help is a quick way to pick up some important ideas to help you keep tabs on your time and time management strategies to put your time to better use whether you're at work, school, or home. Whether you need to get control of personal time management, time management in the workplace, college or at school, after you've gathered our time management tips and time management strategies, take a minute more to relax and smile at time management quotes and maybe find one to add to your time management arsenal.

ROLE OF PERSONAL TIME MANAGEMENT

What is Personal Time?

Who does your time belong to? When you wake up tomorrow, you'll start with exactly 24 hours of personal time. However, most of us have traded part of our 24 hours for benefits. If you work or go to school, you have traded part of your time for education or pay. Personal time is what we call "free time" or the time we haven't already bartered away.

How Do We Spend Our Time?

The average person spends the following amount of time in an average day:

1. 8.5 hours sleeping.
2. 1 hour devoted to personal care.
3. 2.5 hours on household chores (cooking, cleaning, gardening, shopping, etc)
4. 8.5 hours at work and/or school related activities on weekdays and (4 to 5 hours on the weekend).
5. 3 hours caring for others, either those who live with us (children and spouses) or those outside of our homes (elderly relatives, volunteer work).

If you add up the numbers, you'll see that "free time" is really at a premium!

Making Every Minute Count

The trick to managing personal time is first determining how much time you have to manage. Use the example above and put the time you spend sleeping, in personal care, doing chores, at work (or school), and in caring for others during your week to zero in on the personal time you have left to manage.

- Be realistic in categorizing your time. You'll need at least three categories: work (school) time, sleep time, and personal time.
- Personal time spent in relaxation is as important as the rest of your day. Schedule time to read, exercise, meditate... things you'd like to do... on your To Do list.
- Break times at work are personal time. If that's not true for you, then you probably need to learn to say "no". Make use of wasted minutes during lunch hours and breaks. Bring a book to work, take a walk, run an errand.
- Delegate some daily chores to the weekend.
- Learn to multi-task. You can fold the laundry while the potatoes are cooking.
- Divide large tasks into small ones. "Today I'll mow the lawn, tomorrow I'll tackle the weeds."
- Don't be afraid to ask for help and delegate some chores to others. Learn to barter with housemates. "I'll help weed the garden if you'll help wash the car."
- Mark your place. A lot of us waste a good part of our time just finding "where we left off". Keep a notepad or a pad of post-its nearby for emergencies and write yourself a note. Cross finished chores from your To Do List.
- Become listed. A grocery list can keep you from an extra trip to the store when you forget the milk. To Do Lists help you keep your focus on what you need to get done so that you have more time to do the things you want to do!

IMPORTANCE OF TIME MANAGEMENT FOR HIGH SCHOOL STUDENTS

School bells, curfews, household chores. When you're a high school student, it seems that your time gets managed pretty well... by someone other than you! Still you can get control of most of your time now and for the rest of your life, if you take time to pick up some time management skills.

Step 1: Marking Time

Start time management the simple way. Instead of marking off the days of the week, use a calendar to fill in up-coming events. When you schedule something, make sure you also schedule the time it takes to get to and from the event. For instance, if your school day is 8:00 to 2:30 but you have an hour bus ride both ways, then your school day is really 7:00 to 3:30. As well as scheduling school days and social activities, schedule chores.

For instance, if it's your job to take out the garbage or clean the cat box, write it on your calendar. That way, when you're trying to study or in the middle of your favourite TV show, you won't be interrupted by an irate parent. Speaking of TV, if you have a favourite show that you don't want to miss, write it down. Schedule everything for a week or if big events like your birthday are up coming, write them down, too. Use empty calendar boxes (like the ones after day 31) to keep track of future plans. (Next month basketball practice starts– [date]). Now that you know what's in the future, you should have a pretty good handle on the rest of your time. So, if homecoming is on the 6th and the history test is on the 7th, you can schedule extra history study time for the 5th. In addition, make it a point to take good notes that you can quickly review on the morning of the 7th.

Step 2: Use a To Do List

Use a small notebook and jot down things you need to do 1) today, 2) tomorrow, and 3) by the end of the week or later. Prioritize today's list. If today's list is too long, it's time to regroup, break down, and move some items to tomorrow or further into the week. That isn't procrastination; it's time management. Procrastination is when you know you have to get something done, but agonize over doing it as time slips away. For example, if on Monday you get a large assignment that's due Friday, break it into smaller parts and work on it all through the week, making your goal to have most of it done before Thursday's study time.

Step 3: Schedule your time

- Schedule today's "to dos". Make sure you have transferred any important events from your calendar to your list. Also, be sure to schedule some "free time". In addition to being a buffer for tasks that take longer than you expected, scheduling free time can help you deal with interruptions and with unexpected additions to your list.
- As new things come up, add them to your list. As you complete old tasks cross them off.

- If you have evening events— a date, a game, a practice — schedule study time before.

Step 4: Analyze Your Schedule

At the end of the week, take a look back at what you had to do and what you accomplished. See what worked and what didn't work for you. Use both the hits and misses from this week in building a schedule for next week.

Time Pointers

1. Where schoolwork is concerned, make every effort to stay current. In fact, when you get the chance, work ahead! That way when a teacher has a tantrum and assigns two chapters instead of one, you'll have that much less work to do!
2. When you schedule your time, it's a lot easier to say "no" when you need to. "I can't work late, I need to study for a chemistry test" sounds better to your boss than "Nope. Sorry. I have other plans." You can even cut off an interrupting phone call with, "I can't talk right now. Can I call you back at 8:00?"
3. Build some flexibility into your schedule. One way is by scheduling frequent breaks. Another way is to give each "to do" more time than you believe it will take. That way if you need to call a friend for help with an assignment, you can do it at the end of a study time and not feel guilty for taking a few minutes to socialize. A flexible schedule will also help you keep on schedule and help you stay in control of your time.

IMPORTANCE OF TIME MANAGEMENT FOR COLLEGE STUDENTS

For many college students, one of the biggest differences between high school and college is the need to effectively manage your own time. If you began learning time management skills in high school, you have a definite advantage over many college students. Still, you need to make adjustments for the academic environment. Parents aren't around to wake you or nag you about being late. There's no "detention" for being late to class. In fact, most professors won't even know if you're absent or present. Social activities are numerous and unless you're in a dorm with a curfew, you can dance the night away and sleep in when you feel like it. Of course, your newfound freedom can be very expensive short-term with slipping grades and long-term by keeping you from meeting your goals.

The key to effective time management is literally being your own boss. Instead of being accountable to teachers and parents, now you need to be accountable to you! One of the biggest stumbling blocks to time management is procrastination. However, the easiest way to avoid procrastination is to start by memorizing ten little two-letter words; *"If it is to be, it is up to me."* Keep your long-term goals in sight. Map a plan to achieve your goals. You are here. What routes must you take to get to your destination? Schedule everything you know about! Use a calendar to write down class times, work times, social events, and breaks.

When up-coming events span beyond the current month, write them into empty calendar blocks. Start tomorrow at the end of today. Plan each day starting with when you intend to get up. Use a to do list for daily activities. Put scheduled events into their appropriate time slots and prioritize the rest of your list. Work your plan. Often it's easy to stop a task and immediately deal with what we think is a small interruption. However, sometimes small interruptions snowball into big time consumers. Work your day according to your plan. If something new needs attention, wedge it into your schedule or if it is an immediate emergency, make sure you reschedule your current task. Also, be sure to mark your place. Write a note to yourself if need be. Do the tough stuff first.

Once, the worst part of a project is over, the rest will be a breeze! However, if the "tough stuff" is keeping you from getting started, then start with something easy to convince yourself that you can get the job done! Break things down to the ridiculous. Dividing large assignments into smaller parts makes it easier to fit them into your schedule. In addition, you'll benefit from a sense of accomplishment as you finish each phase. It's a lot more satisfying to visualize what you have done than it is to agonize over what remains to do. Rules were made to be bent. Build some flexibility into your schedule. Give yourself extra time to cope with interruptions in your schedule.

As well as time to work, build in some time to play. Scheduling recreational activities and regarding them as important parts of your day gives you something to work towards. There's always tomorrow. Like any other skill, it takes time to learn how to manage your time. Even time management experts have days when their whole schedule falls apart. If yours does, don't quit on time management. Instead, pick up the pieces and start again the next day. Review your schedules at the end of each week to see what did and what didn't work for you. Build on your successes as you develop plans and time management strategies for following weeks.

Bibliography

Albert Hamilton (2004). *Handbook of Project Management Procedures.* TTL Publishing, Ltd.

Apostolou, D.; Karapiperis, S.; Stojanovic, N. (2008). "On Managing Users' Attention in Knowledge-Intensive Organizations". In G.A. Tsihrintzis et al.. *New Directions in Intelligent Interactive Multimedia, SCI 142.* Springer. pp. 239–248.

Burka, Yuen (1983, 2008). *Procrastination: Why You Do It, What To Do About It Now.* New York: Da Capo Lifelong Books.

Davenport, T.H.; Beck, J.C. (2001). *The Attention Economy: Understanding the New Currency of Business.* Harvard Business School Press.

Erickson, T. (2006). From PIM to GIM: personal information management in group contexts. *Commun. ACM* 49, 1 (Jan. 2006), 74-75.

Francis Heylighen & Clement Vidal (2008). *Getting Things Done: The Science behind Stress-Free Productivity",* Long Range Planning 41, no. 6: 585-605.

Frand, Jason; Hixon, Carol (1999). "Personal Knowledge Management : Who, What, Why, When, Where, How?", *Working paper, UCLA Anderson School of Management,*

Galbraith, Jay R. p. 49 ff. (1977). *Organization Design,* Addison-Wesley.

George Stigler (November 1955). "The Nature and Role of Originality in Scientific Progress". *Economica* XXII.

Gruber, Ronald P.; Wagner, Lawrence F.; Block, Richard A. (2000). "Subjective Time Versus Proper (Clock) Time". In Buccheri, R.; Di Gesù, V.; Saniga, Metod. *Studies on the structure of time: from physics to psycho(patho)logy.* Springer. p. 54.

Harold Kerzner (2003). *Project Management: A Systems Approach to Planning, Scheduling, and Controlling* (8th Ed. ed.). Wiley.

Hedberg, Bo (1981). "How organizations learn and unlearn", in: Nyström, P.C. & Starbuck, W.H., *Handbook of Organizational Design,* Oxford University Press.

Huberman, Bernardo A.; Wu, Fang (2008). "The Economics of Attention: Maximizing User Value in Information Rich Environments". *Advances in Complex Systems* 11 (4): 487–496.

Jaldow, Eli J.; Oakley, David A.; Davey, Graham C. L. (1989). "Performance of Decorticated Rats on Fixed Interval and Fixed Time Schedules". *European Journal of Neuroscience* (European Journal of Neuroscience) 1 (5): 461.

James M. Buchanan (2008). "Opportunity cost". *Second Edition*. The New Palgrave Dictionary of Economics Online.

James P. Lewis (2000). *The project manager's desk reference: : a comprehensive guide to project planning, scheduling, evaluation, and systems.* p.185.

Lewis R. Ireland (2006). *Project Management*. McGraw-Hill Professional, 2006.

Lutters, W.G., Ackerman, M.S. & Zhou, X. (2007). "Group Information Management." In William Jones and Jaime Teevan (Eds.), *Personal Information Management* (pp. 236-248), Seattle: University of Washington Press.

Nabeth, Thierry (2008). "User Profiling for Attention Support for School and Work". In Mireille Hildebrandt and Serge Gutwirth. *Profiling the European Citizen*. Springer. pp. 185–200.

Paul C. Dinsmore et al (2005). *The right projects done right!* John Wiley and Sons, 2005.

Rosen, Christine (2008). "The Myth of Multitasking". *The New Atlantis, Spring 2008* 20: 105–110.

Sandberg, Jared (2004-09-10). "Though Time-Consuming, To-Do Lists Are a Way of Life". The Wall Street Journal.

Schraw, G., Wadkins, T., Olafson, L. (2007). "Doing the things we do: A grounded theory of academic procrastination". *Journal of Educational Psychology* 99 (1): 12–25.

Steinle, Bruch, Lawa (1995). Projektmanagement. FAZ Verlagsbereich Wirtschaftsbücher. p.136-143.

Index

P

R

S

T

V

W

■■■